Understanding the
Arizona Constitution

Understanding the Arizona Constitution

Toni McClory

The University of Arizona Press
Tucson

The University of Arizona Press
© 2001 The Arizona Board of Regents
First Printing

∞ This book is printed on acid-free, archival-quality paper.
Manufactured in the United States of America

06 05 04 03 02 01   6 5 4 3 2 1

Library of Congress Cataloging-in-Publication Data

McClory, Toni, 1948–
Understanding the Arizona Constitution / Toni McClory.
p. cm.
Includes index.
ISBN 0-8165-2094-1 (cloth : alk. paper) — ISBN 0-8165-2096-8 (paper : alk. paper)
1. Constitutional law—Arizona. I. Title.
KFA2802.M33 2001
342.791'02—dc21
00-010604

British Library Cataloguing-in-Publication Data
A catalogue record for this book is available from the British Library.

Contents

Illustrations

Figures

Tables

Preface

This book is addressed to three overlapping audiences: students, citizens, and government professionals. My original objective was more limited. I simply needed an introductory textbook for my Arizona Constitution students. In fact, I was in the midst of "beta testing" the first draft when colleagues from other disciplines began stopping me in the corridor. It was an election year, and they had questions about propositions on the ballot. Others, of a more activist bent, wanted to know how bills could be tracked, where statutes and administrative rules could be obtained, and so forth. It occurred to me that it wouldn't be a major stretch to make the book equally useful to a second audience, the engaged citizen. So I expanded topics of special interest to voters and included references to online government resources. For the second time, I thought the task was done. Then I began to receive requests for the manuscript from an unexpected, third source: government professionals. Initially I balked. This was an introductory text, I insisted; it wasn't intended for sophisticated audiences. I knew that the professional reader would require detailed citations and a more nuanced analysis—things that might be off-putting to the general reader. It seemed like an impossible marriage, until I considered endnotes: I could keep the body of the book firmly focused on my primary readership (students) and tell the rest of the story in the back pages. This strategy was later validated when my advanced students also began requesting citations and greater supporting detail. Thus, this book is addressed to the novice as well as to the aficionado; it seeks to be accessible and, at the same time, fairly rigorous.

There are three other editorial emphases that should be explained. First, I have endeavored to blend topicality with history. Topicality is important because this is a profoundly dynamic subject. Teaching the Arizona Constitution is not like teaching geometry. The theorems continually change with new court rulings. And when the voters biennially amend the state constitution, they alter the very axioms. As a result, describing the state's political processes is much like trying to hit a moving target. I have struggled to make the text as up-to-date as publication deadlines allow, but this is a losing game. Inevitably, there will be new developments. Along with topicality, this book heavily emphasizes history. An entire chapter is devoted to the historical underpinnings of the state's government, and linkages to the past are included throughout. This dual focus is not contradictory. Arizona's current political processes cannot be fully understood without this historical backdrop.

Second, throughout the book I emphasize the assumptions and political trade-offs that underlie the state's institutions. To me, the interesting issue isn't that Arizona *has* a part-time legislature, but *why* this is so, and what advantages and disadvantages flow from this arrangement. Accordingly, the book contains multiple pro and con passages designed to stimulate such critical thinking. In fact, many of the points emerged in classroom debates. Not surprisingly, we didn't always agree as to whether a particular consequence belonged in the plus or the minus column. By including these arguments in the text, I am not trying to resolve these issues but rather to similarly engage the reader. Arizona citizenship demands such an analytical stance; the voters must make similar evaluations whenever they vote on ballot measures.

Finally, this book contains a more thorough treatment of the state's judicial branch than is found in most other general texts. I defend this emphasis because the court's role in shaping public policy in Arizona is both significant and poorly understood. Arizona's appellate courts not only "make law"—periodically altering major public and private responsibilities—but also play an aggressive watchdog role, nullifying many high-profile acts of the legislature, other public officials, and the voters. I have discovered that even the judges' more routine functions remain shrouded in mystery. Many people are confused by the difference between civil and criminal trials and wonder how they can reach different outcomes (e.g., the O. J. Simpson case). Others are puzzled about the ruckus over "tort reform." While the latter may seem a bit arcane for an introductory text, Arizona voters have been asked to weigh-in on the subject three times in recent years. I have drawn heavily on my dual careers (law and teaching) to try to present the courts' role in a more complete, accurate, and accessible way.

With such ambitious goals, I obviously required help. In fact, I've been sweating over these acknowledgments for quite a while. There is simply no way to thank all of the people, in government and out, who generously shared their knowledge and insights with me. But I would be remiss if I did not single out a few individuals both for their own contributions and as emblematic of others whom I do not name. At the top of my list is Anthony B. Ching, a constitutional scholar and Arizona's first solicitor general. Tony introduced me to the fascinating stories behind Arizona's political institutions over twenty years ago, and he remains a walking encyclopedia of the state's legal history and lore. He can provide pertinent case references from memory (often with volume numbers) and is always willing to debate any new legal issue that arises. Dr. William Lamkin, along with my other colleagues at Glendale Community College, strongly encouraged this undertaking. Bill also read the manuscript, offered valuable suggestions, and helped me keep the presentation balanced. My POS 222 students at Glendale Community College and Arizona State University West (fall 1998 to spring 2000) deserve special thanks as well. They put up with an early version of the manuscript, caught embarrassing typos, offered many useful editorial suggestions, and warmly encouraged this project.

To procure the raw data that underlies much of the text, I pestered overworked government staffers throughout the state. Belying the public's perception of "bureaucrat," these dedicated workers provided not only the requested data but also rich insights and first-hand recollections. I would especially like to acknowledge the secretary of state's Elections Department, which promptly accommodated all my research requests, and Sandra Claiborne, whom I interrupted the most. Laurie Devine, photo archivist for the Arizona Department of Library, Archives, and Public Records, Robert P. Spindler, archivist for the Arizona State University libraries, and Jean McHale, Public Information Specialist for the Arizona Supreme Court, also deserve special mention. All three helped procure the wonderful images that are reprinted in this book. And Patti Hartmann, Anne Keyl, and Sally Bennett patiently guided me through the final publication stages of this manuscript, along with others at the University of Arizona Press.

Finally, special acknowledgment is owed to the members of my family. They provided far more than the support and forbearance that is typically acknowledged in these pages. Each of my three children also made substantial editorial contributions. Andrew interrupted his own studies to proofread the draft, fruitlessly lecture me on comma placement, and offer thoughtful reactions to the text. Bret, the family's network administrator, facilitated my Internet research by keeping a sophisticated home system humming; he also provided expert assistance with graphics and other technical issues. Emily, the family Web maven, double-checked every URL in the textbook (including those endnotes!), organized the glossary, and provided other assistance with the preparation of the manuscript. However, the person most indispensable to this undertaking has been my husband, Thomas McClory. Tom is a public lawyer who has served the state of Arizona for over twenty years. I continually drew upon his legal expertise and remarkable memory of cases, people, and events. He generously assisted me with all aspects of this project, read the manuscript more times than the marriage contract decently warrants, and picked up the slack at home. I am disappointed that Tom's professional commitments wouldn't permit him to join me as coauthor (it would have been a much wittier text), but I have high hopes for the next edition. It is customary at this point for the author to assume full responsibility for all errors that may remain. I am, of course, solely responsible, but at least with respect to the family members, you know who I'll be blaming.

Understanding the
Arizona Constitution

1

The Arizona Constitution

The Importance of State Constitutions

When people hear the term "constitution," they usually think only of the U.S. Constitution. In fact, all fifty states have their own written constitutions, and two are even older than the nation's.[1] Arizona's constitution became effective in 1912 when Arizona was admitted as the forty-eighth state. Surprisingly, it is not one of the newer constitutions. This is because most older states have jettisoned their original constitutions in favor of newer models. (Louisiana holds the record here; it has had eleven different constitutions since statehood.) Although Arizona has remained loyal to its original charter, the state's constitution has been repeatedly amended. All of this constitutional activity points to one inescapable conclusion: state constitutions *do* matter. Why?

Written constitutions serve at least two major purposes. First, they establish a government by formally defining its powers, responsibilities, and internal structure. For example, the basic organization of Arizona's government is laid out in Article 3 of the state constitution. It declares:

> The powers of the government of the State of Arizona shall be divided into three separate departments, the Legislative, the Executive, and the Judicial; and, except as provided in this Constitution, such departments shall be separate and distinct, and no one of such departments shall exercise the powers properly belonging to either of the others.

Articles 4, 5, and 6 deal with each of the three branches in turn. Thus, if you want to know how old you must be to serve in the state legislature, whether the governor possesses a **line item veto**, or how judges are chosen, you would find the answer in one of these three sections. The remaining articles address such basic matters as the state's official boundaries, its election rules, taxation powers, education system, and local governments. In other words, the constitution is really a blueprint for state government—and the most authoritative guide available.

A second function of written constitutions is to safeguard individual rights from government interference. Arizona's **Declaration of Rights** is found in Article 2. It guarantees freedom of speech, freedom of religion, the right to bear arms, and many other personal freedoms. In modern times, the U.S. Constitution has become the more important source of rights. However, Arizona's Article 2 is not superfluous. Rather, it *supplements* the rights guaranteed to all Americans by the national constitution. More specifically, there are state rights that are simply not found in the U.S. Constitution. For example, Arizona has an express right of privacy. In 1987, the state supreme court used this right to recognize a qualified right to die. This decision preceded national recognition of such a right by three years.[2] Moreover, Arizonans have the power to add new rights to their constitution through the amending process. The voters did this in 1990 when they added special constitutional protections for victims of crime.[3]

Arizona's rights provisions have legal force even when they duplicate rights found in the U.S. Constitution. First, there are often subtle differences in wording. Notably, the state's free speech clause, religious freedom protections, and right to bear arms are all more broadly phrased than their federal counterparts.[4] Second, state courts have the power to interpret state constitutional provisions more expansively than the federal provisions. Arizona's supreme court has done this on several notable occasions.[5] In short, the role of state constitutions in safeguarding personal freedoms, though subordinate to the U.S. Constitution, should not be underestimated.

Finally, a common misconception about constitutions is that they have historic value only—that their importance ceases once the government is established or a new right is added. To the contrary, constitutions serve as a *continuing* limitation on the powers of government. In essence, officials can only do what the constitution permits. An illustration of this principle can be found in the current national debate over **tort** reform. Some Americans believe that jury verdicts are too high. Accordingly, a number of states have passed laws that limit the amount of money that juries can award. However, Arizona's legislators cannot enact such a law because the Arizona constitution

HOW THE CONSTITUTION IS ORGANIZED
The Arizona Constitution currently consists of a preamble and twenty-nine articles. The articles deal with specific subjects, such as education, taxes, and the three branches of government. Most articles are further divided into individual sections. Because the state constitution is so frequently changed, the amendments are not printed at the end of the document as they are with the U.S. Constitution. Instead, Arizona's constitution is periodically republished. The new language is then incorporated into the body of the text, and any superseded language simply disappears. For this reason, it is important to check the "freshness date" of the constitution you are consulting. A current version is always available from the Arizona secretary of state's office and can now be accessed online. (See the online resources at the end of this chapter.)

expressly forbids limits on jury verdicts. The legislature has asked the voters to remove this barrier from the constitution, but the Arizona voters have refused.[6] The idea that the powers of government are thus limited is called **constitutionalism**. It serves as an important check against the abuse of power and is a defining principle of the American system of government.

The Hierarchy of Laws

The Many Sources of Arizona Law

Important as it is, the Arizona Constitution is not the sole authority on state government. Rather, the constitution often leaves key details to another source, the laws. For example, Article 5, section 9 of the constitution reads:

> The powers and duties of the secretary of state, state treasurer, attorney general, and superintendent of public instruction shall be *as prescribed by law* (emphasis added).

"Law" in this context means state **statutes**. As explained in chapters 3 and 4, statutes are enacted by the legislature and, less frequently, by the voters through the **initiative** process. Arizona's statutes address a wide range of subjects and fill many volumes. Among the thousands of statutes in effect, there are laws that pertain to the four major offices listed in section 9, quoted above. Thus, if you wanted to know about the treasurer's office you would have to look in the statutes instead of the constitution. There you would find a curious provision: Arizona's treasurer is required to give formal notice before leaving the state. (This even applies to personal vacations.) The law—which dates back to Arizona's earliest territorial days—reflects a longstanding mistrust of elected officials where public money is involved.[7]

Although statutes fill many of the gaps left by constitutional provisions, they too have intentional holes. The state legislature often leaves the details of governing up to executive branch agencies that possess greater expertise. As discussed in chapter 5, this branch of government has the primary responsibility for seeing that the laws are properly carried out. To accomplish this in a uniform, fair, and efficient way, state agencies promulgate detailed regulations, called **administrative rules.** Sometimes the answer to a specific question about government can only be found in this third body of law.

Unfortunately, our legal inventory is still incomplete. The constitution, statutes, and administrative rules are not the only sources of state law. As explained in chapter 7, local governments—e.g., counties, cities, and towns—have limited authority to make laws too. These local laws are called **ordinances** and **codes.** They typically address matters of public health and safety. For example, nuisance laws, curfews, parking restrictions, and building codes are some of the many issues addressed by local governments.

Lastly, judicial opinions constitute an important, additional source of state law. As explained in chapter 6, **appellate courts** sometimes make new law when they rule in individual cases. Although less accessible to the general reader than the other sources of law described above, court rulings are no less authoritative. For this reason, when we study Arizona government, appellate court opinions must always be considered as well.

Resolving Conflicts between Laws

With so many different lawmaking authorities, conflicts can obviously arise. What happens when a local ordinance conflicts with a state statute or constitutional provision? The answer is that all laws are not equal; the Arizona Constitution stands as the highest law of the state. That means that *its* provisions prevail over any conflicting language in the statutes, rules, and ordinances. The offending provisions are said to be "unconstitutional" and therefore unenforceable. In an analogous fashion, state statutes take precedence over administrative rules and most local ordinances.

Arizona laws must also be considered within the larger, national context. Arizona is a part of a **federal system** that includes the national government

RINGTAILS, BOLA TIES, AND DUELING STATE ANTHEMS

Do you recognize the little animal pictured here? It is a ringtail, the "state mammal." Like other states, Arizona has an official bird (the cactus wren), an official flower (the saguaro blossom), and an official tree (the palo verde). Unlike other states, Arizona also has official neckwear—the bola tie. (If you want to know the identity of the state reptile, fish, amphibian, fossil, and gemstone, you will have to check the statutes!)[8]

Surprisingly, these designations can be quite controversial. Take the state's official song: in 1919, the Fourth Legislature selected Margaret Clifford and Maurice Blumenthal's *Arizona* as the state anthem. Set to a rousing march beat, *Arizona* begins:

Come to this land of sunshine
To this land where life is young.
Where the wide, wide world is waiting,
The songs that will be sung.

In 1982, a Phoenix radio station campaigned for a new state anthem. It favored Rex Allen Jr.'s *Arizona*. The more mellow, country-western song opens:

I love you Arizona
Your mountains, deserts and streams
The rise of Dos Cabezas
And the outlaws I see in my dreams

Country-western fans battled traditionalists in the state legislature. Ultimately, the controversy ended in a draw: the Thirty-Fifth Legislature officially adopted Rex Allen Jr.'s song as the "alternate" state anthem.[9] Battles over state mascots and emblems continue even to this day. (See chapter 3 for a recent brouhaha over a state dinosaur.)

and forty-nine other states. The division between federal and state authority is actually quite complex. States are sovereign entities; they are not subunits of the national government. Both levels of government derive their power from the U.S. Constitution, not from each other. The Constitution gives the national government exclusive power to act in certain areas (e.g., national defense) and reserves regulatory power to the states in other areas (e.g., education, public safety, and health). Furthermore, there are areas where both governments have jurisdiction (e.g., commerce and civil rights).

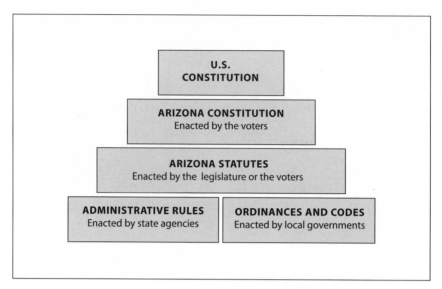

Figure 1.1 The hierarchy of laws

In practice, these constitutional distinctions are often blurred. The national government's spending power has enabled it to indirectly regulate areas that properly belong to the states. It can do this by attaching "strings" to grants and other financial aid. For example, in the mid-1980s the federal government wanted the minimum drinking age to be twenty-one. It lacked the power to order this directly on a nationwide basis. Accordingly, the government threatened to withhold highway funds from states that did not raise their drinking age.[10] Arizona, like other cash-starved states, complied. Today, all fifty states make twenty-one the minimum age for buying alcohol.[11] The national government has used its spending power to regulate many other areas of traditional state authority, including schools.

Conflict is inevitable in any system where power is divided between two separate authorities. Indeed, disputes between the national and state governments have a very long history. However, the **Supremacy Clause** of the U.S. Constitution decrees that in cases where both governments have the authority to act, state law is subordinate to the U.S. Constitution, federal treaties, and duly enacted federal laws.[12] The Arizona Constitution acknowledges this pecking order as well. Article 2, section 3 declares: "The Constitution of the United States is the supreme law of the land." Accordingly, whenever a provision in the Arizona Constitution conflicts with the U.S. Constitution, the state provision is said to be "unconstitutional."

A good example of such federal/state conflict involves Arizona's Official English provision (Article 28). It requires most public business to be conducted in English. The controversial measure was added to the state constitution by the voters in 1988 through the initiative process. However, opponents immediately sued to have it declared unconstitutional. In the end, the Arizona Supreme Court ruled that Official English violated the Free Speech Clause of the U.S. Constitution and was therefore unenforceable.[13] The void language of Article 28 still remains in Arizona's constitution as "deadwood" until the voters remove it.[14] This example illustrates not only the supremacy principle at work, but the need to always consider judicial opinions when reading the Arizona Constitution. The hierarchical relationships among Arizona's statutes, rules, ordinances, and constitution are summarized in figure 1.1.

Amending the Arizona Constitution

Constitutions are supposed to be enduring documents that set forth fundamental principles. The U.S. Constitution fits this description well. It is remarkably succinct (about 8,700 words) and has been formally amended only twenty-seven times. State constitutions differ sharply from this model. Most are fairly long as a result of being frequently amended. Arizona's constitution weighs in at roughly 28,000 words—a bit longer than average—and it has been amended 125 times as of this writing.

There are several reasons why state constitutions are more frequently altered than the U.S. Constitution. First, some citizens wish to restrict the scope of government activity. To do this, they must put barriers in the constitution because states can ordinarily do anything that is not prohibited. In contrast, the situation is reversed for the federal government. Normally, before it can act there must be an express constitutional authorization. Hence, there is less incentive for national amendments.

Second, **interest groups** use the constitution to preserve group privileges. Because constitutions are more difficult to change than ordinary statutes, "locking" something in the constitution prevents lawmakers from easily interfering with matters of importance to these groups. Most state constitutions are filled with specialized tax exemptions and occupational privileges. Compared to its sister states, Arizona is not the worst offender. Nonetheless, examples can be readily found. Article 26 gives real estate salespersons a constitutional right to prepare select legal documents. Ostrich farmers successfully obtained a tax exemption in 1994 for "livestock, poultry, aquatic animals and honeybees."[15] The article dealing with taxation is actually one of the longer sections simply because it contains so many specific exemptions. The issue is not whether these particular measures are wise, but rather whether they belong in a *constitution* (as opposed to statutes, where detailed matters of this type are more appropriately addressed).[16]

Finally, most state constitutions, including Arizona's, can be amended more easily than the U.S. Constitution. In order to change the national constitution, three-quarters of the states (i.e., thirty-eight) must ratify an amendment approved by two-thirds of both houses of Congress.[17] The difficulty of this process is evidenced by the scant number of amendments that have succeeded. Arizona's easier amending procedures are outlined below.

Amending Procedures

The amending process allows constitutional provisions to be added, removed, or altered. In Arizona, it is always a two-step process. First, the amendment must be formally proposed. There are three different ways that this can be

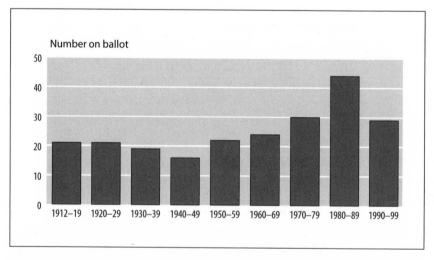

Figure 1.2 Proposed constitutional amendments by decade

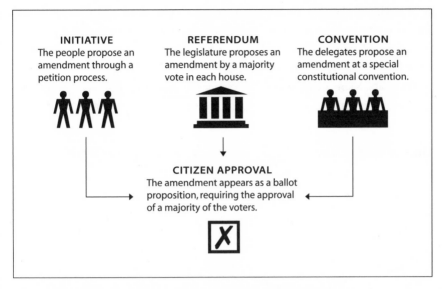

Figure 1.3 Alternative ways to amend the Arizona Constitution

done: (1) the voters can propose amendments using the constitutional initiative process; (2) the legislature can propose amendments using the constitutional **referendum** process; or (3) a constitutional convention can be called to propose amendments. The second step is ratification. No matter how the amendment is originally proposed, it must always be approved by a majority vote of the people. This requirement makes the citizens the ultimate authors of the state's constitution.

The constitutional initiative and referendum processes are detailed in chapter 4, along with other **direct democracy** procedures. These two methods for proposing constitutional amendments have been used frequently throughout Arizona's history. The ink was hardly dry on the state's constitution before amendment fever hit: at the state's very first election in November 1912, five proposed constitutional changes were on the ballot, and all five passed. As of this writing, 226 amendments have been placed before the voters and 125 (55 percent) have been approved. As figure 1.2 indicates, the popularity of constitutional amendments has not diminished over the years.

The third method for amending the constitution—a constitutional convention—has never been used in Arizona. Theoretically, at least, the legislature could call a convention once the people approve its operating rules. If constitutional changes are proposed by the convention delegates, they still must be ratified by voters in the same fashion as referenda and initiatives. Although constitutional conventions were fairly popular with government reformers in the 1960s and '70s, enthusiasm for this procedure has subsided in recent years. Many other states, however, have used this approach to modernize their governments or to revamp overly long and outdated constitutions.

Online Resources

U.S. Constitution:
wwwsecure.law.cornell.edu/constitution/constitution.overview.html

U.S. Supreme Court Opinions:
www.supremecourtus.gov
supct.law.cornell.edu/supct/

Arizona Constitution:
www.sosaz.com/Public_services/Constitution/AZconstitution.htm
www.azleg.state.az.us/const/const.htm

Arizona Revised Statutes:
www.azleg.state.az.us/ars/ars.htm

Arizona Administrative Code:
www.sosaz.com/public_services/Table_of_Contents.htm

Arizona Supreme Court Opinions (recent):
www.supreme.state.az.us/opin/

Arizona Court of Appeals Opinions (recent):
www.state.az.us/co/cindex.htm

Arizona Attorney General Opinions (recent):
www.attorney_general.state.az.us/opinions/opinions_intro.html

Legal Information Institute (state law):
wwwsecure.law.cornell.edu/states/listing.html

2 Constitutional Origins

The Arizona Constitution was written in 1910. Although it has been amended frequently, its core features are very much a product of the distinctive **Progressive** era in which it was written. However, other political forces shaped the constitution as well. European efforts to govern Arizona date back to the sixteenth century. Directly and indirectly, Spanish and Mexican rule, resistance by Native Americans, a lawless frontier period, and an unhappy territorial experience each left a mark on the state's modern government and laws. When it was adopted, the Arizona Constitution was arguably the most radical in the nation. Today, it still offers a real contrast to the U.S. Constitution. To appreciate the differences and understand the logic of the Arizona design, some historical context is necessary.

Arizona's First Governments

The Preterritorial Period

Archaeological evidence establishes that people lived in Arizona for thousands of years before the first Europeans arrived. In fact, Old Oraibi, a Hopi pueblo believed to have been built in A.D. 1150, may be the oldest continuously inhabited settlement in the United States. Arizona's earliest inhabitants lived in small, nomadic groups. As agriculture became more sophisticated in the first millennium A.D., semipermanent settlements began appearing. Eventually, three major cultures emerged: the Anasazi, Hohokam, and Mogollon. They left behind striking architecture and artifacts that suggest a complex social organization. Unfortunately, it is not possible to reconstruct the political institutions of these prehistoric communities with any reliability.[1]

The Spanish period: 1539 to 1821   Spain was the first country to claim sovereignty over Arizona. It established the colony of New Spain on the ruins of the conquered Aztec empire in the early 1500s. Exploration of Arizona began shortly after the first viceroy arrived in Mexico City. A small expedition led by Marcos de Niza was sent to search for the fabled "seven cities of gold." De Niza entered Arizona in 1539.[2] His distant sighting of a glittering city inspired Francisco Vásquez de Coronado to undertake a larger, two-year expedition the following year. De Niza's city turned out to be a Native American pueblo. However, the explorations of de Niza, Coronado, and subsequent explorers provided the first written accounts of Arizona and its indigenous peoples.[3] It also fortified Spain's claim over the entire region.

The early Spanish explorers were followed by Jesuit and Franciscan missionaries, prospectors, and a few hardy ranchers. Permanent Spanish settlements, however, were slow to develop and did not appear until much later. Tubac (1752) and Tucson (1775) are credited with being Arizona's first towns. Actually, they were little more than *presidios,* or forts, and military rule constituted the only real political authority in the region.[4]

Despite Spain's efforts, the colonization of Arizona was never particularly successful. Although other Southwest settlements flourished, at the peak of Spanish control little more than one thousand Hispanics lived in all of Arizona.[5] This was partially due to the region's harsh climate, arid landscape, and limited resources. However, the presence of hostile Native Americans, especially the formidable Apaches, effectively prevented colonization north of the Gila River.[6] Even in the more heavily fortified southern areas, bloody clashes with Apache raiding parties persisted for over two centuries. Only toward the end of Spanish rule did the government gain some measure of control. It instituted a pacification program in 1790 that provided rations, strong liquor, and inferior firearms to the Apaches who settled in "peace camps" adjacent to the forts. The program was a calculated effort to undermine Apache morale. It did bring relative peace to the region for the thirty years that it lasted.[7]

The Mexican period: 1821 to 1848   Political control of Arizona passed from Spain to Mexico when the Spanish government recognized Mexican independence in 1821. Surprisingly, this development had the effect of *reducing* the

Hispanic population in Arizona, because Spain's departure terminated the Apache pacification program. The Apache raids resumed with a vengeance, and the Hispanic population, concentrated in Tucson, dwindled as the settlers abandoned their homes and crops. The new Mexican government simply lacked the financial and military resources to control the Apaches; the region was too remote; and the government was plagued with chronic instability and civil wars. Epidemics and water problems further contributed to the deteriorating conditions on the Arizona frontier.

When Mexico became a federal republic in 1824, southern Arizona was initially made part of the state of Occidente. Although short-lived, the Constitution of Occidente was Arizona's first state constitution. Nominally, at least, it was democratic. The constitution declared that the state's government would be "republican, representative, popular, and federal" and prohibited power from being "centered in one person or group."[8] It established a three-branch government not unlike today's state government and guaranteed many fundamental rights to the citizens. Religious freedom, however, was not one of these rights. The Constitution of Occidente firmly declared that the state's religion would be Roman Catholicism and that "no other whatsoever will be tolerated."[9] In 1831, Occidente was split into two separate states, and southern Arizona became part of the Mexican state of Sonora.[10] (Northern Arizona was essentially an uncolonized no-man's-land, nominally claimed by Mexico but actually controlled by various Native American peoples.)

The reality of political life on the remote Arizona frontier was far more primitive and less democratic than the formal language of the Occidente Constitution suggests. Although Tucson and Tubac now had nonmilitary governments, they were quite rudimentary because the populations were low. (A census taken by the Sonoran government in 1848 reported a mere 249 people living in Tubac and 760 in Tucson.)[11] In the beginning, the local governments of Tucson and Tubac consisted of only an elected mayor (*alcalde*) and a treasurer-attorney. By 1831, the Mexican government had determined that the towns were too small to warrant even a mayor, and the top position was downgraded to justice of the peace (*juez de paz*). Because all the positions required literacy, they tended to be monopolized by a few families on the Mexican frontier.[12] Despite the egalitarian language of the Occidente Constitution, the Spanish political heritage was more elitist. Government in Hispanic Arizona contrasted sharply with the participatory democracies that had long been flourishing in the eastern United States.

Early U.S. control: 1848 to 1863   The United States Congress declared war on Mexico in 1846. Officially, the war was triggered by disputes over the Texas border and private claims of American citizens. In reality the United States was caught up in an expansionist fever known as **Manifest Destiny**. It wanted access to the Pacific Ocean for eastern trade. War became inevitable when Mexico refused to sell California. The uneven military contest ended with the signing of the **Treaty of Guadalupe Hidalgo** on 2 February 1848. In return for $15 million, Mexico ceded more than one-third of its national territory. In addition to acquiring all of Arizona north of the Gila River (Tucson and the rest of southern Arizona remained part of Mexico), the United States acquired the modern states of California, Nevada, Utah, and portions of Colorado, New Mexico, and Wyoming as shown in figure 2.1.

Following acquisition by the United States, Arizona and New Mexico were combined into a single large territory, known as the Territory of New Mexico (fig. 2.2). In contrast, California—with its newly discovered gold—became a full-fledged state almost immediately in 1850. However, Arizoa was a more dubious prize. At the time, it was chiefly regarded as an obstacle on the way to California. Few Americans other than mountain men, prospectors, and soldiers had ever visited the region. Furthermore, the land proved no more hos-

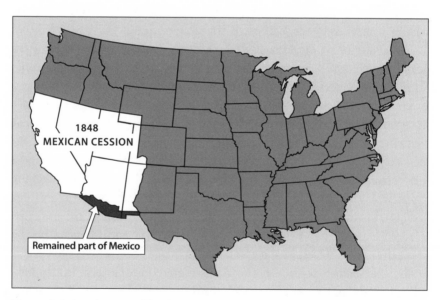

Figure 2.1 Land acquired by the United States in the war with Mexico

Figure 2.2 The Territory of New Mexico

pitable to the American settlers than it had to the Hispanics. Indian wars continued for four more decades.

Despite Arizona's unpromising future, the ink was hardly dry on the Treaty of Guadalupe Hidalgo when the United States pressured Mexico to relinquish even more territory: influential businessmen wanted the additional land to build a southern (all-weather) railroad from New Orleans to San Diego. The favored route along the 32nd parallel was south of the Gila River in Mexican territory. Accordingly, in 1853, railroad promoter James Gadsden was dispatched to secretly negotiate the purchase of additional land. Four of the five deals that Gadsden was authorized to make would have given Arizona beachfront property—that is, access to the Gulf of California.[13] However, Mexican dictator Antonio López de Santa Anna would agree to only a minimal cession of land. The U.S. Senate (which had to approve Gadsden's treaty) wound up reducing the Gadsden deal even further. In the end, the United States paid $10 million for 30,000 square miles of Mexican territory that included Tucson. Many members of Congress viewed the purchase as an exorbitant sum for worthless desert land. One congressman even quoted Kit Carson's description of the territory as "so desolate, desert, and God-forsaken that a wolf could not make a living on it."[14]

The **Gadsden Purchase** thus established Arizona's modern boundary with Mexico. As figure 2.2 illustrates, the southern boundary angles northward to the west to give Mexico a land bridge to Baja California and to deny the United States access to the Gulf of California. Mexican troops left Tucson after the new border was surveyed, and U.S. soldiers formally raised the American flag in November 1856.[15]

While many residents of the Gadsden Purchase welcomed U.S. control,[16] they soon became unhappy with the territorial arrangement. The government was located hundreds of miles away in Santa Fe, and there were no local courts or lawmen to maintain order in the remote region. In addition to continuing Apache troubles, Tucson and other southern settlements became easy prey for fugitives escaping from Mexico and neighboring states. Accordingly, in 1856, the residents began petitioning Congress for separate territorial status. President James Buchanan took up their cause, reporting to Congress in 1859 that Arizona was "practically destitute of government, of laws, or of any regular administration of justice" and that "murder, rapine, and other crimes are committed with impunity."[17]

Congress, however, failed to act. The frustrated residents of the Gadsden Purchase region then took matters into their own hands. They gathered in Tucson and formed their own territorial government in 1860, complete with a constitution, a governor, and other elected officials.[18] It was short-lived. When the Civil War struck, the leaders of the self-proclaimed government applied for admission to the southern Confederacy. Many had come from the South and were sympathetic to its cause. However, the decision to secede was also motivated by frustration with Congress and renewed feelings of insecurity following the sudden departure of federal troops at the onset of the war.

Confederate troops entered Tucson in 1861, and John R. Baylor, an army officer, declared himself governor. His proclamation described conditions in the territory as being "little short of general anarchy" due to the lack of law, order, and protection.[19] Confederate president Jefferson Davis approved Baylor's action, and Arizona was officially made part of the Confederacy on 14 February 1862—coincidentally, fifty years to the day before Arizona became a state. The Confederate flag thus became the fourth national flag to be raised in Tucson.

However, Arizona's Confederate status was also short-lived. A small group of Union soldiers skirmished with Confederate scouts near Picacho Pass in a brief, indecisive battle that resulted in three deaths.[20] (During the Civil War years, the Apaches inflicted more casualties on Confederate and Union troops in Arizona than either army inflicted on the other.) By June 1862, a larger contingent of Union troops had entered Tucson without resistance, placed the city under martial rule, and reclaimed Arizona for the Union. Although the Confederate episode had little effect on the outcome of the Civil War, it arguably delayed Arizona's subsequent admission as a state.

The Territorial Period: 1863 to 1912

The fear that Arizona would again fall into Confederate hands, plus the discovery of precious metals in the region, finally pushed Congress into granting Arizona separate territorial status. On 24 February 1863, President Abraham Lincoln signed the **Organic Act**, which officially established the Arizona Territory. A federal census taken in 1860 reported a mere 2,423 non-Indians living in the entire region. Over seventy percent were male, reflecting the demographics typical of the frontier.[21]

Arizona's territorial government formally began when the first governor, John Goodwin, took the oath of office at Navajo Springs on 29 December 1863. He and a small party of officials arrived under army escort from Santa Fe. They continued on to Fort Whipple, which briefly served as the territory's first capital. (Tucson, the obvious choice, was ruled out because of its Confederate sympathies.) In the summer of 1864, the capital moved to newly founded Prescott, then to Tucson (1867), then back to Prescott (1877), and finally to its permanent home in Phoenix (1889). The frequent moves were instigated by local promoters seeking to spur hometown development. They were usually accompanied by cries of bribery and corruption. (Later on, the U.S. government demanded that Arizona's capital stay put for fifteen years as a condition of statehood.)[22]

The Organic Act expressly contemplated that Arizona's territorial condition would be temporary. After all, neighboring Nevada had become a state in 1864, and California had been a state since 1850. As it turned out, Arizona remained trapped in territorial status for forty-nine years and was the last of the forty-eight contiguous states to be admitted. It was a bad situation, for many reasons.

First, the territory's residents had few political rights. Most notably, they had no say in the selection of the territory's chief officials: the governor, territorial secretary, marshal, district attorney, judges, and Indian agents were all *appointed* by the president of the United States. Adding to the friction, most Arizona residents were Democrats, while the appointed territorial officials were typically Republicans, reflecting the makeup of the federal government during this time. Although the territory had a locally elected legislature, its powers were limited, and its laws were subject to congressional approval. In the final analysis, Arizona was ruled by the federal government. Territorial residents, however, had no say in the election of that government either. Because Arizona was not a state, its residents were ineligible to vote in presidential elections and they had no voting representation in Congress. In many ways the situation resembled colonial America during British rule. Not surprisingly, similar political resentments arose.

Second, the territorial government was weak and at times corrupt. Many of the appointed governors were **carpetbaggers**—opportunists from other states who had no real interest in the territory. They typically got their position as a political favor and did not last long in the job. Given the primitive conditions in the territory—the "governor's mansion" was a simple log cabin (fig. 2.3)— it is not surprising that many of the eastern appointees sought a quick exit. For example, Arizona's first governor was appointed by President Lincoln after losing his House seat from Maine.[23] Within two years, Goodwin left Arizona, never to return.[24] His successor followed a similar course. Some territorial governors, such as John C. Frémont, devoted more attention to private investments than to the job of governing. Frémont (who took the position in 1878 because of financial difficulties) spent most of his brief tenure *outside* of Arizona, pursuing his own business affairs. Frémont's case was certainly extreme. However, the territory's governors often had financial stakes in the mining, railroad, or other commercial ventures that they actively promoted.[25] This led to **conflicts of interest** and allegations of more serious corruption.

Some territorial governors behaved in unorthodox ways, reflecting the primitive conditions of the frontier. For example, when Arizona's third governor, Anson Safford, became enmeshed in an ugly marital scandal, he simply ordered the territorial legislature to enact a law that dissolved his marriage. Safford then promptly signed the bill in his official capacity as governor.[26] The territory's seventh governor, Conrad Zulick, had to be rescued from house arrest in Mexico before he could be sworn in. (He apparently first learned of his **gubernatorial** appointment during his late-night rescue.)[27]

The other two branches of government were no more illustrious. Throughout the territorial period, legislators were accused of embezzlement,

Figure 2.3 The governor's mansion (Prescott, Arizona)

expense account padding, misappropriation of funds, and other financial irregularities. The Thirteenth Legislature became known as the "thieving thirteenth" when a grand jury concluded that it had exceeded its $4,000 operating expense limit by over $46,000.[28] More seriously, territorial legislators were notorious for taking bribes from mining and railroad interests seeking to evade taxes and government regulation. Sometimes governors served as middlemen. For example, Governor Safford once returned $20,000 of a $25,000 payoff to the Southern Pacific Company with a candid note that the legislature was not as expensive to "fix" as the railroad president had anticipated.[29] From the 1880s onward, Arizona's two major railroads and copper companies were able to block nearly all legislation adverse to their interests.

The judicial branch was not above scandal either. Competent judges were scarce and some were simply corrupt. (One justice of the peace purportedly stocked his ranch with cattle that the defendants donated in lieu of exorbitant cash fines.)[30] Judges, like the territorial governors, often had extensive private investments that cast doubt on their impartiality. Many had worked for mining and railroad companies as corporate attorneys before their appointment to the bench. When they enjoined labor strikes, they were perceived as corporate puppets. Above all, the court system was so primitive and understaffed that vigilante justice flourished throughout the territorial period.

Finally, some blame for the poor civic order must be assigned to the citizens themselves. Violence and lawlessness had long been part of Arizona's culture. The territorial period was no exception. When the Apaches were finally subjugated in 1886, rustlers, cattlemen, sheep ranchers, and farmers took up the slack by fighting over land claims and the scarce resources of the open range. In 1887, the lawless Hashknife cowboys (employees of the massive Aztec Land and Cattle Company) drove Mormon farmers from their homes in Heber and Wilford.[31] About the same time, the Pleasant Valley War between cattlemen and sheep ranchers chalked up thirty to fifty casualties. Mining boom towns, such as Tombstone, sprang up overnight and attracted an equally lethal mix of prospectors, speculators, and gamblers. The infamous gunfight at the O.K. Corral shocked the nation; President Chester Arthur even threatened to send federal troops to Cochise County if order were not restored. Saloons and casinos were not confined to mining towns either. They multiplied throughout Arizona Territory and also contributed to widespread public lawlessness. Ethnic clashes among Chinese, Hispanic, and Anglo laborers intensified toward the end of the century and sporadically erupted into violence. Finally, large-scale land and stock frauds were commonplace throughout the territorial period. Undoubtedly, the newspapers and pulp fiction exaggerated Arizona's Wild West reputation. Nonetheless, by the century's end, many Arizonans viewed statehood as the only means of salvation.

The Push for Statehood

Federal Opposition

The U.S. Constitution gives Congress the authority to determine whether a territory should become a state.[32] Arizona began applying for admission as early as 1872. In 1891, it even drafted a state constitution, which Congress ignored. There are several reasons why the federal government remained cool to Arizona statehood right to the very end:

1. Arizona was sparsely populated. The federal census of 1900 reported a mere 122,931 residents. (Statehood advocates argued that the census had overlooked prospectors and persons fleeing to California beaches to escape the summer heat.)[33] In any event, Congress believed there were

simply insufficient people to sustain the burdens of statehood. Some law-makers felt that it would be unfair to give equal voting power in the U.S. Senate to such a small population. (The average state population at this time was over one million.)

2. The region's long-term economic prospects were not promising. Congress viewed Arizona's agricultural industry as "precarious" due to its dependency upon irrigation systems that had already reached their limits. (The federal government's ambitious Reclamation Act to bring water and hydroelectric power to the West was not enacted until 1902; the Roosevelt Dam was not completed until 1911.) Many in Congress viewed Arizona as a giant mining camp that was likely to disappear when the ore played out.[34]

3. Arizona's politics were out of sync with Washington, D.C. At the turn of the century, most Arizona voters were conservative Democrats, reflecting their southern origins. The federal government, however, was controlled by Republicans. Not surprisingly, Congress was unenthusiastic about admitting a state that would presumably send two Democratic senators to Washington. In addition, the territory's strong support for free silver in the great monetary controversy of the day was also unpopular with the Republican majority. Finally, the Civil War was still fresh in people's memories, and the territory's former disloyalty did not help its statehood cause.

4. Arizona's demographics did not fit Congress's Anglo-Saxon, Protestant ideal. Many voiced concerns about the high percentage of Arizona residents who were non-English-speaking Hispanics. Nearly one-fourth of the population was foreign-born—a figure well above the national average.[35] Additionally, most of the state's residents were Roman Catholic, and a sizeable number were Mormon. This was at a time when national prejudice against both religions ran high.

5. The Arizona statehood movement had a powerful opponent in Senator Albert J. Beveridge. The Republican from Indiana was the chairman of the U.S. Senate's committee on territories. In 1902, he toured Oklahoma, New Mexico, and Arizona to determine whether these remaining territories were finally ready for statehood. According to frustrated local accounts, he spent a total of three days whizzing through Arizona and seeking out the worst features of the region. Beveridge was apparently shocked by the territory's arid terrain, by the saloons in Bisbee, and by

the region's high illiteracy rate (purportedly 29 percent).[36] He also was disturbed by widespread political corruption within the territory—a concern that was reinforced when a bribery attempt was later made to win his own support on statehood.[37] Not surprisingly, Beveridge's initial report to the U.S. Senate painted an unflattering picture of Arizona. It singled out the territory's saloons and gambling houses, which, Beveridge noted, operated day and night and even on Sundays.[38] Simply put, Beveridge regarded Arizona as morally unfit for statehood.

Beveridge successfully killed statehood bills in 1902 and 1903. However, as pressure continued to mount, he supported a compromise plan to admit Arizona and New Mexico as a single state. The "jointure" proposal resolved the issue of insufficient population. More cleverly, it eliminated Congress's fear of a Democratic state because New Mexico was more populous *and* Republican. To placate Arizona, Beveridge proposed that the new state be called "Arizona the Great," and he delivered a rousing speech that lauded its potential.[39] Although New Mexicans favored the jointure idea, Arizonans were furious. When President Theodore Roosevelt supported the plan, angry Phoenix officials changed the name of Roosevelt Street to Cleveland Street in protest.[40] (It was subsequently changed back.) The issue of joint admission was put to the residents of both territories in 1906. Although New Mexicans approved, Arizona voters wound up rejecting joint admission by a decisive margin.[41]

Congress Passes the Enabling Act

By the end of the decade, even Senator Beveridge could not stop the push for statehood. In 1910, there were 204,354 people living in the territory—not a large number, but more than the population of three existing states.[42] Arizona and New Mexico's disenfranchised status was becoming a national embarrassment. Accordingly, Congress passed the **Enabling Act,** which set forth specific conditions for attaining statehood. The Enabling Act imposed many conditions that were similar to the enabling acts of other western territories. For example, it required the territory to draft a constitution. This, of course, was reasonable. However, at least two requirements were atypical.

First, the Enabling Act required Arizona's constitution to be personally approved by the president even though the U.S. Constitution does not give the president a role in the admission of new states. Nonetheless, the Republican majority in Congress wanted President William Howard Taft, a fellow

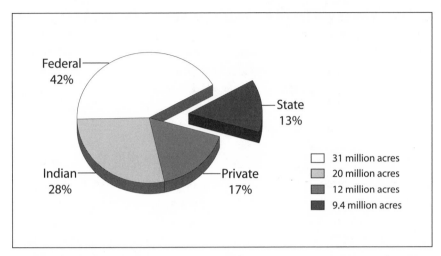

Figure 2.4 Arizona land ownership (2000). Source: Arizona State Land Department.

Republican, to serve as an additional check on the anticipated radicalism of the Arizona Democrats. As detailed below, this requirement nearly proved fatal to Arizona's prolonged quest for statehood.

Second, the Enabling Act imposed unprecedented restrictions on the state's management of public lands. Prior to statehood, the federal government owned most of the land in Arizona. (As figure 2.4 reflects, it remains the state's largest landowner by a wide margin.) However, it was the national government's longstanding custom to transfer a portion of its land to the state when it achieved statehood. Unfortunately, by 1910, many of the older states had already squandered their valuable land dowries, selling off the land at corruptly low prices.[43] Senator Beveridge did not want the same thing to occur in Arizona. Accordingly, although the federal government generously gave the state over twelve million acres—more land than was given to any state other than Alaska—it sharply restricted the state's use and disposition of the land.[44] The bulk of these restrictions are still in force today, and they continue to generate controversy.

The Enabling Act designates the vast majority of the land as school trust land. This means that the state must manage the land for the exclusive benefit of its public schools. It may sell or lease the land, but all proceeds must go into a special school account. Controversy arises whenever the state wants to use the land in a way that would not earn maximum income for the schools. For example, it cannot simply convert the land into a public park. And when the highway department needed some trust land for a right of way, the U.S. Supreme Court ruled that the state had to pay for it.[45] In essence, it was required to buy the land from itself—at full market value. The issue has become heated once again as environmentalists seek ways to preserve some state trust lands from development without having to pay prohibitive purchase prices.

The Enabling Act also imposes strict procedures that the state must follow when selling or leasing trust land. This is to prevent the state from giving away the land at corruptly low prices. In recent years, state officials have complained that the restrictions are too rigid. In particular, they have wanted to be able to "swap" parcels of public land for private land. They claim that having the power to trade will enable the state to acquire valuable land without having to pay high purchase prices. Although the federal government relaxed its ban on swaps years ago, Arizona voters have thus far refused to go along.[46] (Their approval is *also* needed because Enabling Act restrictions are embedded in the Arizona Constitution and the constitution can be changed only with voter approval.)[47] Apparently, modern Arizonans share Senator Beveridge's distrust of state land management. It should be noted, however, that as a result of the stringent restrictions, Arizona retains more of its original trust land (9.4 million acres) than any other state.[48]

The Framers of the Arizona Constitution

Arizona voters elected fifty-two men to draft the state's constitution in 1910. Just as the Republican Congress had feared, forty-one were Democrats. More significantly, most of the Democrats were sympathetic to the Progressive and labor agendas.

The Progressive agenda   Progressivism was a **bipartisan** national reform movement that emerged in the late 1890s. It primarily attracted white, middle-class citizens. Progressives contended that government had become hopelessly corrupted by monopolistic corporations, trusts, and wealthy individuals. They advocated sweeping structural changes to give ordinary citizens greater political rights. Five specific political reforms were especially high on the Progressive agenda:

1. The **secret ballot** (to enable employees to vote without undue pressure from their employers).
2. The **direct primary** (to enable the citizens, rather than the party elite, to select the candidates for the ballot).
3. The initiative (to enable the citizens to make their own laws).
4. The referendum (to enable the citizens to reject laws passed by the legislature).
5. The **recall** (to enable the citizens to remove elected officials from office before the end of their terms).[49]

The labor agenda   During roughly the same period, a national labor movement was also calling for political change. It attracted different classes of people: principally blue-collar workers, minorities, recent immigrants, and the poor. The movement's major objective was to improve working conditions through legislation. At the time, the workplace was virtually unregulated. There were few wage, hour, child labor, or safety laws anywhere in the country. Moreover, in the aftermath of the Industrial Revolution working conditions were generally harsh. And the conditions in Arizona's mines—the territory's major industry in terms of employment—were among the worst.[50]

In most parts of the country, the Progressive and labor movements were fairly separate. However, they briefly allied in Arizona when the state constitution was being drafted. To prevent labor organizers from sending their own delegates to the constitutional convention, the Democrats promised to support *both* the labor and the Progressive cause. Interestingly, the labor movement was influential in Arizona for only the brief interlude that happened to coincide with the writing of the state's constitution. Both before and since 1910, internal conflicts and a powerful employers' lobby effectively reduced labor's political clout. (The infamous deportation of striking mineworkers from Bisbee in 1917[51] and the passage of a **right-to-work** amendment to the constitution in 1946[52] solidified Arizona's reputation as an "anti-labor" state.) In short, for organized labor, 1910 was an anomaly.

The constitutional convention of 1910   The fifty-two delegates who gathered at the territorial capital in Phoenix chose George W. P. Hunt to serve as the convention's president. Hunt had only an eighth-grade education and had arrived in Arizona by burro seeking gold in the summer of 1881. He became a successful small businessman and served in the territorial legislature. In a period of considerable corruption, Hunt had a reputation for honesty and supporting the cause of the common man. Upon statehood, he became Arizona's first governor and went on to win a record six more terms in office.

The framers began drafting the constitution in October. While they labored, newspapers in Arizona and around the country closely monitored their activity. The new constitution was a blank slate; it offered a unique opportunity for putting the entire Progressive agenda into effect. This worried many prominent public officials. Just the year before, President Taft had visited Arizona and ominously warned the territory not to pursue too radical a course. Some newspaper editorials and political cartoons took the warning seriously and fretted that the framers were jeopardizing statehood for a "radical, socialistic constitution." The majority of delegates stubbornly ignored these warnings. On 9 December 1910 they formally completed their task, voting in favor of their constitution by a nearly **partisan** vote of 40 to 12.

The Constitution of 1910

In many respects, the constitution that the framers produced was quite traditional. They borrowed heavily from such obvious sources as the U.S. Constitution and the constitutions of sister states. For example, it is no coincidence that Arizona has three separate branches of government and a two-chambered legislature. And much of Arizona's Declaration of Rights (Article 2) was lifted from the constitution of Washington state. However, in other respects the constitution *was* radical and original. First, it was arguably the most Progressive of the day: the secret ballot, the direct primary, the initiative, the referendum, and the recall *all* were adopted, along with many other structural features designed to reduce the power of elected officials and increase the role of the citizenry.[53] An elected **Corporation Commission** with sweeping regulatory powers was established to oversee the railroads, and the constitution firmly declared that "monopolies and trusts shall never be allowed in this state."[54] Hunt quite aptly pronounced it a "people's constitution."[55]

Second, the Democratic drafters also kept their pledge to labor. They included an entire article devoted to protecting the interests of workers. Article 18 guaranteed an eight-hour work day for government workers, restricted child labor, banned employment contracts that gave employers immunity for their **negligence,** and directed the legislature to enact workers' compensation laws. For their day, these were cutting-edge reforms. The constitution also

Figure 2.5 The constitutional convention (Phoenix, 1910)

established a state mine inspector to monitor the safety of the state's largest industry. Significantly, the framers made it an *elective* office to ensure that the people—as opposed to the mines' **lobbyists**—would be choosing the watchdog. Finally, they included several provisions in the constitution to ensure that injured workers and others would have full recourse in the courts.[56]

The Progressive and labor influences are unmistakable. However, the state's deeper past left its mark on the constitution as well. For example, multiple English-language requirements were mandated by a U.S. Congress that was uneasy with Arizona's Hispanic heritage.[57] Nonetheless, evidence of Spanish rule can still be found in the state's law. For example, the new constitution tersely rejected English water law,[58] just as the first territorial legislature had done in 1865. English rules had never taken hold in Arizona because of the territory's Spanish origins as well as its arid conditions.[59] Other Hispanic legal influences can still be found in the statutory and **common law** of the state. The clearest example is Arizona's **community property** law. Community property gives married women coequal ownership of marital property. It comes from the Roman legal tradition and was brought to the Southwest by

Spain. In contrast, most American states inherited the more paternalistic property laws of England.[60] These states generally did not give married women comparable rights until recent times.

Arizona's Confederate sympathies (a quarter of the constitution's framers were originally from the South) may have been responsible for several racist proposals that were openly debated at the state constitutional convention. For example, the framers seriously considered a provision that would have mandated separate schools for whites and African-Americans. The measure narrowly failed only because some delegates felt that it did not cover enough minority races, and others believed the territory's statutes already adequately mandated segregated schools.[61] Similarly, although the framers also rejected a proposed ban on interracial marriage, it too was deemed underinclusive and unnecessary because the ban was already part of the state's marriage statutes.[62] Finally, the delegates debated labor provisions that would have discriminated against immigrants and non-English-speaking workers. In the end, they decided to ban noncitizens from public works projects but rejected broader prohibitions.[63]

Arizona's prolonged conflict with Native Americans also left its mark on the state's constitution and laws. The federal government brought an end to the Apache wars in 1886. However, the Enabling Act sharply limited Arizona's authority over Indian affairs.[64] Today, Arizona must coexist with twenty-one tribal governments, as well as with a substantial, continuing federal presence. Not surprisingly, this has produced many intergovernmental conflicts over such matters as taxation, land use, water rights, law enforcement, and natural resources. The ongoing controversy over reservation casinos is but the latest manifestation of this tension.[65]

Arizona's territorial experience also left its mark on the state constitution. The period's rampant corruption helped make the Progressives' case for reform. However, it also inspired remedies targeted at specific local scandals. For example, one constitutional provision prohibits public officials from accepting free rail passes—a routine practice of the territorial period.[66] The problem of absentee governors, such as Frémont, was addressed with an unusual remedy: whenever Arizona governors leave the state, all their powers temporarily pass to the official next in line of succession (typically the secretary of state). The provision takes effect even when the governor travels on official state business.[67] The constitution also prohibits the legislature from

Figure 2.6 Official seals. Arizona's first territorial seal featured the territory's natural beauty and included a giant saguaro in the foreground. The seal adopted upon statehood emphasized Roosevelt Dam and burgeoning industries.

enacting "special laws" that apply only to particular persons, businesses, or localities. The examples listed in the constitution are traceable to specific territorial abuses. For example, subsection 1 prohibits the legislature from granting divorces—evoking the Governor Safford scandal. Another subsection bars the legislature from "granting to any corporation, association, or individual, any special or exclusive privileges, immunities, or franchises." Again, this was a routine occurrence during the territorial period.[68]

It would be misleading, however, to suggest that the Arizona Constitution was solely influenced by the region's colorful past. To the contrary, most of the framers were very oriented toward the future. They wanted to overcome the state's desert image and recast Arizona as an irrigated oasis and modern industrial state. This is best captured by the surprisingly lengthy debate over the state's official seal. As shown in figure 2.6, the seal depicts Roosevelt Dam, irrigated fields and orchards, a quartz mill, a miner, and grazing cattle.[69] Conspicuously absent was the cactus that graced the first territorial seal,[70] or other symbols that would identify Arizona with the Southwest. There was applause when the new seal was defended as an effort "to get away from cactus, Gila monsters, and rattlesnakes" and depict the *industries* that would put Arizona on the map.[71] After heated debate, the delegates wound up dumping the cactus by a vote of 28 to 11.

Finally, in at least one key respect, the forward-looking framers lost their nerve. Despite intense lobbying, they denied women the right to vote (except in school elections). By this time, most of the other western states had already given women the vote. Wyoming had even established women's **suffrage** in 1869 when it was still a territory. One explanation for Arizona's resistance is that the territorial women had been vigorously lobbying the convention for the prohibition of alcohol. Presumably, the framers feared that the state would go dry if women were allowed to vote.[72]

The Taft Veto and Its Aftermath

Although the people of Arizona approved the 1910 constitution by a margin of more than 3 to 1, the federal government was less enthusiastic. Congress reluctantly sent the constitution on to President Taft for review. Taft carried out his prior threat. He was hostile to most of the direct democracy provisions of the Progressive agenda. However, Taft vetoed Arizona statehood over a *single* feature that he found especially offensive: the citizens' right to recall judges from office before the end of their terms. Taft believed that the recall of judges would destroy the independence of the judiciary. More specifically, he argued that

1. Recall would put pressure on judges to make popular, rather than proper, decisions. (Taft reasoned that judges are not like other elected officials; they are supposed to apply the law and protect the rights of minorities even when such outcomes are not favored by the majority.)
2. Recall would be unfair to judges. (Taft objected because citizens could precipitously remove a judge on the basis of a single unpopular decision when their passions were running high. Taft favored **impeachment** and periodic elections over recall, because the former allowed a hearing and the latter allowed the judge's entire tenure to be taken into consideration.)
3. Recall would be abused by powerful interest groups and the media. (Taft reasoned that these entities had the resources to stir up the people against judges who were opposed to their agendas.)
4. The threat of recall would discourage honorable persons from becoming judges. (Taft reasoned that the prospect of arbitrary removal would make the office less attractive to principled individuals.)

Interestingly, Taft knew that his veto was futile: that Arizona could always reinstate the judicial recall once it attained statehood. Nonetheless, he felt so deeply about the issue that he single-handedly obstructed the territory's prolonged campaign for admission. Taft's veto statement remains one of the most unusual vetoes of any president, and it stands as a striking rebuttal to the philosophy of Progressivism. (The entire veto is reproduced in the Appendix.)

After Taft's veto, Arizona voters agreed to remove judicial recall from the constitution. With this single alteration, the state constitution was then endorsed by both Congress and Taft. Arizona officially became the nation's forty-eighth state on 14 February 1912. When the news arrived by telegraph, jubilant Arizonans celebrated statehood with sirens, fireworks, and parades.[73]

The story, however, does not end in February. A presidential election took place the following November. Four men were running for the office: Taft (who was seeking a second term), Woodrow Wilson (a Democrat), Teddy Roosevelt (who was now running as a Progressive with Arizona's old nemesis, Senator Beveridge), and Eugene Debs (a socialist). Arizona voted in the presidential election for the very first time. The state gave Taft the fewest votes of the four and helped Wilson win the election.

Figure 2.7 President Taft signs Arizona's statehood bill

On the state level there were other interesting developments at the 1912 election. Arizona voters decisively approved a constitutional referendum to restore judicial recall to the state's constitution![74] The vote pointedly signaled the state's independence from Washington. Additionally, the issue of female suffrage was put on the ballot as well. The male voters approved this amendment by a 2 to 1 margin. Thus, although Arizona women did not have the full suffrage from the *very* beginning, they did have it nine months later—and well ahead of the Nineteenth Amendment to the U.S. Constitution in 1920. Altogether, Arizonans made five changes to their brand new constitution, launching an amending habit that continues to this day.

Online Resources

Treaty of Guadalupe Hidalgo:
www.yale.edu/lawweb/avalon/diplomacy/guadhida.htm

Arizona Enabling Act:
www.azleg.state.az.us/const/enabling.pdf

Arizona Department of Library, Archives and Public Records:
www.dlapr.lib.az.us/archives/index.html (History and Archives Division)
www.dlapr.lib.az.us/archives/azcollinks.htm (links to Arizona history web sites)

Arizona Historical Society:
w3.arizona.edu/~azhist/general.htm (Southern Arizona Division)
www.tempe.gov/ahs/ (Central Arizona Division)
w3.arizona.edu/~azhist/nadgeneral.htm (Northern Arizona Division)

Arizona State Museum:
www.statemuseum.arizona.edu/

Sharlot Hall Museum:
www.sharlot.org/

Journal of Arizona History:
www.library.arizona.edu/swetc/jah.html

3 The Legislative Branch

A common misconception about the Arizona State Legislature is that it is a clone of the U.S. Congress. Certainly, it resembles that body in many ways. For example, the main functions of the two legislatures are quite similar. Both bodies make laws and propose constitutional amendments, control public spending, and monitor the other two branches of government. Nonetheless, there are some significant differences. The men who drafted Arizona's constitution in 1910 were reformers. Their goal in designing the state's legislative branch was to fix perceived weaknesses in the Congress, not duplicate them. Above all, they sought to make the legislative branch more responsive to the average citizen. Whether they succeeded is quite debatable. But in trying, they did create a legislature that differs from the federal model in many interesting ways. Accordingly, this chapter will explore the structure and function of the Arizona legislature, emphasizing the underlying logic of its distinctive features.

Legislative Structure

We can study the state legislature from different vantage points. At the farthest distance it resembles most of the world's lawmaking bodies in two fundamental respects. First, it is a collective decision-making body. That means that it can take official action only when a majority or more of its ninety members agree. (In contrast, officials in the executive branch and many judges have the power to act alone.) Second, it is a representative body. Arizona legislators are elected from small districts throughout the entire state.

This enables the legislative branch to reflect the diverse interests of different regions and constituencies.

As we move in closer, the state legislature bears a strong resemblance to the U.S. Congress. Most strikingly, it is **bicameral,** or two-chambered. Even the names of Arizona's two houses are copied: the smaller chamber is called the senate and the larger chamber is called the house of representatives. Like Congress, the state houses operate fairly independently of each other but must concur in order to pass laws. Although this duplication is somewhat inefficient, it provides a check against hasty or corrupt legislation. (With the sole exception of Nebraska, all of the nation's states have bicameral legislatures.)[1]

It is only in the close-up view that the distinctive features of the state legislature begin to emerge. This is not surprising. When Arizona drafters sat down to design the legislative branch, they did not have a totally free hand. The U.S. Constitution required them to create a "republican form of government."[2] Today, we call this type of government a **representative democracy** (see chapter 4). The Progressive drafters of Arizona's constitution were not as enthusiastic about representative democracy as were the nation's Founding Fathers. Arizona's drafters favored a greater role for the citizenry. However, they feared that if they deviated too much from the national norm, Congress would reject Arizona's statehood application. Accordingly, as outlined below, they made many subtle changes that were designed to make state legislators more accountable.

Legislative Elections

Length of terms   In Arizona, all state legislators have simultaneous two-year terms. This contrasts with the federal government (where senators serve for staggered six-year terms) and most state governments (where senators serve for four years). Short, simultaneous terms can make a legislature more responsive to the people in at least two ways. First, they permit voters to dismiss all the **incumbents** at once, thus producing an immediate change in government. Arizonans can do this at the **general election,** which takes place in November of every even-numbered year. All seats in the state legislature are up for reelection at this time. Second, short terms encourage legislators to be more attuned to their constituencies. In essence, they are continually running for reelection. A legislator on such a short leash can't afford to act too independently of the voters' wishes. (In contrast, a U.S. senator has far greater freedom in the early years of the term. Unless an issue is unusually salient, constituents will not even remember their senator's vote down the road at reelection time.)

Short legislative terms have some downsides, however. A degree of experience, stability, and continuity are sacrificed when both houses have short terms. The other two branches of government—which have longer terms—tend to take advantage of the situation. Permanent legislative staffers and lobbyists become more powerful. Frequent elections also place added fund raising burdens on legislators. This in turn, increases the influence of interest groups (the primary source of campaign money). Finally, some argue that it is not desirable to make the legislature *too* responsive to the citizens' will, since voters can be uninformed, short-sighted, or impulsive. This is one reason why the nation's Founding Fathers counterbalanced short terms in the House with long terms in the Senate.

Term limits   In 1992, the voters added **term limits** to the state constitution.[3] No legislator may now serve more than four consecutive terms (i.e., eight years). This is not a lifetime ban, as it is in California. An Arizona legislator only has to sit out a two-year term and the cycle begins anew. Alternatively, the legislator could simply run for the other house. The fact that the two chambers have identical electoral cycles makes this quite feasible.

Term limits remain controversial. Proponents argue that the limits will bring fresh blood and new ideas into the legislature; increase electoral competition by creating more open races; remove career politicians who become too detached from the needs of the people; lessen the impact of campaign contributions (which ordinarily go to incumbents); and loosen the grip of lobbyists and special interests who develop cozy relationships with longtime legislators.

Critics counter that term limits infringe upon voter choice. They also argue that the limits deprive the legislature of experienced legislators; increase the power of the other two branches of government and staffers; reduce the number of qualified people who are willing to serve; undermine legislative leadership; make legislators less accountable in their final terms; and increase the grip of special interests (who provide services needed by inexperienced lawmakers). The verdict on term limits is still out, because the limits have only recently kicked in.[4]

Despite the popularity of term limits, legislative "careerism" has not been a major problem in Arizona. When the state's voters overwhelmingly approved the limits, they may have been confusing the state legislature with the U.S. Congress.[5] During the 1990s, turnover in the state senate ranged from 23 to 40 percent, and in the house, from 20 to 53 percent. Only five legislators retained their seats throughout the entire decade.[6] Arizona incumbents, like their counterparts in Washington, do enjoy an electoral advantage when they run for additional terms. However, unlike their federal counterparts, they do not tend to make a career out of legislative service. To the contrary, Arizona seems to have a greater problem in getting people to run for the office than in retiring them. In 1998, *no* party candidates bothered to run for two house seats. (Write-ins were ultimately elected.)

The district system and gerrymandering   State senators and representatives are now elected from thirty equally populated legislative districts across the state. Each district elects one senator and two representatives, giving the senate a total membership of thirty and the house, sixty. The current district system has been in effect since 1966. Prior to that time, various systems were used.[7] However, none of the former approaches accurately apportioned the legislators with respect to population.

With the passage of time, the situation only grew worse. After 1953, Arizona senators were elected on a countywide basis, with every county receiving exactly two senators apiece. This arrangement gave the sparsely populated rural counties far more representation than the heavily populated urban areas. For example, immediately prior to the adoption of the new districting system in 1966, the 663,510 people living in Maricopa County had as many senators (two) as the 7,736 people living in Mohave County. Similar voting disparities in other states spawned legal challenges that eventually reached the U.S. Supreme Court in the early 1960s. In a series of famous decisions known as the reapportionment cases, the U.S. Supreme Court ruled that unevenly populated voting districts violated the U.S. Constitution's Fourteenth Amendment and the principle of "one man, one vote."[8] The states were accordingly ordered to (1) redraw their legislative districts to ensure that every voting district had the same number of people and (2) repeat the process after every decennial census to keep the apportionment fair over time.

Efforts to comply with the Supreme Court's rulings produced an intense partisan battle in Arizona. Republicans and Democrats could not agree as to how the new district boundaries should be drawn. Ultimately, three federal judges wound up dividing the state into thirty equally populated districts when no single plan proved acceptable to all parties.[9] The court's solution was officially made part of the state constitution in 1972.[10]

Redistricting had two immediate and profound political consequences in Arizona. First, with the new districts in place, legislative power shifted from the rural counties to Maricopa County, where it has permanently remained. Today, more than half the state's thirty districts are wholly located in this county. Second, legislative control switched to the Republican party, which won majorities in both houses for the first time in the state's history. This partisan shift occurred because Arizona's rural counties were (and remain) predominately Democratic. When they lost seats in the legislature, so did the Democratic party. The results were the most dramatic in the state senate, where the party breakdown shifted overnight from a 26 to 2 Democratic advantage to a 16 to 14 Republican edge.[11]

Although redistricting solved the problem of numerical unfairness, it didn't cure the problem of **gerrymandering**. Simply put, there is more than one way to divide the state into evenly populated districts. Gerrymandering occurs when the boundaries are deliberately drawn to give an unfair electoral advantage to one particular party, group, or individual. (The term comes from an 1812 Massachusetts political cartoon—which indicates that the practice is neither new nor unique to Arizona.) The Republican and Democratic parties are the primary contenders in Arizona's decennial gerrymandering wars. However, incumbent legislators get involved too. They seek to draw the boundaries of their *own* districts in a way that will optimize their personal reelection chances. Finally, minority groups push for the creation of districts that will elect more minorities ("**majority-minority districts**").

There are many ways to gerrymander. Two of the more common techniques are **fracturing** and **packing**. Fracturing involves splitting the opposition into multiple districts to dilute its voting strength. Packing involves confining the opposition to a few super-strong districts that "waste" votes and simultaneously remove the opposition from many more surrounding districts. The advent of computers has made these and other gerrymandering techniques easier than ever. Arizona's legislature has had the responsibility of redistricting since 1966.[12] Each of its decennial maps has generated lawsuits and controversy. For example, in 1971, the legislature carved the Navajo Reservation into three separate districts, thereby diluting the Navajos' voting power. A federal judge commented that "the Indians were done in" and overturned this blatant gerrymander.[13] The court, however, rejected the Democrats' claims that the map gave the Republicans an unfair advantage. Amazingly, the map adopted in the following decade brought the San Carlos Apaches into court, complaining that *their* community had been unfairly fractured into three districts. This was overturned as well.[14]

Finally, the federal government was partly to blame for the state's gerry-mandered 1990s map. The U.S. Justice Department forced Arizona to create more Hispanic-dominated districts to help Hispanics win office.[15] The map did accomplish this result. However, it had the effect of helping Republicans as well. This is because Hispanics tend to be Democrats; packing them into super-strong Hispanic districts therefore reduced the number of Democrats in surrounding districts. Such gerrymandering has recently been condemned by the U.S. Supreme Court in cases from other jurisdictions. The cases hold that the states may no longer redistrict primarily on the basis of race or eth-nicity even if the motive is to increase minority voting power.[16] The rulings will impact the drawing of the next district map following the 2000 census.

One has only to look at the district map in figure 3.1 to see unmistakable evidence of gerrymandering. Properly drawn districts are supposed to be con-tiguous, compact, and aligned with natural neighborhoods. However, in the greater Phoenix area, the 1990s map violates all three of these principles. In central Phoenix, you would expect to see neat rectangles because neighbor-hoods largely follow the city's gridlike street structure. Instead, the seventeen districts zigzag in ways that defy natural boundaries. One district (district 20) is even located in two separate places. These districts were carefully drawn to help the majority party retain its edge, to give an advantage to certain, power-ful incumbents in both parties, and to create a few districts with higher His-panic populations.

The evidence of gerrymandering is also shown by the numbers. To have perfectly competitive races there should be an equal number of Republicans and Democrats in each district. Of course, this isn't achievable in the real world for several reasons. First, the state as a whole may simply have more members of one party than another. This is the case in Arizona, where Repub-licans have had an edge since 1985.[17] Second, Republicans and Democrats are not distributed evenly throughout the state. There are areas that are strongly aligned with a single party. Accordingly, if the map makers draw compact, contiguous districts that respect community boundaries, most districts will not have identical numbers of Democrats and Republicans.

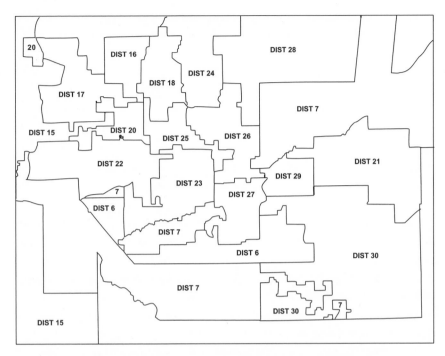

Figure 3.1 Legislative districts in the greater Phoenix area (1990s map)

However, Arizona's maps have been drawn to deliberately *exaggerate* the number of lopsided districts in the state. For example, when the map for the 1990s was drawn, the difference between Republican and Democratic voter registration was roughly three percentage points.[18] Yet, 24 out of 30 districts had more than a 12-point party difference, and the average district spread was 24 points. This helped Republicans win more seats than their proportionate strength in the general voting population. For example, by the decade's end, Republicans held 62 percent of the seats in the legislature, even though they represented only 45 percent of the voting electorate.

Finally, gerrymandering does greater harm than simply giving the successful practitioners undeserved seats. Because it artificially creates "safe" districts, it reduces overall electoral competition. That is, when a party has a lopsided numerical advantage in a district, candidates from the opposing party do not bother to run. (It makes little sense to waste time and money on a campaign that is doomed to fail.) As indicated in table 3.1, state senate elections provide disturbing evidence of this phenomenon. In the 1998 general

Table 3.1 Senate Races without Opposition from the Other Major Party

Year	Unopposed Seats
1990	27%
1992	50%
1994	73%
1996	43%
1998	63%

election, 19 out of 30 senate races had *no opposition* whatsoever from the other major party. Moreover, in seventeen of these same races, the candidates had no primary opposition either. In essence, the majority of Arizona's senators attained their offices simply by filing an application with a few hundred nominating signatures.

Lack of electoral competition is undesirable for many reasons. It allows less qualified candidates to gain office. It causes voters to lose interest in the election and depresses turnout. This, in turn, negatively impacts other races and issues on the ballot. Finally, lack of competition reduces the accountability of legislators to their constituencies. A legislator who is assured of retaining his or her seat has less incentive to respect the wishes of the voters. In short, the Progressive commitment to electoral accountability becomes fairly meaningless when the elections themselves are uncontested.

Arizona's Citizen Legislature

The drafters of Arizona's constitution had a low opinion of career politicians. They believed that the state would be better served by a part-time legislature made up of civic-minded citizens. The **citizen legislature** they designed offers many contrasts to professional legislative bodies like the U.S. Congress.[19] It is fostered by short terms, minimal qualifications, short sessions, and low compensation.

Qualifications   The qualifications for holding legislative office in Arizona are not onerous. The Progressives did not want to create barriers that would limit the office to elites. To serve in either house of the legislature, you need

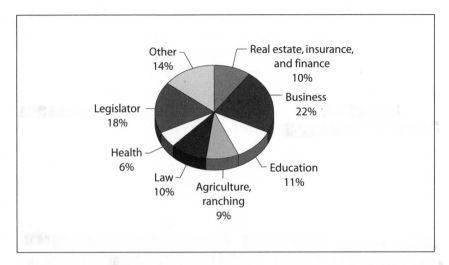

Figure 3.2 Legislative occupations. Adapted from Arizona News Service, *Guide to the 44th Legislature, 2d Regular Session* (Phoenix, 2000).

only be twenty-five years old,[20] a U.S. citizen, an Arizona resident (three years), a county resident (one year), a registered voter, and English proficient.[21] (The registered voter requirement bars felons and legally incapacitated persons from holding office.)

Of course, such formal qualifications reveal little about the actual composition of the state legislature. While Arizona legislators tend to be older, better educated, and more well off than the state's population as a whole, the legislature is not a body of elites. In contrast to the U.S. Congress, the typical state legislator is a small business owner—not a lawyer or professional politician. Many Arizona legislators lack college degrees, and those with degrees are more likely to have attended state institutions than ivy-league schools. The Arizona legislature has always attracted a comparatively high number of women. Today, 36 percent of its membership is female, one of the highest ratios in the nation. To some degree, therefore, the Progressives succeeded in making the legislature more egalitarian.

Sessions   Serving in the Arizona legislature has always been a part-time occupation. In the beginning, the legislature met for only a few months in the winter of every other year. The biennial schedule perfectly accommodated the independent rancher—arguably the drafters' prototype of the ideal citizen legislator. The rancher could leave his homestead in the hands of others during the slow winter season, come to Phoenix, do his civic duty, and return home in short order. To better serve the state's growing needs, the legislature began meeting on an annual basis in 1950. Its two official annual meetings are called **regular sessions**. Each begins on the second Monday in January and typically lasts until late April (roughly one hundred days). The hundred-day rule is not fixed by the constitution; it results from longstanding tradition and the internal rules of each chamber.[22] The state's part-time legislators are usually quite eager to return to their home districts and primary occupations.[23]

The state constitution recognizes that emergency situations requiring legislative action might arise at other times of the year. It therefore allows for an unlimited number of **special sessions.** Special sessions can be initiated by the governor or the legislature at any time. If the governor initiates the session, the legislature can only enact legislation on the specific subjects mentioned in the governor's call. By contrast, if the legislature initiates the session, there is no restriction as to subject matter.[24]

In recent times, there have been an average of three special sessions a year. The governor initiates most of them, and they are usually brief. The legislature might be summoned in the summer or fall to extend an expiring law, to correct a legislative oversight, or to appropriate money for some unforeseen need. Generally, lawmaking of this type can be accomplished in a few days or even a few hours. Most special sessions occur during the "off season" when the legislature is not normally meeting. However, they can be also called in the middle of an ongoing regular session. The governor does this to focus the legislature's attention on a matter deemed important.[25] While the legislature is in a special session, it cannot conduct other business. For example, it is customary for the state's budget to be enacted in such a special session, because this complex undertaking benefits from the legislature's full attention.

Calling a successful special session requires political skill on the part of the governor. Although the legislature must meet when the governor issues a call, it is not obligated to pass any legislation. For this reason, the governor has to proceed delicately. An unsuccessful or prolonged special session can be costly, disruptive, and embarrassing to the governor's leadership skills. A politically savvy governor will rarely call a special session unless he or she is reasonably confident that sufficient votes are lined up to pass the desired legislation.

PROPOSITION 300

RECOMMENDATIONS OF THE COMMISSION ON SALARIES FOR ELECTED STATE OFFICERS AS TO LEGISLATIVE SALARIES HAVE BEEN CERTIFIED TO THE SECRETARY OF STATE AND ARE HEREBY SUBMITTED TO THE QUALIFIED ELECTORS FOR THEIR APPROVAL OR REJECTION.

DESCRIPTIVE TITLE:
PROVIDES FOR AN INCREASE IN THE PRESENT SALARY OF STATE LEGISLATORS FROM $15,000 PER YEAR TO $24,000 PER YEAR AS RECOMMENDED BY THE COMMISSION ON SALARIES FOR ELECTED STATE OFFICERS.

"SHALL THE RECOMMENDATIONS OF THE COMMISSION ON SALARIES FOR ELECTED STATE OFFICERS CONCERNING LEGISLATIVE SALARIES BE ACCEPTED? ☐ YES ☐ NO."

SUCH RECOMMENDATIONS IF APPROVED BY THE ELECTORS SHALL BECOME EFFECTIVE AT THE BEGINNING OF THE NEXT REGULAR LEGISLATIVE SESSION WITHOUT ANY OTHER AUTHORIZING LEGISLATION.
CURRENT LEGISLATIVE SALARY $15,000
SALARY PROPOSED BY SALARY COMMISSION $24,000

PROPOSITION 300

A "yes" vote shall have the effect of raising state legislators' annual salaries to $24,000.	YES ☐
A "no" vote shall have the effect of maintaining state legislators' annual salaries at $15,000.	NO ☐

Figure 3.3   A salary proposition on the ballot (1996)

Finally, it should be emphasized that legislators perform services even when the legislature is not in session. Most bills must be drafted well before the session begins. (A hundred-day session does not allow much slack time.) **Interim committees** meet in the summer and fall to study complex issues that might require legislation. Constituents and interest groups demand services from legislators on a year-round basis. In short, although serving in the Arizona legislature is not a full-time job, it consumes considerably more than one hundred days a year.

Legislative salaries   To foster the concept of a citizen legislature, the Progressives favored low legislative salaries. They hoped that this would attract public-spirited candidates instead of individuals seeking office for personal gain. More importantly, they wanted legislators to be part of the same private-sector world as their **constituents**. Accordingly, the constitution set the first legislative salaries at $7 a day with a $420 cap.[26] This was meant to reimburse lawmakers for their expenses—not serve as a living wage. However, putting an actual dollar amount in the constitution had a secondary effect: it invited the *citizens* to control legislative salaries because the voters are required to approve all constitutional changes.[27] As a result, legislators rarely received a raise. By 1970, the annual salary had risen to only $6,000 a year. Many felt that this was inadequate compensation and that a better system was needed. The constitution was accordingly amended.

Ironically, the solution that was adopted in 1970 has turned out to be scarcely more effective in increasing legislative pay.[28] A five-member commission now makes salary recommendations for all elected officials. The commission's members are private citizens appointed by the leaders of the three branches of government. They study the legislators' workload and comparable pay scales. When the commission recommends a raise for legislators, the raise must be approved by the voters.[29] The salary recommendation therefore goes on the ballot as a numbered proposition, as shown in figure 3.3. If a majority of the voters vote "yes," the raise takes effect at the start of the next regular session. To date, the salary commission has recommended a legislative

Table 3.2   Voter Response to Legislative Salary Propositions

Year	Current Salary	Proposed Salary	Voter Response
1972	$6,000	$10,000	No
1974	$6,000	$10,000	No
1976	$6,000	No recommendation	N/A
1978	$6,000	$9,600	No
1980	$6,000	$15,000	Yes
1982	$15,000	$18,900	No
1984	$15,000	No recommendation	N/A
1986	$15,000	$20,000	No
1988	$15,000	$25,000	No
1990	$15,000	$24,000	No
1992	$15,000	$19,748	No
1994	$15,000	$19,750	No
1996	$15,000	$24,000	No
1998	$15,000	$24,000	Yes
2000	$24,000	$30,000	Pending

pay raise on twelve separate occasions. The voters have gone along only *twice*. As shown in table 3.2, for eighteen years, legislative salaries were stalled at $15,000. In 1998, the voters finally approved an increase to $24,000 a year. At the same time they rejected a legislative proposal that would have revamped the salary system and reduced the citizens' role.

The per diem issue   The annual salary is not the legislature's only public compensation. Like their counterparts in most other states, Arizona legislators also receive a **per diem** (travel and subsistence reimbursement) that they—not the voters—control. Under current law, legislators outside of Maricopa County receive an extra $60 per day while engaged in formal legislative business; Maricopa legislators receive $35 per day.[30] This extra compensation, along with the legislators' mileage reimbursements, has generated controversy. Some view it as a way of circumventing the will of the electorate. Others question the propriety of a per diem for Maricopa County legislators, who are not required to work away from home. And some allege that legislative leaders have abused the system.[31] Although the voters voted to eliminate the current per diem system in 1998, the Arizona Supreme Court ruled that the matter was not properly on the ballot.[32] The controversy remains.

Evaluating the citizen legislature   Although the citizen legislature is found in most states, it has come under increasing attack. Reformers regard it as an outdated concept and contend that states would be better served with professional (full-time, well-paid, well-staffed) legislatures. More specifically, they contend that part-time lawmakers lack the time and expertise to address the complex issues confronting modern state governments. The "amateur" lawmakers tend to rely too heavily upon lobbyists and special interests for help. The critics argue that part-time lawmakers are more easily corrupted because of their low pay and long hours. (They point to "Azscam," a sting operation that led to the indictment of seven Arizona legislators in 1991. Lawmakers were captured on videotape promising to legalize gambling in exchange for surprisingly small sums of money or other benefits.) Citizen legislatures have pro-business and pro-development biases. These occupations are overrepresented in the legislature (see figure 3.2) because they have flexible hours that can accommodate part-time legislative service. (Additionally, a lawmaker's private business is likely to profit from the contacts that can be made as a legislator.)[33] Citizen legislatures have more conflicts of interest because most lawmakers hold two jobs. When the lawmakers vote on matters affecting their own livelihoods, public confidence is eroded. Finally, the critics contend that citizen lawmakers are more arrogant because they regard themselves as "volunteers" who are not committed to long-term political careers.[34]

Nevertheless, citizen legislatures have many passionate, modern-day defenders. Proponents view it as a more democratic system. They argue that citizen lawmakers better understand the needs of ordinary citizens because they live and work in the private sector along with their constituents. In contrast to professional politicians, they are not immune from the regulatory environment that they create. Citizen legislatures attract members who are more civic-minded than politically ambitious. The lawmakers are more likely to stand up to special interests and "do the right thing" because they are not committed to long-term political careers. Supporters argue that when lawmakers vote on matters affecting their own livelihoods, they bring added expertise to the vote. Citizen legislatures tend to be more diverse, attracting women, minorities, retired persons, and others who have traditionally avoided full-time political careers. The legislatures have higher turnover rates, which retard the abuse of power and encourage fresh approaches. Part-time legislatures enact fewer laws, which leads to less bureaucracy and government regulation. Lastly, citizen legislatures are cheaper.

Legislative Organization

Nominally, all legislators have equal lawmaking power. No vote counts more than any other, and a consensus is always needed for final, official action. However, without leadership and strong organization, it is doubtful that the legislature could function at all, let alone accomplish its business in a mere one hundred days. Accordingly, the state legislature is organized around three powerful elements: leaders, **standing committees**, and the majority party.

Legislative leaders   Each chamber of the legislature chooses its own officers and makes its own operating rules.[35] The leader of the senate is called the **president**, and the leader of the house is the **speaker**. Officially, these two officers are chosen by a majority vote of their respective chambers at the start of each new two-year term. In reality, however, the leaders are preselected in a private **caucus** by the members of the **majority party** alone. The two presiding officers wield more power than their counterparts in the U.S. Congress. Their authority lies in four main areas:

1. *Parliamentary powers:* The presiding officers chair the meetings of their chambers, set the agendas, decide who gets to speak, and rule on procedural disputes.

2. *Administrative powers:* The presiding officers hire and supervise legislative staff, handle per diem and other personnel matters for legislators, and manage the chambers' facilities. Even the latter power is not as innocuous as it seems. For example, in recent years one speaker "banished" a reporter from the house for writing newspaper articles that were critical of the speaker. A senate president allowed the chamber's doors to be locked to prevent members from leaving during an important vote.[36] Needless to say, both actions were widely criticized; nonetheless, they exposed the raw power that these leaders routinely exercise.

3. *Appointive powers:* The presiding officers assign the members to committees and pick the chairperson of each committee. Conversely, they have the power to summarily remove legislators from committees and demote chairpersons. As outlined below, by merely threatening to use these powers, the presiding officers can sometimes influence the voting behavior of fellow lawmakers.

4. *Referral powers over bills:* The presiding officers assign bills to committees for study and determine when (or whether) a vote on the bill will be taken. As explained below, these powers enable them to speed a bill's passage through the legislature, kill it outright, or hold the bill hostage for desired changes.

In addition to the president and speaker, the majority party chooses two floor assistants in each chamber, a majority leader and a majority whip. Together with the committee chairpersons, they form the dominant leadership structure in the legislature. The **minority party** organizes itself as well. Each chamber chooses a minority leader, minority whip, and assistant minority leader. Their primary job is to maintain party unity. Without such organization and unity, minority members would be fairly powerless in the Arizona legislative process.

Standing committees   The state legislature could not possibly accomplish the task of studying roughly a thousand bills in one hundred days without significant division of labor. Standing committees serve this function. These committees are semipermanent, although the number, names, and responsi-

Table 3.3 Standing Committees in the Arizona Legislature (1999–2000)

Senate Committees	House Committees
Appropriations	Academic Accountability
Commerce, Agriculture & Natural Resources	Agriculture
Education	Appropriations
Family Services	Banking & Insurance
Finance	Children & Family Integrated Delivery System
Financial Institutions & Retirement	Counties & Municipalities
Government & Environmental Stewardship	Economic Development
Health	Education
Judiciary	Environment
Rules	Federal Mandates & State's Rights
Transportation	Government Operations
	Government Reform
	Health
	Human Services
	International Trade, Technology & Tourism
	Judiciary
	Natural Resources
	Program Authorization Review
	Public Institutions & Universities
	Rules
	Rural & Native American Affairs
	Transportation
	Veterans & Military Affairs
	Ways & Means

bilities of these committees occasionally change. Currently, as indicated in table 3.3, there are eleven standing committees in the senate and twenty-five committees in the house. (The house always has more committees because it is a larger body.) The sizes of the committees vary, and legislators serve on more than one committee. The typical senate committee has nine members; the typical house committee has six. Standing committees focus on specific subject areas, as indicated by the committee name. This enables the members to develop expertise and to better coordinate the laws in a particular area. During the regular session, the standing committees meet on fixed weekly schedules to study proposed legislation.

Standing committees aren't the only committees used by the legislature. There are also special joint committees created by statute. Unlike standing committees, these committees include members from both houses and often meet when the legislature is not in session. One example is the powerful **Joint**

Legislative Budget Committee (JLBC).[37] It monitors the state's fiscal affairs and proposes a biennial budget for the state. The legislature also creates ad hoc committees that exist for a limited time and purpose. For example, when the house and senate pass different versions of the same bill, a **conference committee** is appointed to work out a compromise. Similarly, when the legislature decides to conduct an investigation, it may establish a special committee for this limited purpose as well. Finally, interim committees are created to study particular issues when the legislature is not in session. In short, the bulk of the legislature's work takes place in small committee rooms—not in gatherings of the entire chamber.

The majority party   The majority party is the single most powerful organizing force in the state legislature. Its authority rests upon legislative tradition rather than constitutional provisions or formal rules. Nonetheless, it controls the legislature's operations in three major ways: (1) the presiding officer is always a member of the majority party; (2) committee chairs are members of the majority party; and (3) every standing committee is carefully composed so that the majority party makes up the majority of each committee. (The ratio of Republicans to Democrats on each standing committee usually mirrors the party's strength in the chamber.) This organizational structure enables the majority party to potentially control the entire agenda and all vote outcomes. That is, as long as party members stand together, minority party members might as well be absent.

Of course, in the real world, party members do not always think alike. This is where "party discipline" comes into play. The party's position on important matters is worked out in caucuses, where the members debate, wheel, and deal. During the session, such caucuses may meet one or more times a week. Once there is consensus, the leadership can use various sanctions to encourage party unity. For example, as noted previously, a rebellious legislator can be summarily removed from a committee before he or she can cast an adverse vote. A disobedient chairperson can be dethroned. Often the mere threat of reassignment is sufficient to produce the desired voting behavior. The party leadership can also play "tit for tat," threatening to kill the dissenting legislator's pet bills unless the legislator cooperates with the party's agenda. (A legislator who cannot enact bills for constituents is less likely to be reelected.)

Despite these and other disciplinary tools, the party leadership is rarely completely successful in keeping all of its members in line. Accordingly, when the majority party is short votes, it must appeal to minority members. However, if the minority party is well disciplined, it can leverage these situations into opportunities to advance its own agenda. That is, it will refuse to help out unless the majority party agrees to support some of *its* bills. While the two major parties do not take stands on every matter coming before the legislature, party membership powerfully controls most legislative outcomes.

Legislative Functions

The Lawmaking Process

The chief job of the state legislature is to make and revise the laws of the state. At any given time, there are thousands of statutes in effect. Some of these are criminal laws that prohibit specific behaviors and impose penalties for violation. The vast majority of statutes, however, are noncriminal in nature. They address such varied subjects as adoption, banking, inheritance, labor, marriage, public health, taxation, etc. In fact, more than six hundred laws pertain to education alone—from teacher qualifications to pesticide spraying at public schools.

Approximately three hundred new laws get enacted each year (see figure 3.4). Many wonder why lawmaking is such a continuing process; superficially it would seem to be more of a one-time project. One answer is that society changes. New social problems trigger public demand for new legislative solutions. For example, in recent years, the state has enacted criminal laws addressing domestic terrorism, drive-by shootings, harassment, and computer fraud. However, most of the laws enacted each year are not new measures but instead are revisions to existing laws. They are needed because lawmaking is not an exact science. Time and experience reveal errors in existing statutes and suggest better approaches. While constant overhaul of the laws is certainly undesirable—it breeds confusion and disrespect for law— excessive rigidity creates problems too. The lawmaking process in Arizona attempts to strike a balance between these two pitfalls.

The constitution makes the legislature's task appear fairly simple. It merely requires that a proposed law, or bill, be approved by a majority or more of the members in both houses and signed by the presiding officers.[38] In actual practice, however, the lawmaking process is far more complex. There are multiple ways that bills can fail within the Arizona legislature; most bills die before an

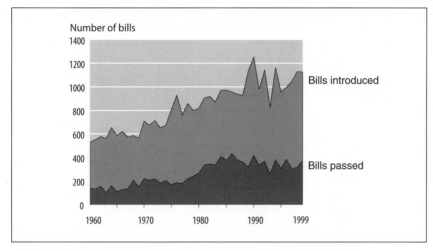

Number of bills

Figure 3.4 Total number of bills, 1960–1999. (Excludes special sessions.)

official vote is ever taken. Conversely, successful bills must ordinarily traverse the five major stages outlined below:

Introduction   Proposed laws, called **bills,** can originate in either house of the legislature. Only a senator or representative, however, can formally introduce a bill. This legislator is called the bill's **sponsor;** successful bills usually have multiple sponsors (see figure 3.5). Legislators do not think up the ideas for most bills themselves. Rather, the ideas come from various sources including the governor, state agencies, local governments, citizens, and interest groups. The actual writing of the bill is usually done by the legislature's professional staff at the request of the sponsoring legislator. Typically, this takes place before the session begins.

A legislator does not have an entirely free hand in inventing new laws. As noted in chapter 1, statutes must conform to the provisions of the U.S. and state constitutions because these supersede ordinary laws. In addition, the state constitution contains specific prohibitions on lawmaking that have no counterparts in the federal constitution. For example, as noted in chapter 2, legislators cannot enact "special laws" for the benefit of particular individuals or entities.[39] Arizona's constitution also requires that every bill be limited to a single subject, as reflected in its title.[40] This prevents legislators from sneaking bills through the system by burying them within other measures. It also dis-

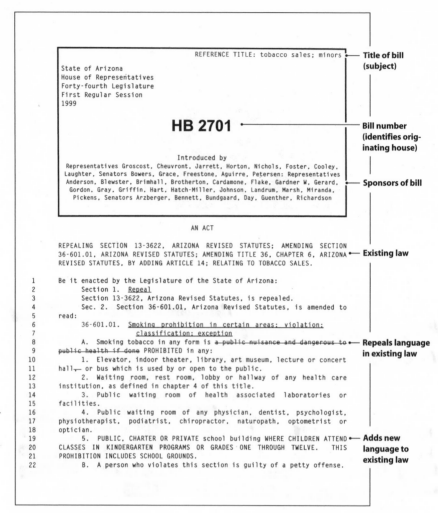

Figure 3.5 A typical bill

courages **riders.** (A rider is an unrelated measure that is attached to a more popular bill in order to secure its passage. They are quite common in the U.S. Congress.) The Arizona Constitution is also fairly strict with respect to **appropriation** (spending) bills. These bills must always be separate from other types of legislation.[41] And, except for the **general appropriation bill** (which addresses all the state's major departments), they must also be confined to a single subject. This prevents much of the **log rolling** that takes place in Congress. That is, unlike their federal counterparts, Arizona's legislators cannot tack pet spending projects or other unrelated items onto a bill as quid pro quo for their votes. The restriction enables the state to better control spending and live within its budget.

Committee review in the first chamber   Once a bill is introduced, it embarks on a course that resembles a labyrinth filled with dead ends and quicksand at every turn. As shown in figure 3.6, nearly two-thirds of all bills fail to make it through this process. This is intentional; the system is designed to retard the passage of new laws. Thus, as explained below, there are many more ways to kill a bill in the legislature than to pass it.

At the start of the legislative session all bills go to the presiding officer of the chamber in which the bill is introduced. The speaker or president then assigns the bills to standing committees for detailed study. Typically, the presiding officer will refer a bill to committees that deal with the bill's subject matter. For example, a bill to lengthen the school year would be assigned to the education committee. The bill might also be assigned to the appropriations committee for consideration of its fiscal impact. All bills will also be assigned to the chamber's **rules committee** for technical scrutiny. These standing committees do not simultaneously study the bill. Rather, bills normally proceed through committees in the order dictated by the presiding officer. Most importantly, *if a bill ceases to advance through the chamber it is effectively dead.*[42] Bills that begin in the senate can even die at the starting block: senate rules permit the president to kill a bill by not assigning it to any committees for study. The bill is said to be "held."[43] (House rules currently require all bills to be assigned to committees, but this can be a mere technicality. The speaker can easily assign the bill to a committee whose chairperson has agreed to "hold" the bill.)

The graveyard for most bills is the standing committee (see figure 3.6). The committee's chairperson can kill a bill by simply refusing to schedule it for a committee hearing. When this occurs, we say that the bill has been "held in committee." Although procedural devices exist for dislodging bills, as a practical matter the chair's discretion is rarely challenged. This powerful prerogative enables legislative leaders to screen bills that are frivolous, that are flawed, or that simply lack sufficient majority party support. It is an arguably necessary power given the huge number of measures that are introduced each session, and the severe time constraints under which the legislature operates.

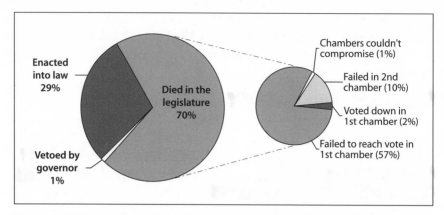

Figure 3.6 Bills in the 43rd Legislature, 1st Regular Session (1997). A total of 1,045 bills were introduced during the session; only 300 became law.

If a bill is not held, it is scheduled for a brief public hearing before the committee. During this hearing, the members debate the merits of the bill and usually propose changes or formal amendments. At the discretion of the chairperson, the bill's sponsors, outside experts, lobbyists, and interested citizens may testify for or against the bill. When the hearing is concluded the committee ordinarily takes a vote. However, the chairperson or the committee itself can hold the bill at this juncture by refusing to take a vote. This prevents the bill from further advancing through the legislature and effectively kills the measure. If a standing committee decides to vote on a bill, it has three major options:

1. It can vote *do pass*, meaning that the committee has studied the bill and approves it in its original form.
2. It can vote *do not pass*, meaning that the committee disapproves of the bill. (In contrast to holding the bill back, this option allows the bill to proceed, although it carries the committee's express disapproval.)
3. It can vote *do pass as amended*. This means that the committee supports the passage of the bill only with the specific amendments proposed by the committee. (It is a common vote outcome, because close scrutiny of the bill usually reveals some flaws or unpopular aspects.)

Committee votes operate on the principle of majority rule. This means that if party members vote as a unified block, the majority party can control all committee outcomes, because they outnumber the minority party on every committee. This significantly reduces the likelihood that the minority party's bills will advance.

If a bill makes it through the first assigned committee it proceeds to the next. However, every chairperson and committee along the way has exactly the same holding and amending powers. Accordingly, it is not unusual for a bill to survive the first committee only to die in the second or third. Ultimately, the hardy survivors wind up in the chamber's rules committee. All bills are required to go to this committee before they reach the floor for a final vote. Theoretically, the committee is supposed to review bills only to determine whether they are constitutional and in proper form. However, in actual practice, policy considerations can influence the committee's action. Accordingly, the rules committee and its chairperson are especially powerful because they can potentially hold (kill) *every* bill in the chamber.

Passage by the first chamber   If a bill survives scrutiny by the standing committees it returns to the presiding officer. It is then put on the calendar for consideration by the entire chamber. However, the speaker or president can hold the bill at this juncture too. This occurs when proposed amendments have undermined support for the bill; it may also be the result of increased lobbying efforts. If the presiding officer allows the bill to proceed, it goes before a special meeting of the entire chamber known as the **Committee of the Whole** or "cow." Here the bill is debated along with the various amendments proposed by the standing committees. New amendments can also be offered by legislators from the floor. This gives members who were not on the standing committees the opportunity to participate in shaping the legislation. If cow approves the measure, the bill is scheduled for the official vote. This vote is usually anticlimactic. As figure 3.6 indicates, most bills that make it to this point pass.

Review and passage by the second chamber   Passage by one chamber, however, is not the end of the story. The bill must still successfully traverse the second house—where the process begins anew! It goes to the presiding officer, who normally assigns it to a single standing committee, plus the rules committee, for study. Although the process is thus streamlined, the same pitfalls exist: the bill can be held back, further amended, or voted down. And a death in the second chamber generally kills the measure, despite its success in the

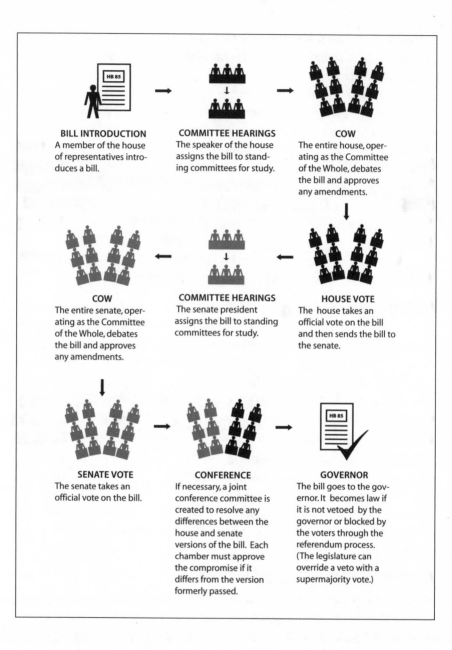

BILL INTRODUCTION
A member of the house of representatives introduces a bill.

COMMITTEE HEARINGS
The speaker of the house assigns the bill to standing committees for study.

COW
The entire house, operating as the Committee of the Whole, debates the bill and approves any amendments.

COW
The entire senate, operating as the Committee of the Whole, debates the bill and approves any amendments.

COMMITTEE HEARINGS
The senate president assigns the bill to standing committees for study.

HOUSE VOTE
The house takes an official vote on the bill and then sends the bill to the senate.

SENATE VOTE
The senate takes an official vote on the bill.

CONFERENCE
If necessary, a joint conference committee is created to resolve any differences between the house and senate versions of the bill. Each chamber must approve the compromise if it differs from the version formerly passed.

GOVERNOR
The bill goes to the governor. It becomes law if it is not vetoed by the governor or blocked by the voters through the referendum process. (The legislature can override a veto with a supermajority vote.)

Figure 3.7 A bill becomes law. In this simple example, the bill begins in the house of representatives. However, bills can start in the senate as well. The only requirement is that both houses must ultimately approve the bill in the identical form.

first chamber. Only if the second chamber approves the bill in *exactly* the same form as the originating chamber does the bill finally leave the legislature and proceed to the governor.[44] It is quite common, however, for a bill to be amended in the second chamber. This means that the two houses did not approve the identical version of the bill. Accordingly, the originating house must take another vote to determine whether it approves of the changes. If it does not, a joint conference committee is created to negotiate a compromise. The bill is said to have "died in conference" when this committee cannot come up with mutually agreeable language. However, if a compromise is achieved, it must be formally approved by both houses. Only then does the measure finally leave the legislature and proceed to the governor for review.

Approval by the governor or legislative override   The governor's power to **veto** bills is examined in chapter 5. However, a gubernatorial veto does not completely kill a bill. The legislature can **override** a veto by repassing the bill by a higher majority (see table 3.4). Such overrides are extraordinarily rare in Arizona. Not only are supermajority votes difficult to achieve, but the legislature often adjourns before the vote can even be taken. Under these circumstances, the governor's veto kills the bill. Nonetheless, having the override power gives the legislature the final say over legislative matters.

Legislative voting rules   Voting rules in the Arizona legislature are more complex than in the U.S. Congress. Usually, only a **simple majority** (i.e., one more than half) is required for legislative action. This means that sixteen senators and thirty-one representatives are needed for the passage of most bills.[45] The simple majority rule ensures that the numerically larger side always prevails in cases of disagreement. However, there are circumstances where the state constitution requires a higher, **supermajority** vote for legislative action.

Supermajorities (two-thirds or three-fourths votes) are difficult to achieve. Not only do they put a greater strain on party loyalty, they usually require bipartisan support (i.e., unless one party holds more than two-thirds of the seats). As a practical matter, this makes such votes more costly because a well-organized minority party will often demand some favors in exchange for its votes. Proponents of supermajorities argue that weightier matters should require a higher level of commitment. (This is why the criminal justice system imposes the highest degree of commitment of all—jury unanimity—on decisions that could result in imprisonment or death.) Supermajority votes are also popular with voters because they tend to put the brakes on legislative

Table 3.4 Voting Rules in the Arizona Legislature

Type of Bill	Votes Needed to Pass	Votes Needed to Override
Ordinary bills	Simple majority	Two-thirds
Bills with emergency clauses	Two-thirds	Three-fourths
New tax bills	Two-thirds	Three-fourths
Bills altering voter-approved laws	Three-quarters	Not addressed

action. However, some political theorists contend that these high vote requirements are undemocratic. That is, that they enable a small (and possibly misguided) minority to defeat the will of the majority. As summarized in table 3.4, there are four special circumstances in the lawmaking context where a supermajority vote is needed:[46]

1. *Emergency bills:* A two-thirds vote is needed to pass any bill with an **emergency clause.**[47] An emergency clause is a legislative declaration that public health or safety requires the immediate enactment of the measure. Attaching this clause to a bill has two important consequences: (1) the bill takes effect immediately (i.e., as soon as it is signed by the governor or the legislature votes to override a governor's veto); and (2) the bill cannot be blocked by the people using the referendum process. These two effects are more fully discussed in chapter 4.
2. *New tax laws:* A two-thirds vote is needed to pass bills that create new taxes or raise existing ones.[48] The voters imposed this requirement on the legislature in 1992, using the initiative process. The intent was to make it harder for the legislature to raise taxes.
3. *Modifications of voter-approved laws:* A three-fourths vote is now needed to alter laws that have been approved by the voters through either the initiative or referendum processes. Moreover, the amendment must "further the purposes" of the original legislation.[49] This supermajority requirement was added by the voters in 1998 and is discussed in chapter 4.
4. *Veto overrides:* A supermajority vote (two-thirds or three-fourths, depending upon the circumstances) is required to enact a bill that has been vetoed by the governor.[50]

DINOSAUR WARS IN THE ARIZONA LEGISLATURE

The legislature's battle over an official state dinosaur in 1999 gave the state's schoolchildren an unintended lesson in the politics of the lawmaking process. At the request of a nine-year old constituent, Senator John Huppenthal of Chandler introduced a bill declaring the dilophosaurus the official state dinosaur. The 20-foot, poison-spitting carnivore was featured in the movie *Jurassic Park*. The proposed law would add the dinosaur to the other state emblems mentioned in chapter 1. Senator Huppenthal thought that Arizona's schoolchildren could monitor the bill's progress through the legislature. He anticipated smooth passage.[51]

Instead, the bill was mired in controversy from the very start. Southern Arizona legislators vigorously opposed the dilophosaurus. They wanted the honor to go to the sonorasaurus—a gentle plant-eater found only in southern Arizona. (The critics pointed out that the dilophosaurus was not unique to the state and that its bones had been carted off to California.) Accordingly, when the bill came before the first standing committee, opponents introduced an amendment to strike "dilophosaurus" and substitute "sonorasaurus." The ensuing dispute caused the bill to be held in the committee.

Senator Huppenthal, however, refused to give up. Near the end of the session, he dramatically revived his dinosaur bill by using a parliamentary trick known as a "strike all" amendment. More specifically, the senator struck the contents of a totally unrelated bill and put his dinosaur measure into its empty shell. The ploy nearly worked. By a vote of 24 to 6, the full senate approved a compromise that diplomatically honored *both* dinosaurs. The measure then went to the house of representatives. Unfortunately for Arizona's schoolchildren, the controversy reignited in the second chamber. In the end, the house majority whip blocked a vote on Senator Huppenthal's well-intentioned measure. The bill thus died in the house, leaving Arizona without an official dinosaur!

Evaluating the lawmaking process   The state's lawmaking process is admittedly complex. This account hasn't even covered the more subtle ways that a bill can die or be resurrected in the state legislature.[52] The essential characteristics of the lawmaking process, however, can be summarized as follows:

1. The process is highly efficient. It allows ninety part-time legislators, operating on an extremely tight time schedule, to review more than a thousand bills a year. This is no mean feat! Critics, however, contend that the legislature's reviewing process is too superficial and that all of the state's needs are not being adequately addressed.

2. The process is conservative. That is, the system is intentionally designed to make it easier to kill bills than to pass them. This retards hasty or mis-

guided measures, discourages excessive regulation, and keeps the laws from changing too frequently. Critics counter that needed legislation often falls by the wayside and that delayed response to problems also has serious social costs.

3. The process promotes moderate legislation. Few bills, apart from minor corrective measures, are ever enacted in their original form. That is, to garner sufficient votes for passage, the bill's sponsors are forced to compromise with the bill's opponents. As a result, the law that emerges in the end is not necessarily the best approach, but it is usually the least controversial. Critics charge, however, that watered-down legislation is not always desirable and that tough social problems sometimes require more aggressive solutions.

4. The system gives a few individuals—the leaders and committee chairs—great power. These persons may not be able to single-handedly pass a bill, but they usually have the power to defeat one.[53] Defenders argue that the system would bog down without giving someone the ability to prioritize and screen bills. They also note that the leaders are usually carrying out the wishes of the majority (as negotiated in party caucuses). Finally, defenders cite parliamentary rules that theoretically allow the leadership to be overruled by the rank and file. Critics attack the leaders' power as being undemocratic. They also contend that it makes the process more corruptible. That is, if a special interest wants to kill a particular measure, it has to "persuade" only one or more key figures, as opposed to a majority of the legislature.

5. The process is highly partisan. If the majority party can maintain tight discipline, it can (a) prevent the opposition from defeating or altering its bills and (b) prevent the minority party from passing any bills of its own. Party rule promotes efficiency and ideological consistency. It keeps the members from going in ninety different directions on every issue. It also furthers accountability to the electorate. The voters know what they are getting; if they disapprove of one party's stewardship, they can always give the other party a chance to govern. Critics charge, however, that the partisan system essentially deprives 40 percent or more of the state's citizens of meaningful legislative representation; that good ideas are ignored simply because they come from the wrong party; and that less-ideological approaches are preferable.

Fiscal Powers

The state legislature is said to have "the power of the purse." This means that it decides how most of the state's money will be spent. However, before the legislature can appropriate money for a specific purpose, it must first raise funds. These two interrelated tasks—revenue-raising and spending—constitute a critical part of the legislature's continuing responsibilities.

Raising revenues   Over ten billion dollars a year is currently needed to keep the state's institutions and programs running. Arizona raises nearly six billion of that sum itself; the federal government contributes the rest. These revenue levels make Arizona a significant component of the national economy. If the state were a private business, its level of revenues would put it on the "Fortune 500" list.[54]

Raising sufficient revenues to provide uninterrupted government service is no simple task. Taxes constitute the principal way that the state gets the money it needs. However, it also derives funds from user fees (such as university tuition), from the interest earned on its investments (including school trust lands), from the state lottery, and from various other sources. When the state needs large sums for major capital projects—e.g., building highways—it typically borrows the money through the sale of bonds. All of these fiscal options involve difficult policy choices, but none provokes more controversy than taxes.

Arizona's tax policies have long been controversial. During the territorial period, the government relied mostly upon property taxes. However, the wealthiest property owners—the mines and railroads—paid little or no taxes. In 1906, Senator Beveridge complained that Arizona had over $400,000,000 in taxable property, yet the tax rolls listed less than $50,000,000.[55] (It was not uncommon for railroads to be given twenty-year tax exemptions as an incentive to build in the territory.) The Progressives attempted to put a stop to such practices. Arizona's constitution therefore contains multiple provisions that ban preferential tax treatment.[56] For example, the main fiscal section, Article 9, opens with the words

> The power of taxation shall never be surrendered, suspended, or contracted away. All taxes shall be uniform upon the same class of property . . . and shall be levied and collected for public purposes only.

These constitutional prohibitions cured the worst abuses of the territorial period. But they did not eradicate all controversy over taxes. Today, Arizona's state and local governments rely upon a mix of income, sales, property, vehicle, and other taxes. No tax is perfect, and each impacts different groups of people in different ways. However, Arizona's direct democracy procedures (see chapter 4) have enabled the taxpayers to periodically attack specific taxes and revenue policies. Over sixty tax measures have appeared on the ballot since statehood—more than any other single subject. Two measures in particular have made the legislature's current revenue-raising job especially difficult.

First, in 1980, Arizonans put stringent limitations on residential property taxes. State and local governments are now barred from increasing annual valuations or taxes beyond certain constitutional ceilings.[57] The amendments were spawned by a grassroots taxpayer revolt that began in California a few years earlier. Although Arizona's state government had already reduced its dependency on property taxes prior to the 1980 vote,[58] local governments—counties, cities, school and other districts—still derive most of their revenue from these taxes. Living within the 1980 limits continues to be a major challenge for them.

Second, the citizens added a supermajority requirement to the constitution in 1992. It now takes a two-thirds vote before the legislature can impose any new taxes, raise existing taxes, or eliminate tax deductions and exemptions.[59] This citizen initiative was approved by over 70 percent of the voters. As intended, the provision makes it much harder for the legislature to get revenue from new sources. (Arizona is now one of fourteen states with such a supermajority tax limitation.)

As figure 3.8 reveals, most of the state government's revenue currently comes from sales tax. Arizona relies more heavily on this type of tax than forty-two states.[60] Sales tax is politically attractive to state legislators for many reasons. Because it is often paid in small increments, the burden is less visible to taxpayers. Private businesses collect the tax for the state, thereby reducing collection costs. Above all, the tax can be passed on to tourists, who don't vote. However, sales tax has downsides as well. The tax tends to be regressive—that is, it takes a larger share of the income of the poor.[61] It is also more sensitive to fluctuations in the economy. (For example, during the 1980s, the state had repeated budget crises. To make ends meet, state agencies even had to return funds that had already been appropriated. A "rainy day" savings

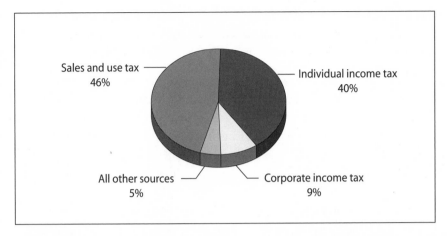

Figure 3.8 General fund sources: where the money comes from (FY 2000). Source: Arizona Joint Legislative Budget Committee.

fund has been implemented to provide a cushion against future fluctuations.) Finally, sales taxes can be circumvented through out-of-state purchases, an increasing worry for state officials as Internet sales gain in popularity.

When the state needs more cash than it can raise through taxes, it must borrow. However, the constitution imposes barriers here as well. Notably, it limits the state's maximum debt to $350,000.[62] This limit was put in the constitution in 1912 when the dollar was worth considerably more. A rigid application of the debt ceiling today would bar many legitimate undertakings. Accordingly, the courts have sanctioned a variety of "workarounds." For example, court decisions have held that the state's retirement system does not violate the debt limitation. The state has also been allowed to finance major capital projects through the sale of revenue bonds, which are also interpreted as being outside the debt proscription. Lease-purchase agreements constitute another creative financial device that enables the state to circumvent the unrealistic limit.[63] (Currently, the three state universities are constructing buildings collectively costing more than $140,000,000 through such lease-purchase agreements.)[64]

In summary, it has become harder for the state to raise revenues over the years. At the same time, the demand for public services has grown. Polls show that Arizonans want improved schools, long-term incarceration for inmates, better health care, and more rigorous environmental enforcement. All of these undertakings are extremely costly. The continuing challenge for state and local governments is to come up with sufficient funds in the face of restrictive constitutional provisions and strong taxpayer resistance.

The appropriations process   Public money cannot be spent unless the expenditure is first authorized by law.[65] This constitutional mandate puts the legislature in charge of most spending decisions because it is the state's law-making branch. State agencies and institutions all compete for the limited available funds. When the legislature appropriates money, it is really determining the state's priorities. Figure 3.9 shows how the state's money is currently being allocated.

The state constitution distinguishes between two types of legislative appropriations: (1) the operating needs of state agencies and institutions (called the "general appropriation") and (2) all other needs that arise from time to time (called "supplemental appropriations"). Supplemental appropriations are handled through the normal legislative process. That is, a bill authorizing a specific appropriation is introduced, studied by committees, voted upon, and sent to the governor.[66] In contrast, the general appropriation bill is handled somewhat differently, as described below.

The general appropriation bill is really the state's operating budget because it appropriates funds for more than one hundred state agencies and institutions. If it is not passed in a timely manner, the universities, schools, courts, prisons, and other state institutions would simply run out of money and have to shut down. Accordingly, passing this bill—which is now done on a biennial basis—is one of the legislature's most important tasks. In many states, legislatures have surrendered most budget responsibilities to the governor's office. This is not the case in Arizona. Arizona's general appropriation bill relies on significant input from the governor, but it is very much a legislative product.

By law, the governor is required to submit a proposed operating budget to the legislature every two years.[67] However, the legislature's own Joint Legislative Budget Committee (JLBC) prepares a proposed budget as well.[68] The two rival budgets then undergo intense scrutiny in the legislature. Individual components of the budgets are debated in committees, subcommittees, party caucuses, and public hearings. State agencies and institutions, such as the universities, often lobby for higher appropriations. In the end, each legislative chamber votes on the final budget recommendations of its own appropriations committee. Typically, the official legislative adoption of the general

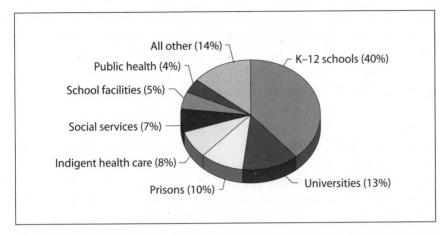

Figure 3.9 General fund appropriations: where the money goes (FY 2000). Source: Arizona Joint Legislative Budget Committee.

appropriation bill occurs in a special session called just for this purpose. Once the bill is approved by both houses, it goes the governor for approval or veto. As with all appropriation bills, the governor can exercise the more powerful line item veto. This enables the governor to reject individual appropriations within the bill while approving the remainder (see chapter 5). Additionally, because the general appropriation bill is necessary to the support of government, it is exempt from the referendum process (see chapter 4).

Although the legislature has significant control over public spending, its power is not absolute. First, the constitution imposes various spending restrictions. For example, unlike the federal government, the state's annual budget must be balanced.[69] In addition, in 1978, the voters added a provision that restricts state appropriations in any fiscal year to 7 percent of the state's total personal income.[70] Intended to combat "big government," the provision is highly complex, contains exemptions, and is not easy to apply.

Second, the legislature has very little authority over "earmarked" funds. These are revenues that are dedicated to special uses by constitutional or statutory provisions. For example, the constitution decrees that gasoline taxes must go into a separate fund for street and highway needs.[71] The legislature is not free to apply these tax revenues to other purposes. Federal funds are usually earmarked as well. Of special interest, however, are recent efforts by citizens to earmark funds to eliminate legislative discretion. For example, a 1994 citizen initiative raised taxes on cigarettes as an antismoking measure. However, the initiative directed that the taxes go into a special fund for indigent health care, antismoking research, and antismoking education. The citizen measure pointedly stressed that the funds were *not* subject to legislative appropriation.[72] It turned out that the tobacco tax generated far more revenues than anticipated. The legislature concluded that the excess money could be better spent on the construction of a new state health lab. It accordingly passed legislation authorizing the diversion of funds. This angered the citizens who sponsored the original initiative. They circulated a referendum petition to block the legislature's action. However, after enough signatures were collected to put the matter on the ballot, the legislature backed down. It quietly repealed the measure on its own, extinguishing the referendum. In 1996, another initiative similarly earmarked a portion of the state's lottery revenues for specified health programs. Clearly, the practice of earmarking funds is popular with the voters. However, government experts criticize this trend. They argue that earmarking introduces too much rigidity into the system and prevents the legislature from allocating resources to best meet the needs of all the citizenry.

Government Oversight Powers

The state legislature also plays an important watchdog role. It has various powers to ensure that state officials are properly performing their duties and that state programs are meeting their objectives:

Impeachment powers   The impeachment process enables the legislature to remove executive branch officials and judges from office before the end of their terms. It is an extreme remedy. Each chamber performs a separate constitutional function in this two-stage process. First, the house of representatives conducts a formal investigation when credible allegations of official misconduct arise. At the end of the investigation, the house takes a vote to decide whether or not the official should be impeached. To "impeach" a public official means to formally *accuse* the official of specific wrongdoing. Like the term "indict" in the criminal context, it simply triggers a trial; it does not determine whether the official is guilty of the charges. A vote of impeachment, therefore, merely requires a simple majority vote.[73]

The Arizona Constitution states that an official may be impeached for "high crimes, misdemeanors or malfeasance in office."[74] Interestingly, the parallel provision in the national Constitution[75] does not include the term "malfeasance"—which means misconduct. When Evan Mecham became the first governor in the state's history to be impeached, he sued the state legislature, arguing that the charges against him did not constitute impeachable offenses. (Mecham was accused of obstructing justice, making false statements in connection with campaign filings, and misusing public funds. The latter charge arose from his

Figure 3.10 Former governor Evan Mecham

loan of $80,000 in a state protocol fund to his own Pontiac dealership.) The Arizona Supreme Court, however, rejected Mecham's contentions. It held that it is up to the legislature to determine what constitutes an impeachable offense.[76]

Although an impeachment vote is merely the first step in the process, it does have serious consequences if the governor is the one being impeached. The state constitution requires that the governor temporarily step down at this juncture.[77] Thus, when 46 members of the house voted to impeach Governor Mecham on 5 February 1988, Secretary of State Rose Mofford immediately became the acting governor. (This is another difference between the state and federal processes. When President William Clinton was impeached by the U.S. House of Representatives in 1998, he remained in office.)

After an official is formally impeached, the process moves to the senate. The chief justice of the supreme court presides over a trial on the house's charges unless the chief justice is being impeached. (Another justice would be chosen in such circumstances.) In many ways an impeachment trial resembles any other trial: witnesses are summoned to testify, evidence is introduced, and attorneys make legal arguments. However, because it is a *political* trial, the official is not entitled to all of the procedural protections applicable in criminal cases (see chapter 6). The senate serves as the jury. When the trial is over, it takes a vote to determine whether the official should be convicted. Unlike the vote to impeach, this vote requires a two-thirds majority.[78]

The impeachment trial of Governor Mecham raised several novel constitutional questions. One involved the appropriate penalty. The language of the constitution is arguably unclear. It states that judgment in such cases

> shall extend only to removal from office and *disqualification to hold any office of honor, trust or profit in the state* (emphasis added).[79]

Everyone agreed that a senate conviction would have the effect of removing the governor from office. The dispute centered on the disqualification issue. This portion of the constitution is known as the **Dracula Clause** because it metaphorically puts a stake through the heart of the officeholder, preventing him or her from haunting the state again. Some senators argued that disqualification automatically accompanies a vote to convict. Others contended that it is an additional, *discretionary* penalty—to be levied only if the senate so chooses. In the end, the senate chose the latter interpretation and opted to take two separate votes. Governor Mecham was convicted of two of the house's three impeachment charges.[80] He was therefore removed from office and permanently replaced by the secretary of state, Rose Mofford, under the constitution's succession rules.[81] However, when the senate took the second vote on the issue of disqualification, the vote fell short. (Several key Democrats refused to support disqualification, presumably for political reasons.) Thus, Mecham was removed but not "dracula-ized." This allowed him to run for governor in the very next election, but he lost in the Republican primary.[82]

Impeachment is a rarely used procedure. (Governor Mecham's impeachment trial attracted national attention because it was the first time in sixty-one years that any governor in the country had been impeached.) No other state official has ever been removed through Arizona's impeachment process. It is fortunate that the process is rarely invoked. The Mecham trial lasted five weeks, not counting the house investigation that preceded it. This was a significant interruption for a hundred-day session. It delayed the passage of bills and took a major toll on the state's part-time lawmakers, many of whom declined to run again.

Legislative expulsion   The impeachment process does not apply to legislators. Instead, the constitution gives each chamber the power to expel its own members by a two-thirds vote.[83] In 1991, Senator Carolyn Walker was removed from the senate through this very means. Walker was one of the seven legislators involved in the Azscam bribery scandal. Unlike the others, she refused to resign her seat even after she was criminally indicted. The senate expelled her.

Other governmental oversight powers   Impeachment and expulsion are rare events. The legislature continuously monitors the state's large **bureaucracy** in more routine ways. First, its fiscal powers give it important leverage over all state agencies and departments. The legislature can effectively kill a program by simply refusing to fund it. Second, state agencies and programs are subjected to **sunset review**. This is a process that forces the legislature to reevaluate the efficacy of these programs on a periodic basis. That is, when an agency or program is created, it is given an automatic termination date. If the legislature doesn't vote to renew the agency or program before that date, the agency or program simply dies. Third, the legislature has the power to conduct investigations into any matter of governmental concern. It can hold formal hearings and subpoena witnesses to testify. Refusal to testify can result in contempt charges and imprisonment for the duration of the legislative session.[84] Finally, the senate approves high-level appointments made by the governor. This applies to most state agency heads and the members of state boards and commissions. If the senate rejects the governor's nominee (this rarely occurs), the governor is required to nominate a new person.

Other Legislative Powers

Most of the legislature's time is devoted to the lawmaking, appropriations, and oversight functions described in this chapter. The following additional responsibilities, although infrequently exercised, are nonetheless significant:

1. *Proposing state constitutional amendments:* The legislature periodically proposes amendments to the state constitution using the constitutional referendum process (see chapter 4). Proposed amendments are processed in the legislature in much the same way as ordinary bills and require only a simple majority vote for passage. However, when they are approved by both houses, they must always go to the people for a vote, rather than to the governor for approval or veto.

2. *Redistricting:* Since the mid-1960s, the legislature has been responsible for drawing the map for state and federal voting districts. It does this after each decennial census. Some argue that the function should be taken away from the legislature and given to a body that does not have a direct stake in the outcome. As of this writing, a constitutional initiative is circulating that would transfer redistricting to an independent citizen commission.[85]

3. *Amendments to the U.S. Constitution:* The legislature approves or rejects amendments to the U.S. Constitution on the rare occasions when such amendments are sent to the states for ratification.[86]

Online Resources

Arizona State Legislature:
   www.azleg.state.az.us/ (home page)
   www.azleg.state.az.us/legtext/bills.htm (bills)
   www.azleg.state.az.us/members/members.htm (members)
   www.azleg.state.az.us/maps/state.htm (district map)
   www.azleg.state.az.us/committes.htm (committee schedules and agenda)
   www.azleg.state.az.us/jlbc.htm (JLBC)
   www.azleg.state.az.us/srules.htm (senate rules)
   www.azleg.state.az.us/hrules.htm (house rules)

Arizona Bill:
   www.azleg.state.az.us/members/hbillaw.pdf

Arizona Legislative Council, *Arizona Legislative Bill Drafting Manual:*
   www.azleg.state.az.us/council/bdmwog.pdf

Arizona Legislative Council, *Arizona Legislative Manual:*
   www.azleg.state.az.us/council/legman.pdf

Gnant, Randall, *The Legislative Process in the Arizona Senate:*
   www.azleg.state.az.us/bill3law.htm

National Conference of State Legislatures:
   www.ncsl.org/ (home page)

4 Direct Democracy

Arizona's direct democracy procedures have no counterpart in the national government. Few states give their citizens as much power either.[1] The initiative, referendum, and recall have been part of Arizona's constitution since statehood. They remain just as popular with the voters today. In 1998, Arizonans amended the constitution to make the procedures even stronger. Nevertheless, as explained below, direct democracy procedures continue to generate controversy in theory as well as in practice.

The Theory of Direct Democracy

The term "democracy," which comes from the Greeks, can be loosely translated as "rule by the people." For nearly two thousand years, the term referred to a government in which the citizens *literally* ruled themselves. The most famous example of such a system was the government of ancient Athens, which flourished in the fifth and fourth centuries B.C. Approximately forty times a year the citizens of this city-state would assemble, debate, and make all major governmental decisions themselves.[2] Most government positions were filled by lot; ordinary citizens would simply take turns.

When America's Founding Fathers met in Philadelphia to establish a new government in 1787, they were fully aware of the Athenian model. However, they deliberately rejected it. A primary reason was the country's vast size. The Greek city-state was so small that all of the eligible citizens could assemble in one place. In contrast, even when America consisted of only thirteen colonies, this was not physically possible. Size, however, wasn't the only concern. Many of the Founding Fathers did not believe that ordinary citizens would make the best rulers. For example, James Madison and Alexander Hamilton, writing in the *Federalist Papers*, described pure democracy as a form of mob rule. They argued that democracy was likely to generate decisions based upon passion rather than reason; produce demagogues and divisive factions; trample the interests of minorities and the wealthy; and ultimately lead to civil or foreign wars that would destroy the country.[3]

For these and other reasons, the Founding Fathers favored a "republican form of government" over democracy.[4] Today we call their design a representative democracy and refer to the Greek version as a direct democracy or a "pure democracy." In a representative democracy, the citizens do not actually govern. Instead, representatives govern on their behalf. The representatives, however, must be accountable to the people in some fashion. (The most common mechanism of accountability is election to a fixed term of office.)

Madison believed that representative democracy was superior to direct democracy for several reasons: (1) it would allow the people's raw opinions to be "refined" through the representative process; (2) it would enable popular government to be extended over a larger territory; and (3) the larger territory would prevent the emergence of dangerous factions that could trample personal liberties or destroy the state.[5]

Many modern political theorists share these views. However, harsh economic conditions in the 1880s spawned a **Populist** movement in America that was highly critical of representative government. Essentially, the Populists believed that the political system was serving the interests of big business and neglecting the interests of farmers, workers, debtors—in short, "the little guy." At the century's end, the more broad-based Progressive movement (see chapter 2) took up many of the Populists' themes. The Progressives were especially critical of state and local governments. They believed that these governments were being controlled by corrupt party bosses, political machines, and powerful corporate interests.

Both the Populists and Progressives concluded that radical change was necessary. Specifically, they wanted to engraft elements of direct democracy onto the representative structure. Their thinking was that this would allow ordinary citizens to better control government. Thus, in the late 1890s the Progressives began aggressively promoting the initiative, referendum, and recall. South Dakota became the first state in the nation to adopt the initiative and referendum in 1898; eight other states quickly followed suit in the next decade; and Oregon added recall to the mix in 1908.[6]

When Arizona included six direct democracy procedures in its constitution of 1910, it was therefore in the vanguard but not setting precedent. However, in contrast to its predecessors, Arizona's adoption of direct democracy required the approval of the federal government because Arizona was applying for statehood.[7] The framers of Arizona's constitution were acutely aware of the risks. A lawsuit challenging Oregon's initiative was already pending in the U.S. Supreme Court.[8] The plaintiffs in that case were arguing that the initiative violated the U.S. Constitution's guarantee of a "republican form of government." Nonetheless, Arizona's framers refused to abandon direct democracy. As chronicled in chapter 2, their stubbornness led to Taft's veto of Arizona statehood. His veto, however, was targeted at a single direct democracy provision, the judicial recall. Arizona removed the provision, became a state, and promptly reinstated it. Meanwhile, the U.S. Supreme Court refused to rule on the constitutionality of the initiative in the Oregon case, holding that it was a "political question" for Congress to decide. Fortunately for Arizona, that ruling was issued five days after the territory had become a state! Today, the initiative, referendum, and recall are firmly established in Arizona.

How the Procedures Work

Arizona has five separate initiative and referendum procedures, which are summarized in table 4.1. Most voters don't differentiate them, because they all appear on the ballot as numbered **propositions.** There are, however, some fundamental differences. Initiatives allow the voters to approve or reject measures that have been *drafted by the citizens themselves.* In contrast, referenda enable the voters to approve or reject measures *drafted by the legislature.* The remaining differences turn on what the measure seeks to alter (either the constitution or the statutes) and who triggers the ballot process (either the voters or the legislature).

The Initiative

The constitutional initiative   The constitutional initiative allows the people to make changes to the state's constitution, bypassing elected officials alto-

Table 4.1 A Summary of Arizona's Initiative and Referendum Procedures

Procedure	What the Procedure Does	Signatures[a]
Constitutional initiative	Allows the voters to approve or reject constitutional amendments proposed by the voters	15%
Statutory initiative	Allows the voters to approve or reject new statutes proposed by the voters	10%
Constitutional referendum	Allows the voters to approve or reject constitutional amendments proposed by the legislature	None
Statutory referendum (by voter petition)	Allows the voters to approve or reject new statutes passed by the legislature	5%
Statutory referendum (by legislative referral)	Allows the voters to approve or reject new statutes proposed by the legislature	None

[a] Number of petition signatures needed to qualify the measure for the ballot. (Percentage refers to the total vote for governor in the prior election.)

gether. The voters can use this process to add, modify, or simply remove language in the constitution. Only fifteen states besides Arizona give citizens such power.

A successful constitutional initiative must survive two separate stages: petition and ballot. The petition stage begins with the drafting of the initiative. Any registered voter in Arizona can write a constitutional amendment on a petition form supplied by the secretary of state.[9] The measure can be typed or handwritten, crafted in perfect "legalese," or written in ungrammatical prose. Because this is entirely a people's process, no legal or editorial assistance is provided by the government. The petition is then circulated among registered voters. An initiator needs to collect supporting signatures equal to 15 percent of the state's last vote for governor. This currently equates to roughly 150,000 signatures, although the precise figure changes after every gubernatorial election. As a practical matter, successful petitioners must collect considerably more than the constitutional minimum to allow for the 20 percent that are typically invalidated. The initiator can begin collecting signatures any time after a general election, but all petitions must be returned to the secretary of state four months prior to the next election. This deadline gives petitioners a maximum of twenty months to complete the task. (A petitioner who fails to collect sufficient signatures can try again during the next general election cycle, but the signatures do not carry over.)

The constitution's signature requirement is intended to filter out proposals that are frivolous or that lack widespread public support. However, critics contend that it imposes too high a barrier. (In comparison to other states with constitutional initiative processes, Arizona's signature requirement is somewhat steep. For example, California requires only 8 percent; Massachusetts, 3 percent.) Nowadays, in order to collect enough signatures, most successful initiative campaigns must use paid circulators—a major obstacle for many grassroots efforts. There have been recent attempts to amend the constitution to lower the signature requirement, but, ironically, these initiative efforts have failed to attract sufficient signatures to make it to the ballot! If the secretary of state determines that there are enough valid signatures,[10] the second stage of

Figure 4.1 A constitutional initiative on the ballot. This measure, approved by the voters in 1996, required serious juvenile offenders to be tried as adults.

the initiative process commences. The proposed amendment goes to the voters at the next general election. The amendment appears on the ballot as a numbered proposition, with "yes" or "no" voting options (see figure 4.1). If more people vote yes than no, the measure becomes part of the constitution.[11]

The vast majority of constitutional initiatives die during the petition-circulating phase. Supporters simply fail to collect enough valid signatures to make it to the ballot. Even if they get past this hurdle, passage is not assured. Between 1912 and 1998, fifty-seven constitutional initiatives appeared on the ballot; of these, only twenty-five (43 percent) were approved by the voters. Nonetheless, many of Arizona's citizen-initiated amendments have been noteworthy. Some changed the basic rules under which the government operated. For example, citizen initiatives gave women the right to vote (1912); created merit selection for judges (1974); added a supermajority requirement for new taxes (1990); imposed term limits on elected officials (1992); and made it harder for officials to alter voter-approved measures (1998). Other citizen initiatives reacted to social concerns of the day. For example, the initiative pro-

Figure 4.2 Prohibition. Four constitutional initiatives on the ballot between 1914 and 1932 dealt with the prohibition of alcohol.

cess was used to prohibit alcohol and later repeal the prohibition (1914, 1932); to make Arizona an antiunion, "right-to-work" state (1946); to declare English the official language of the state (1988);[12] to add victims rights to the constitution (1990); and to punish juvenile offenders more severely (1996).

The statutory initiative   The statutory initiative allows ordinary citizens to write and enact laws. Only sixteen other states give the citizens such power.[13] Except for the lower signature threshold, the process is identical to the constitutional initiative. Any registered voter can propose a new statute. It can be a criminal law, an education law, a tax law, etc. Alternatively, the initiative can repeal or modify an existing statute. The only constraint is that a citizen-initiated law must conform to the Arizona and U.S. constitutions just like any other law.[14] As with constitutional initiatives, what you see is what you get; the government does not provide any legal or editorial assistance to citizen lawmakers.

The signature requirement for statutory initiative petitions is 10 percent of the state's last vote for governor. Currently this equates to roughly 100,000 signatures. As figure 4.3 indicates, most initiatives do not make it past this first stage. Moreover, an initiative that survives the petition stage has only cleared the first hurdle. It still must win the approval of a majority of the voters. Accordingly, it goes on the ballot at the next general election as a numbered proposition. If it is passed by the voters, the citizen-initiated law goes into the statute books to be enforced by public officials like any other state law.

From the very beginning, the legislature and the voters have clashed over statutory initiatives. In 1914, the voters added a provision to the constitution that was intended to prevent the legislature from *ever* altering voter-approved measures. However, the Arizona Supreme Court effectively nullified this barrier by interpreting it narrowly.[15] Nonetheless, the legislature would usually tread carefully. It would typically wait a few years—that is, until voter memories had dimmed—before tinkering with citizen-initiated laws. However, the Forty-third Legislature was not so deferential. It boldly went after several high-profile measures enacted by the people. Most notably, it gutted a controversial marijuana initiative approved by the voters only months before.

An upset citizen group, calling itself the "Voter Protection Alliance," launched a counterattack in 1998. It used the constitutional initiative to make voter-approved measures virtually immune from legislative alteration. As a result of this initiative, Arizona's constitution now unambiguously states that (1) the governor cannot veto any measure approved by the voters; (2) the legislature cannot repeal any measure approved by the voters; and (3) the legislature can modify a citizen-approved measure or divert earmarked funds only if the modification "furthers the purpose" of the citizen measure and is passed by *three-quarters* of the members of both houses.[16] These restrictions will make it extremely difficult for the legislature to overrule the people on statutory matters in the future. They indicate that the Progressive spirit is alive and well in Arizona. (Whether it is desirable to have laws that are so insulated from alteration remains to be seen. Citizen-initiated laws, like those enacted by the legislature, are rarely perfect in their first incarnation.)

Between 1912 and 1998, eighty-five statutory initiatives made it to the ballot, but only thirty-three (39 percent) were approved by the voters. This low number demonstrates that the vast majority of the state's laws are made by elected officials and not by the citizens. Although citizen-initiated laws are relatively rare, they are interesting and often quite controversial. For example, the voters have used this process to restrict the employment of noncitizens

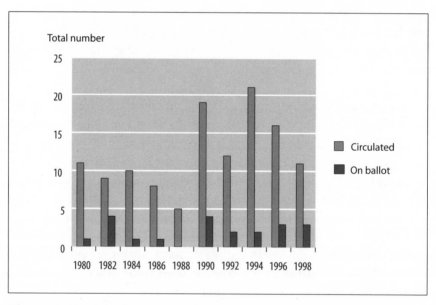

Figure 4.3 Number of statutory initiatives circulated and on the ballot. Source: Arizona Secretary of State, Election Department.

USING THE INITIATIVE TO FIGHT FOR A SCHOOL NAME [17]

There used to be only one public university in Arizona—and the University of Arizona wanted to keep it that way. Its upstate rival was created on the same day in 1885, but Tucson got the university; Tempe instead got a teacher-training school, originally called the Arizona Territorial Normal School. Over the years, the U of A used its political clout to prevent its Tempe rival (later named Arizona State College) from adding "university" to its name. The fight became serious in the mid-1950s. Multiple bills were introduced in the legislature to authorize the name change to reflect the school's expanded offerings. Two thousand Tempe students marched to the state capitol, but the bills still stalled. (This was before redistricting, and Maricopa County was badly underrepresented.) In 1958, the frustrated college president, Grady Gammage, decided that a grassroots initiative campaign was the only hope. Even though the petition was filed late in the election cycle, students and alumni managed to collect double the needed signatures in a mere two months' time. Once the measure passed the ballot hurdle, an enthusiastic advertising campaign kicked in. Billboards, bumper stickers, a barnstorming airplane, and a 30-second spot by TV celebrity Steve Allen were all enlisted in the cause. On election day, students manned the phones and went door-to-door to turn out the vote. That night they packed the Memorial Union to anxiously await the results. Voters in Maricopa County resoundingly supported the name change by a vote of 105,152 to 15,854. It was no surprise that Pima County voters rejected the measure, but the margin was a lopsided 9 to 1. Overall, however, the measure passed by 72,460 votes. The letters "ASU" were lit on the Tempe Butte for the first time, the Sun Devil band played, and exultant students hoisted President Gammage in the all-night victory celebration. Arizona State College was now Arizona State University.

(1914);[18] to abolish and then reestablish the death penalty (1916, 1918); to change the name of Arizona State College to "Arizona State University" (1958) (see box); to create a state lottery (1980); to impose strict limits on campaign contributions (1986); to levy a higher cigarette tax (1994); to ban steel-jawed animal traps (1994); to permit the medical use of marijuana and other controlled substances (1996); to authorize public financing of election campaigns (1998); and to make cockfighting a crime (1998). At the same time, the voters rejected citizen initiatives that would have legalized gambling (1942, 1952); desegregated public schools (1950); imposed a nuclear freeze (1982); required beverages to be sold in returnable containers (1982); and banned abortion under most circumstances (1992).

The Referendum

The constitutional referendum   The constitutional referendum is the most common route to constitutional change. In this process, the legislature proposes the amendment. Although each chamber has to independently approve it, only a simple majority is needed. Once the amendment passes, it goes to a vote of the people. Ordinarily this vote occurs at the next regularly scheduled general election. On rare occasions the legislature has called a special election instead. In either event, the amendment appears on the ballot as a numbered proposition and is voted on in the same fashion as other ballot measures. It should be noted that the governor plays no role in this process. In fact, the governor cannot veto any initiative or referendum.[19]

Over the years, the legislature has proposed constitutional amendments on a variety of different topics. For example, in 1994, the legislature concluded that the state needed a lieutenant governor. (Arizona is one of the few states that lacks this office.) The legislature drafted the necessary constitutional language and sent it to the people for approval. The voters, however, decisively rejected the proposition by a margin of nearly 2 to 1. Between 1912 and 1998, the legislature sent 169 constitutional amendments to the voters this same way, and 100 (59 percent) were approved. As the numbers indicate, Arizona voters do not always rubber-stamp their legislature, although the legislature's amending success rate is higher than the people's.

The statutory referendum by citizen petition   Arizona citizens have the power to block laws passed by the legislature. Most new statutes do not take effect immediately. Rather, they remain on hold for ninety days after the legislative session adjourns. This waiting period gives the citizens an opportunity to launch a statutory referendum. Any registered voter can do this by circulating a petition that targets a specific law or part of a law. The voter must obtain supporting signatures equal to 5 percent of the state's last vote for governor. (Currently this equates to roughly 50,000 signatures.) Although this is a much smaller number than that required for initiatives, the shorter time-period (ninety days) makes this task relatively difficult.

If enough valid signatures are collected, the targeted law does not take effect with the other laws passed during the same legislative session. Instead, it remains on hold until the next general election. The challenged measure then appears on the ballot as a numbered proposition. Voters are asked to decide whether or not it should be approved. If the majority of voters vote "yes," the referendum fails. This means that the voters have sided with the legislature, and the law belatedly takes effect. If the majority of voters reject the proposition, the referendum has succeeded. In essence, the people have "vetoed" the law. Significantly, there are three types of laws that *cannot* be blocked by the people through this process:

1. *Laws with emergency clauses.* The legislature can insulate any law from the referendum simply by attaching a paragraph to the bill that declares that the law is immediately needed to "preserve public peace, health, or safety."[20] (It does not have to be true.) However, as noted in chapter 3, emergency bills require a higher two-thirds vote to pass. This prevents the legislature from easily abusing the exemption. Of course, real emergencies that require a quick governmental response do occur. Without the exemption, needed governmental action (e.g., emergency relief funds) would be delayed for at least ninety days.

2. *Laws necessary to the support of government.* The state's general appropriation bill and other funding bills needed to keep government running are also exempt from the referendum.[21] Without this exemption, a small, cranky minority could temporarily shut down all state institutions, including prisons and schools.

3. *New tax laws.* Tax laws are also exempt from the voter-triggered referendum.[22] This exemption is presumably based upon the fear that 5 percent of the voters could always be found to block a tax. It should be noted, however, that citizens still have the power to repeal a tax *after* it takes

effect using the initiative process. (This may not always be practical with short-term taxes, such as the Bank One Ballpark levy, which expire before the initiative process could be successfully completed.)

Between 1912 and 1998, only thirty-four referenda by petition reached the ballot, and the voters sided with the legislature half the time. Superficially, this would suggest that the people's referendum is not a very powerful tool. However, the potency of the procedure cannot be judged by these figures alone. The mere *threat* of a referendum can operate as a significant deterrent on legislative behavior. For example, in 1995, at the behest of Governor Fife Symington, the legislature passed a controversial bill giving the governor the power to fire appointees to state boards. (As explained in chapter 5, these persons cannot be removed by the governor—a fact that reduces the governor's overall control of the executive branch.) Citizens opposing the expansion of gubernatorial powers launched a referendum and obtained enough signatures to put the measure on the 1996 ballot. However, the voters never got the chance to vote. Instead, the legislature quietly repealed the bill prior to the election. Similarly, when the legislature attempted to divert cigarette tax revenues that had been earmarked by a citizen initiative (see chapter 3), a group calling itself "Stop the Raid!" also collected enough signatures to force a referendum. Once again, the legislature chose to repeal the bill on its own, rather than to allow the referendum to proceed. In both of these examples the referendum process was well under way; it is impossible to estimate how often the legislature alters its course simply because a referendum is threatened or anticipated.

The statutory referendum by legislative referral   The final of the five procedures is the rarest. From statehood through 1998, the legislature has referred only nineteen proposed statutes to the people. The process is fairly straightforward. Whenever the legislature passes a bill, it has the option of sending it to the voters instead of the governor. If it chooses this course, the measure is held until the next general election (i.e., unless a special election is called). The proposed statute then appears on the ballot like any other numbered proposition with "yes" and "no" options. If a majority of the voters approve it, the law takes effect. Otherwise, it is killed by the peoples' vote. The legislature almost always uses the traditional lawmaking process, sending its bills to the governor. This is the quicker and less costly route. However, the referendum gives the legislature a way of circumventing an anticipated gubernatorial

REFERENDA WARS: KING DAY AND THE SUPER BOWL

Arizona's referenda procedures got a real workout during the state's six-year struggle to create a Martin Luther King Jr. state holiday. Paid holidays in Arizona are normally established by statute. However, in 1986, Governor Bruce Babbitt simply declared an MLK holiday by executive decree after the legislature balked. (Arizona was one of a few states that lacked such a holiday.)

Babbitt's term expired before the January observance took place. His successor, Evan Mecham, repealed the holiday as one of his first acts in office.[23] The controversial repeal helped launch a recall effort against Mecham six months later. It also brought Arizona unwanted national attention and hurt the state's ongoing effort to lure the Super Bowl to Tempe. Accordingly, when Mecham was ousted from office in 1988, Governor Rose Mofford was able to persuade the legislature to legally establish a King holiday. However, because the lawmakers didn't want state workers to get an additional day off, their measure eliminated Columbus Day. This upset Italian-American voters. They quickly collected enough signatures to trigger a referendum. The holiday measure was put on hold until all the voters could decide the issue at the next general election in 1990.

In the meantime, entertainers and national conventions began boycotting Arizona. When the legislature came under increasing pressure from the tourism industry, it decided not to wait for the outcome of the referendum. Instead, it passed a new holiday law that restored Columbus Day and established King Day as an additional paid holiday. Governor Mofford promptly signed the new bill into law. However, before this second attempt could take effect, another coalition of voters collected sufficient signatures to trigger a referendum!

When the 1990 election rolled around, Arizona voters were thus confronted with two conflicting holiday propositions on the same ballot.[24] Not surprisingly, this created voter confusion. Heavy-handed lobbying by the National Football League on the eve of the election only worsened the situation. The NFL's commissioner publicly threatened to remove the 1993 Super Bowl from Tempe if one of the two measures didn't pass. This antagonized many voters who resented the outside interference in state affairs. In the end, both holiday proposals failed, although the second measure lost by a mere 17,882 votes.

The NFL followed through on its threat. The 1993 Super Bowl was yanked from Arizona and played in Pasadena instead. The national boycott of the state intensified, causing the legislature to go back to the drawing board. This time, the legislature crafted a new law that made room for King Day by combining Lincoln's and Washington's birthday into a single holiday. And instead of sending the bill to the governor—the usual course—it opted to refer the measure directly to the people using the statutory referendum. The third time was the charm. In November 1992, Arizona voters approved the King holiday by a wide margin. The Super Bowl was played in Tempe in 1996.

veto. More typically, it uses the statutory referendum when an issue is of great public interest or likely to produce an angry voter backlash—circumstances that were both present in the prolonged debate over the creation of a Martin Luther King Jr. holiday (see box).

Evaluating the initiative and referendum   Initiatives and referenda have appeared on the Arizona ballot at a fairly constant rate since statehood. Nonetheless, the procedures generate as much controversy today as they did back in 1910. Modern critics contend that the citizen measures produce poorer laws because they do not undergo the scrutiny that takes place in the traditional legislative process. They point to the legal challenges that these laws often spawn and argue that such court cases waste public resources.

Another common criticism is that citizen measures are too extreme. Initiators are not forced to make compromises in order to win passage. Consequently, the voters are often given all-or-nothing choices instead of a preferred middle ground. The 1996 "medical marijuana" initiative is a good illustration. While polls showed that many voters favored a relaxation of the law with respect to marijuana, the measure on the ballot actually extended to heroin, PCP, and 113 other hard drugs.

Citizen measures often target minorities and unpopular groups, thereby exacerbating social tensions. For example, Arizonans used the process to restrict the hiring of noncitizens (1914), and to pass an "Official English" amendment (1988). Both of these were subsequently declared unconstitutional by the courts. During the 1990s, initiatives targeted at homosexuals and illegal aliens were circulated but failed to make the ballot. (They did pass in California and Colorado.)

Another criticism is that the procedures are too costly for ordinary citizens to use. Even when enough signatures can be collected, supporters may not be able to afford the advertising needed to win passage. For example, a 1992 grassroots initiative to ban steel-jawed animal traps was favored in opinion polls until the National Rifle Association (NRA) funded a $1.4 million media campaign against it.[25] Conversely, big businesses, trade associations, unions, and professional organizations can exploit the processes for their own economic advantage.[26] In contrast to citizens, they can afford to hire petition circulators and advertise. In fact, this is how Arizona got the lottery in 1980. An out-of-state gaming company was seeking to expand its own business. When the company couldn't talk the legislature and governor into allowing gambling, it financed a successful initiative campaign. The 1994 battle over tort reform (see chapter 6) is another example. One side, calling itself "People for a Fair Legal System," was really the insurance industry; the other side, "FAIR," was an organization of personal injury lawyers. Both groups had direct economic stakes in the controversy and disseminated misleading advertising about the complex ballot measures. Similarly, the tobacco industry was the real force behind the "No More Taxes Committee" that opposed a 1994 anti-smoking initiative.

A related criticism is that initiatives and referenda permit wealthy outsiders to influence or alter the state's laws. For example, three millionaires joined forces and collectively contributed more than $3 million to the two successful ballot campaigns that changed Arizona's drug laws in 1996 and 1998. Two of the millionaires didn't even live in Arizona. (The threesome succeeded in changing the laws of four other states as well.)[27]

Another concern is that elected officials are increasingly using the procedures to augment their own power. For example, when Governor Symington couldn't persuade the legislature to enact his juvenile justice proposals, he launched a citizen initiative. The governor was able to use his high-profile position to easily win passage of the measure in 1996. Governor Jane Hull and Superintendent of Schools Lisa Keegan have threatened similar action as a way of increasing their leverage with the legislature. This practice alters the delicate checks and balances between the two branches of government.

The increasingly popular tactic of "counter-propositions" threatens the integrity of the initiative process. Counter-propositions are rival measures sponsored by opponents of an initiative. They lengthen the ballot, confuse the voters, and increase the likelihood that the two competing measures will both fail—which is often the outcome most desired by the opponents. In recent years, the state legislature has also begun using this tactic. In 1998, it referred three measures to the voters to counter citizen initiatives; in 2000, it referred an antisprawl measure because the Sierra Club was sponsoring a more aggressive initiative. (In fairness, the legislature defends this practice, saying that it is merely responding to voter concerns and providing a more reasonable alternative.)

Finally, critics of direct democracy procedures argue that voters do not always make the best legislators. Ballot measures can be quite complex. Yet they are often enacted or rejected on the basis of inadequate information and misleading media sound-bites. Some ballots contain more than a dozen propositions, severely taxing the ability of the voters to make informed choices. And in contrast to the legislature, voters do not have the entire picture when they vote on an issue being pushed by one particularly vocal group. That is, they do not have to balance the needs of all the other competing constituencies.

Despite these criticisms, the initiative and referendum remain quite popular with most citizens. Defenders of the procedures argue that initiatives provide the only reliable way of reforming government, particularly when the proposed measures are not in the legislators' own self-interest. For example, Arizona's stringent campaign contribution laws and term limits provisions were enacted by the citizens; it is doubtful that either would have been approved through the traditional legislative process.

Direct democracy procedures also give citizens a way to counter the influence of powerful interest groups, such as the tobacco industry, that hold sway over the legislature. For years, this lobby was able to block the enactment of tougher antismoking legislation. In 1994, Arizona citizens did an end run around this lobby by using the initiative process. Similarly, voters have used referendum procedures to kill special interest legislation that would have otherwise taken effect.

Supporters also argue that initiative and referendum procedures make the government more responsive. The procedures don't even have to be used. The mere threat of a petition process can prompt the legislature to address issues that it would otherwise prefer to ignore (e.g., antigrowth measures), or cause it to refrain from taking action contrary to the public interest.

Initiatives also enable ignored or powerless groups to take their case to the people. For example, women gained the right to vote in Arizona through this means in 1912. In 1996, the Salt River Pima-Maricopa Indians used the initiative process to win the right to operate casinos. The small tribe, which had little political clout, simply took its "fairness" argument to the voters after the governor refused to negotiate.

Direct democracy enthusiasts argue that the critics underestimate the common sense of the electorate. Many issues on the ballot are fairly straightforward and well within the competence of the voters to decide. They also note that big money does not always determine election outcomes. For example, in 1994 the tobacco industry spent more than $4.7 million in a fruitless attempt to defeat the cigarette tax initiative, and State Farm Insurance donated nearly $3.5 million to push a tort reform initiative that did not pass.[28]

The steel-jawed trap initiative, although initially defeated by NRA money, did eventually pass two years later, after it was slightly revised.

Finally, supporters argue that ballot measures foster a more engaged electorate and a healthier democracy. They stimulate interest in elections, educate the citizens, focus attention on issues, as opposed to candidate personalities, permit social solutions to come from a broader pool, and provide a safety valve for alienated citizens.[29]

The Recall

Recall permits Arizona voters to remove state and local officials from office before the end of their terms. Like other direct democracy processes, it has both a petition stage and an election stage. Any registered voter can begin the process by circulating a petition for the recall of a specified official. The petition must set forth the grounds for removal in two hundred words or less.[30] The only constraint is that no recall can be started until after the official has served six months in office. (An exception exists for legislators, who can be targeted a mere five days after the first session begins.)

The signature requirement for recall petitions is the steepest of all of Arizona's direct democracy procedures. It requires 25 percent of the total number of votes cast in the last election for the targeted office. (For example, over 250,000 signatures currently would be needed to launch a recall effort against the governor.) If sufficient petition signatures are obtained, the official is given five days to resign. If he or she refuses, a special recall election is called by the secretary of state. Any qualified person can run against the incumbent in this election. Whoever gets the most votes wins the office. If the incumbent wins, the recall effort has failed. The official cannot be recalled again during the term unless the recall petitioners pay the expenses of the preceding election.

It is instructive to compare recall to impeachment, the more traditional means of removal in this country (see table 4.2). Most obviously, recall is a peoples' process, whereas impeachment is not. With recall, an election campaign, rather than an evidentiary trial, determines whether the official will remain in office. If the governor is the target, there are two other important differences. First, the governor remains in office throughout the recall process. (In contrast, with impeachment the governor temporarily loses power at the moment the house votes to impeach.) Second, following a successful

Table 4.2 Contrasting the Impeachment and Recall Processes

Differences	Impeachment	Recall
Who starts the process?	The house of representatives by a simple majority vote.	Twenty-five percent of the citizens by petition.
Who decides the outcome?	The senate by a two-thirds vote following an evidentiary trial.	The voters, voting in a special recall election.
Who gets the office?	If the governor is the target, the office passes to the constitutional successor (usually the secretary of state); if another official is the target, a successor is appointed (usually by the governor).	The winner of the recall election gets the office. If the incumbent wins, he or she retains the office and the recall fails.

recall, an outsider—i.e., the person who wins the election—inherits the office. In contrast, when the governor is convicted of impeachment charges the office passes to the constitutionally designated successor. This will ordinarily be the secretary of state, assuming that the officeholder was elected to the office and not appointed.[31]

Because the signature requirement is so steep, serious recall efforts are a rarity on the state level. No statewide official has ever been removed from office by this means.[32] And despite President Taft's concerns, only one superior court judge has been recalled from office (for erratic behavior). Instead, most recalls occur at the local level and involve city council or school board members. (The same 25 percent requirement applies. However, because the electorate is smaller, and voter turnout is much lower, the signature requirement is more easily met.)

Arizona's recall procedures garnered national attention in 1988 when Governor Evan Mecham was simultaneously subjected to separate recall, impeachment, *and* criminal proceedings. Six months to the day after the governor assumed office in 1987, citizens began circulating recall petitions for his removal. Meanwhile, in early 1988, the house of representatives voted to impeach the governor (see chapter 3). While the impeachment trial was still pending in the senate, recall supporters defied the odds and collected over 300,000 petition signatures within four months. This was far more than needed to trigger a recall election. When Governor Mecham refused to resign, the secretary of state scheduled a recall election for May. Several prominent candidates began campaigning against the governor. In April, however, Mecham was convicted of impeachment charges in the senate and removed from office. Secretary of State Rose Mofford thereupon became governor under the constitution's succession provision. (Mecham was later acquitted of all criminal charges by a superior court jury.)

The controversy, however, did not end with Governor Mecham's removal. Some voters wanted the recall election to still go forward. Mofford was a Democrat, and many Republicans were unhappy with their party's unexpected, midterm loss of the governor's office. Others simply wanted to be able to choose Mecham's successor from among the candidates who were already campaigning. When the attorney general issued a legal opinion that the recall election could not be stopped, the matter went to court. In the end, the state supreme court cancelled the recall election. The court acknowledged that it was forced to improvise because there was no precedent for the triple constitutional threat faced by the governor.[33] As a result of the ruling, Governor Mofford remained in office for the balance of Mecham's term, and gubernatorial control abruptly switched from the Republican party to the Democrats.

Evaluating the recall process   Although initiative and referendum procedures have slowly gained support in the past century, recall (at least on the state level) still remains fairly controversial. Most states have not adopted this procedure. Critics of recall contend that it undermines representative government by making elected officials too timid to make principled and tough decisions. The process can be abused by political rivals and disgruntled factions who refuse to accept the majority's electoral choice. Special interests can also exploit the process for their own ends. Even when recall is not successful or fully completed, it creates divisiveness and distracts elected officials from their duties. This, in turn, may deter capable individuals from running for office. Critics also contend that recall is inferior to impeachment because (1) it permits the public to react too quickly to a single unpopular decision; and (2) it does not afford the officeholder a forum for a reasonable hearing. Finally, recall can be costly to both the taxpayers (who pay for the extra election) and the officeholder (who may be forced to campaign twice for the same office).

In rebuttal, supporters of recall argue that recall enables the electorate to remove incompetent, corrupt, or unresponsive officials without excessive delay. It provides for *continuous* accountability, making elected officials more sensitive to the public interest on every decision. Recall allows the citizens to act when the legislature may be too corrupt to impeach. It serves as an important safety valve for disaffected voters. Finally, defenders argue that the high petition signature requirement and restriction on multiple recall elections prevent the process from being abused.

Online Resources

Arizona Secretary of State:
    www.sosaz.com (home page)
    www.sosaz.com/election/ (Election Department)

5 The Executive Branch

The job of the executive branch is to carry out ("execute") the laws and judicial decrees of the state. It is a huge responsibility. More than 62,000 people work for this branch of government, in addition to multiple elected officials. This makes the executive not only the largest of the three branches of state government, but also Arizona's biggest employer by a wide margin.

Most people don't realize the range of services that the executive branch provides. Nor do they think of university professors (or football coaches for that matter) as executive branch employees. However, these individuals get their paychecks from the state, along with highway engineers, park rangers, correctional officers, prosecutors, social workers, and many other professionals. Arizona's executive branch operates prisons, medical facilities, and three universities. It oversees the public school system and certifies all of those teachers. It constructs, maintains, and polices state highways. It manages vast natural resources and public lands. It provides assistance to the needy and unemployed. It licenses accountants, barbers, chiropractors, contractors, dentists, nurses, pharmacists, physicians, psychologists, real estate brokers, veterinarians, and many other occupations. It regulates corporations, day care centers, hospitals, insurance companies, liquor sellers, nursing homes, and other private businesses. It issues hunting, fishing, and drivers' licenses. It operates a lottery. It preserves the vital records of the state's residents. It handles the state's legal affairs. It oversees elections. It promotes tourism and economic development. And this list is incomplete.

Coordinating such a range of responsibilities is no easy task. However, like most of its sister states, Arizona has a "weak" executive branch. That is, neither the governor nor any other official has overarching management authority. Instead, power in the executive branch is carefully restricted by the constitution and fragmented among many elected officials and quasi-independent boards. The design of Arizona's executive branch reflects the deep mistrust of its Progressive framers. They were uneasy about executive power for several reasons. First, the executive branch enjoys considerable discretion in how policies are carried out; the framers worried that this discretion could be easily abused. Second, the framers feared all concentrations of power. They knew that when power is consolidated in a few hands, it is more easily corrupted. Finally, Arizona's territorial officials did not give executive power a particularly good name. However, the framers faced a dilemma. Most large organizations also need strong leadership, which implies firmness, single focus, and quick response. These are traits that committees and collective bodies typically lack. For this reason, large organizations generally favor the pyramid structure that the framers wound up rejecting. In the end, they consciously sacrificed a degree of efficiency for greater safety. Although some of their efforts have been undone by modern amendments, Arizona's executive branch still remains weak by deliberate design.

Executive Branch Structure

A Plural Executive Branch

Multiple elected officials   Arizona has a **plural executive branch**. Instead of concentrating power in a single elected head (like the U.S. president), there are multiple elected officials. The voters separately elect a governor, secretary of state, attorney general, state treasurer, superintendent of public instruction, state mine inspector, and corporation commissioners. The total number of officials has changed slightly since statehood. Originally, the voters also elected a state auditor, but this office was eliminated as an elective position in 1968. In addition, there have been proposals to expand the corporation commission from three elected members to five.[1]

Having so many elected officials increases the level of conflict and disunity within the executive branch. Because the officials are elected independently of each other, they can be of different political parties. For example, from 1990 through 1994, Arizona had a Republican governor and a Democratic secretary of state; in 1998, the voters elected a Republican governor and a Democratic attorney general. Members of different parties, of course, have ample reason not to cooperate with each other. Conflicts also occur even when the officials are of the same political party. They may be rivals for some future office or may simply have different policy views. For example, in the mid-1990s, Governor Fife Symington and Superintendent of Public Instruction Lisa Graham Keegan advocated diametrically opposing approaches to educational reform. The governor could not "fire" the superintendent or insist that she promote his policies. As an independently elected official, the superintendent could rightly claim that *she* had been chosen by the voters to set the state's school policies. Later on, the school superintendent and Governor Hull wound up taking opposite sides in a major lawsuit challenging school funding.[2] Arizona's attorney generals have also clashed with the state's governors, irrespective of party affiliations. (Attorney generals often harbor ambitions of being governor themselves, making them potential political rivals.) Tensions between these two offices can be particularly disruptive because the attorney general's legal support is needed to implement most executive branch policies. Not surprisingly, when Attorney General Robert Corbin began criminal proceedings against Governor Evan Mecham (a fellow Republican) in 1988, turmoil within the executive branch reached record levels. While this was undeniably an extreme situation, the plural design of Arizona's executive branch promotes internal conflicts and rivalries. This in turn reduces the power of the governor and the branch as a whole.

Many quasi-independent boards and agencies   The organization of the state's bureaucracy further limits the governor's control. The executive branch is divided into more than one hundred separate departments and agencies. Many of these are headed by a single person, who is subject to the governor's control. However, other agencies are headed by multiperson boards that are highly independent. Board members are typically part-time "citizen administrators" drawn from the professions that they regulate. For example, the Arizona Board of Medical Examiners (BOMEX), which oversees the state's physicians, is required to have eight doctors, one nurse, and three members of the general public.[3] Although the governor appoints the members of most boards,[4] they generally serve for fixed terms and cannot be removed by the governor.[5] The governor, accordingly, has limited ability to control decision making by these agencies. Moreover, as table 5.1 reflects, some important executive responsibilities are controlled by such quasi-independent boards.

Evaluating the executive branch   The plural design of Arizona's executive branch is not unique. Nearly all states elect multiple officials instead of fol-

Table 5.1 Major State Boards and Commissions

Accountancy	Industrial Commission
Barbers	Medical Examiners ("BOMEX")
Chiropractic Examiners	Nursing
Community College	Opticians
Corporation Commission[a]	Parks
Cosmetology	Pharmacy
Dental Examiners	School Facilities[c]
Education[b]	Regents[d]
Executive Clemency	Veterinary Medical Examiners
Funeral Directors and Embalmers	

[a] Members are elected.

[b] The superintendent of public instruction is a member of the board.

[c] The superintendent of public instruction is a non-voting member of the board.

[d] The governor and superintendent of public instruction are ex-officio members of the board.

lowing the unitary structure of the national government. The large number of quasi-independent boards, however, makes Arizona's governor weak in comparison to most sister states. Public administration experts generally criticize this design. They argue that a plural executive branch deprives the state of strong leadership, and that it is prone to too many conflicts and internal rivalries. Accountability is also reduced because elected officials can blame each other for failures. The state would be better off, the critics contend, with a single official who could be held responsible. Finally, a plural executive branch puts more elected politicians, as opposed to expert professionals, at the helm of major state departments.

However, most Arizonans still share the Progressives' contrary views on this issue. Over the years, the voters have rebuffed proposals to consolidate or strengthen the governor's powers. Defenders of the plural design counter that a plural executive branch provides needed checks against abuse of executive power. It also insulates sensitive regulatory agencies from excessive political pressure. (For example, without relative independence, parole board decisions could be easily politicized by governors seeking to score points with the voters.) Finally, a plural executive branch is more democratic, enabling the citizens to elect the heads of key departments (such as education) and allowing citizens to serve on more boards and commissions.

Terms and Elections

Length of terms   The constitution originally gave the governor and other executive officers two-year terms like legislators. This was intended to further reduce executive power by putting such officials on a short leash. At the constitutional convention, short terms were touted as "one of the guarantees of democratic government."[6] In 1968, however, the voters concluded that two-year terms were *too* short. (This is one of the few times when they heeded the advice of public administration experts.) Accordingly, the constitution was amended to give the five major offices four-year terms.[7]

When the executive terms were lengthened, the state had to decide whether the four-year electoral cycle should coincide with the U.S. presidential term. In the end, Arizona decided to follow the practice of most states and have its executive officers elected in even-numbered, *off*-presidential years (2002, 2006, 2010, etc.) (see figure 5.1). This arrangement has advantages as well as disadvantages. On the plus side, it focuses more attention on state issues and prevents national presidential politics from unduly influencing state election outcomes. On the minus side, as shown in figure 5.2, **voter turnout** is much

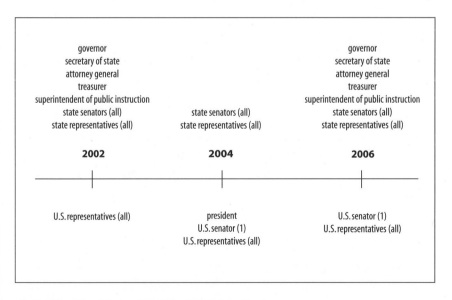

Figure 5.1 The Arizona and U.S. election cycle

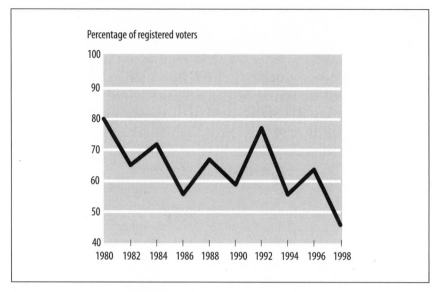

Figure 5.2 Voter turnout in Arizona general elections. Source: Arizona Secretary of State, *Official Canvass*, 1980–1998.

lower in off-presidential years. (Even in presidential election years, Arizona's voter turnout is well below the national average.)[8] The result is that the state's top officials are chosen by a small segment of the voting age population.

Term limits   Prior to 1992, Arizona executive officials could hold office for an unlimited number of terms. Arizona's first governor, George Hunt, remains the gubernatorial record holder, having won seven (two-year) terms. In 1992, Arizona voters imposed term limits. (The state treasurer had always been subject to term limits—reflecting the framers' heightened concerns over the management of public money.) Currently, the five major executive branch officers can serve no more than two consecutive terms in office, or eight years.[9]

Qualifications

In keeping with their Populist sympathies, the Progressive drafters of Arizona's constitution intentionally kept the qualifications for executive office relatively low. The governor and the state's four other major officers need only

THE POLITICAL SOLUTION THAT BACKFIRED

How do you determine who wins an election when more than two candidates run? For seventy-six years, Arizona's constitution provided a straightforward answer: whoever gets the most votes. This is known as a plurality rule. However, in 1988, Arizonans had second thoughts about this simple rule. They were reacting to the political trauma caused by the impeachment and recall of Evan Mecham (see chapters 3 and 4). Some blamed the state's plurality rule. It was observed that Governor Mecham had won the office in an unusual three-way race where the votes were distributed as follows:

*Evan Mecham (R) =	40%
Carolyn Warner (D) =	34%
Bill Shulz (I) =	26%

In other words, Mecham never had the support of a majority (i.e., one more than half) of the voters. In fact, it could be argued that 60 percent of the electorate wanted anybody but Mecham. A majority rule would have prevented this situation from occurring. Accordingly, the voters decided to amend the constitution to require a runoff election between the top two vote-getters if nobody got a majority of the vote. This would ensure that the winner would always have the support of at least half of the state's voters. It seemed like a good idea—at least to the 56% of the electorate that supported the constitutional change. Unfortunately, disaster struck at the very next gubernatorial election. There shouldn't have been any need for a runoff, because this was only a two-candidate race. However, the election was extremely close, and seven write-in candidates (including a prominent Mecham supporter) siphoned off a scant 11,731 votes in an election where more than one million votes were cast. The final breakdown was as follows:

*Fife Symington (R) =	49.7%
Terry Goddard (D) =	49.3%
All write-ins combined =	1.0%

Even though Symington got the most votes, he did not win the election under the constitution's brand new majority rule. The state was required to conduct a runoff election that was a virtual replay of the original election. Symington won the runoff and became governor. However, the duplicate election cost the taxpayers several million dollars. It also financially burdened the candidates with double campaign expenses, subjected the voters to a campaign that never seemed to end, raised issues of unfairness over the specter that the two elections would come out differently, and delayed the gubernatorial transition for several months—disrupting state government. At the next general election in 1992, chagrined Arizonans quietly amended the constitution back to the original plurality rule! The lone runoff election remains an anomaly in Arizona history—and an interesting lesson in unintended political consequences.

be twenty-five years old, U.S. citizens (ten years), Arizona residents (five years), registered voters, and English-proficient.[10] This contrasts with thirty-nine states that require their governors to be at least thirty years old.[11]

Until 1988, the state constitution also stated that the top five executive officers had to be male. This provision was actually an oversight that had no legal effect. When women were given the right to vote in 1912, the amendment

Figure 5.3 Historic firsts. Arizona made history when it elected women to all of the top executive branch offices in 1998. The new officeholders were sworn in by Justice Sandra Day O'Connor (the first woman to serve on the U.S. Supreme Court and a fellow Arizonan). Also joining them on inauguration day was former representative Polly Rosenbaum, who served in the Arizona legislature for a record forty-six years, until she lost her first election at age 95. (From left to right: Superintendent of Public Instruction Lisa Graham Keegan, Attorney General Janet Napolitano, Governor Jane D. Hull, Rosenbaum, O'Connor, State Treasurer Carol Springer, and Secretary of State Betsey Bayless.)

expressly included the right to hold all public offices.[12] The drafters simply forgot to remove the male qualification that was located in another section of the constitution. The gender qualification was belatedly deleted in 1988 after Rose Mofford became the state's first female governor following Evan Mecham's ouster. Actually, Mofford was not the first to break the gender barrier in the executive branch. Elsie Toles was elected superintendent of public instruction in 1920, and Ana Frohmiller served as the elected state auditor for twenty-four years. Frohmiller, who crusaded against government waste, was the first female state auditor in the country. She was narrowly defeated in her bid for governor in 1950. However, these historic firsts were trumped by Arizona's 1998 election. Jane D. Hull became the first woman to be elected governor. However, the voters set national precedent when they chose women to fill *all five* of the state's top executive offices (see figure 5.3).

Executive Compensation

The same salary commission that makes recommendations for legislative salaries (see chapter 3) also makes recommendations for elected executive officials and judges. However, the follow-up process is quite different. The recommendations for these officials do *not* go to the voters for approval. Rather, they initially go to the governor, who has the authority to raise, lower, or completely reject the proposed increases. The governor's recommendations are then transmitted to the legislature. If the legislature does nothing, the salary recommendations automatically take effect.[13] This arrangement conspicuously reverses normal legislative practice; ordinarily the legislature must take action in order to make a change. Clearly, the process was designed to give the legislature political "cover." (Every legislator can tell constituents, "I didn't vote for a pay raise.") The process also puts the governor in the awkward position of reviewing the salary for his or her own office.[14] However, if approved, the raise would not take effect until the next term, and fiscally conservative governors have overruled the salary commission's recommendations from time to time. For example, in 1994, Governor Symington rejected pay increases for all elected officials despite the fact that the salaries then were quite low. In 1999, Governor Hull similarly declined to forward the salary commission's recommendation of a $50,000 gubernatorial raise to the legislature.[15]

Table 5.2   Salaries of Arizona's Elected Executives (2000)

Office	Annual Salary
Governor	$95,000
Secretary of state	$70,000
Attorney general	$90,000
State treasurer	$70,000
Superintendent of public instruction	$85,000
State mine inspector	$50,000
Corporation commissioner	$73,000

As indicated in table 5.2, executive salaries are currently well above legislative salaries. This is because the executive positions are full-time and the voters are not involved in the salary-setting process. Interestingly, members of the governor's own staff, and more than 800 state employees, receive higher salaries than the governor. (Currently, the University of Arizona's head basketball coach is the highest paid state employee with an annual salary of $562,230.)[16]

Removal

The constitution provides two alternative ways to remove executive branch officials from office before the end of their terms: impeachment (by the legislature) and recall (by the people). These processes are described in chapters 3 and 4 respectively.

Succession

When an executive office becomes vacant the governor appoints a replacement. However, if the *governor* becomes incapacitated, the constitution's succession rules apply. The constitution distinguishes between temporary incapacity (e.g., a short-term disability, temporary absence from state, or impeachment) and permanent incapacity (death, resignation, conviction of impeachment charges, or a permanent disability). In either case, the secretary

Table 5.3 Arizona's Governors since Statehood

1912	George W. P. Hunt (D)	1952	J. Howard Pyle (R)
1914	George W. P. Hunt (D)	1954	Ernest W. McFarland (D)
1916	George W. P. Hunt (D)[a]	1956	Ernest W. McFarland (D)
1918	Thomas E. Campbell (R)	1958	Paul J Fannin (R)
1920	Thomas E. Campbell (R)	1960	Paul J. Fannin (R)
1922	George W. P. Hunt (D)	1962	Paul J. Fannin (R)
1924	George W. P. Hunt (D)	1964	Samuel P. Goddard (D)
1926	George W. P. Hunt (D)	1966	Jack Williams (R)
1928	John C. Phillips (D)	1968	Jack Williams (R)
1930	George W. P. Hunt (D)	1970	Jack Williams (R)[c]
1932	Benjamin B. Moeur (D)	1974	Raul H. Castro (D)
1934	Benjamin B. Moeur (D)		Wesley Bolin (D) (1977)[d]
1936	Rawglie C. Stanford (D)		Bruce Babbitt (D) (1978)[e]
1938	Robert T. Jones (D)	1978	Bruce Babbitt (D)
1940	Sidney P. Osborn (D)	1982	Bruce Babbitt (D)
1942	Sidney P. Osborn (D)	1986	Evan Mecham (R)
1944	Sidney P. Osborn (D)		Rose Mofford (D) (1988)[f]
1946	Sidney P. Osborn (D)	1990	Fife Symington (R)
	Daniel E. Garvey (D) (1948)[b]	1994	Fife Symington (R)
1948	Daniel E. Garvey (D)		Jane D. Hull (R) (1997)[g]
1950	J. Howard Pyle (R)	1998	Jane D. Hull (R)

[a] Thomas E. Campbell served one year before the court declared Hunt the election winner.

[b] Technically, Garvey became "acting" governor upon the death of Osborn and was denied the governor's compensation. The constitution was amended five months later to make it clear that the successor officially becomes governor.

[c] Terms were lengthened to four years as a result of a 1968 constitutional amendment.

[d] Bolin became governor when Raul Castro resigned to become U.S. ambassador to Argentina.

[e] Babbitt became governor upon the death of Bolin.

[f] Mofford became governor upon the impeachment and removal of Mecham.

[g] Hull become governor when Symington resigned following a federal criminal conviction.

of state ordinarily assumes the powers of the office. If it is a permanent incapacity, the secretary of state officially becomes the governor and appoints someone to fill the vacated office of secretary of state.[17] As table 5.3 indicates, the succession clause has come into play four times in Arizona's brief history as a state. The most recent occasion was in the summer of 1997, when Governor Fife Symington resigned following a federal criminal conviction. Secretary of State Jane D. Hull became governor. On one occasion the attorney general became governor because the secretary of state was ineligible.[18] The number of non-elected governors prompted some to argue that the state needed a lieutenant governor (an office found in forty-two other states). A constitutional referendum to create such an office was put on the 1994 ballot. However, the voters resoundingly rejected the change, presumably concluding that it would be a tax-supported office with insufficient responsibilities.

The Governor's Powers

The public expects the governor to provide strong leadership. He or she is supposed to offer effective solutions to the state's problems, forcefully manage the state's bureaucracy, take charge in times of crisis, and represent the state on important ceremonial occasions. In short, the governor is viewed as the state's presidential equivalent. Unfortunately, the constitution and statutes do not give the Arizona governor the powers to fully realize these expectations. Although the office does possess significant administrative, legislative, and judicial powers, these formal powers are limited in multiple ways. In addition, the plural structure of the executive branch undermines the governor's monopoly on leadership. Nonetheless, if a governor is politically astute—and outside forces cooperate—a governor can be the most powerful person in state government.

Administrative Powers

The governor's primary job is to manage the state's bureaucracy and coordinate the many executive branch responsibilities listed at the start of this chapter. The constitution and statutes give the governor various means to do this.

Appointment powers   One way that the governor exerts influence over the state bureaucracy is through the power to appoint. The governor selects the heads of most state agencies and fills vacancies on boards and commissions. This enables the governor to install persons who share the governor's political philosophy and policy views. For example, if the governor wants the state's prisons to emphasize punishment over rehabilitation, he or she will pick a corrections head of similar mind. There are, however, various limits to the governor's appointment powers. First, most appointments must be approved by the senate, although this is largely a formality. The senate rarely rejects a governor's choice. Second, the governor cannot "clean house" by filling every top position in the state at once. Although the governor can usually replace the heads of top departments at will, independent board members typically serve for staggered, fixed terms. This means that a governor inherits appointees from his or her predecessor and must wait until a term expires before a replacement can be appointed. Third, constitutional and statutory provisions sometimes limit the governor's choice by imposing highly specific qualifications on appointees or requiring the governor to choose from a short list prepared by others. Finally, appointees do not always remain loyal to the governor's agenda once they get the job. Without commensurate removal powers, the governor cannot maintain total control.

Removal powers   The governor's removal powers are also limited. Some appointees can be fired by the governor for any reason whatsoever. These include the heads of most large agencies such as the Arizona Department of Corrections. They serve at the "pleasure" of the governor. This permits the governor to control how their agencies operate. If the agency refuses to follow the governor's directives, the head can be summarily replaced with a more obedient director. However, most state personnel are not removable by the governor except for "cause"—which means incompetence or wrongdoing, not disagreements over policy. These include the heads of a few important agencies (e.g., the banking department), the members of virtually all boards and commissions, and most of the 62,000 civil service workers who make up the state's bureaucracy. Finally, the governor cannot fire the other eight elected members of the executive branch—several of whom head large agencies with significant public policy responsibilities.

Fiscal powers   As described in chapter 3, the governor is a major participant in the state's budget process. The governor is required to submit a proposed operating budget to the legislature requesting specific dollar amounts for all state agencies, boards, and programs. The legislature has the final say, and agencies can independently lobby the legislature for funds. Nonetheless, the governor's backing is often critical to their success. In addition, the governor possesses a powerful line item veto (discussed below) that enables the governor to strike particular items from appropriation bills approved by the legislature. The governor can use these fiscal powers to pressure otherwise independent agencies to tow the line.

Military powers   The constitution makes the governor the commander-in-chief of the state's military forces (the national guard). Ordinarily, this authority would warrant little more than a footnote. Unless a natural disaster requires deployment, most governors simply appoint a military head and have little further contact with the guard. However, Arizona's governors have exercised their military authority in more unusual ways.

Arizona's first governor, George W. P. Hunt, interpreted his commander-in-chief status quite literally. On occasion he camped out with the guard during training maneuvers.[19] Other governors deployed the national guard in controversial ways. For example, in 1934, Governor Benjamin Moeur took on the federal government by ordering the state's guard to block construction of the Parker Dam. (He opposed the dam because it diverted Colorado River water to California.) Moeur actually sent one hundred armed personnel to the dam site and managed to delay construction for nearly a year.[20] Although the

Figure 5.4 George W. P. Hunt. Arizona's first governor served a record seven terms in office.

deployment was plainly illegal—the federal government could have nationalized the guard at any time—Moeur was able to extract some concessions from the federal government on water issues.

In 1953, Governor Howard Pyle sent over a hundred armed highway patrol officers into Colorado City (then known as Short Creek) to end polygamy in the remote community. Arriving in the middle of the night, they arrested ninety-six men. Community leaders protested on grounds of religious persecution, the newspapers criticized the governor's use of force, and a backlash from the raid contributed to Pyle's defeat in the next gubernatorial election.[21]

A few decades later, Governor Bruce Babbitt sent the national guard into Morenci to restore order in the strike-torn mining community. Although Babbitt's deployment rested on firmer legal grounds than Governor Moeur's, it remains controversial to this day. Labor sympathizers still contend that Babbitt unfairly sided with the mine owners and prematurely ended a a lawful strike for improved working conditions.

Finally, in November 1995, Governor Fife Symington copied Moeur's strategy when he used the national guard to protest the federal government's ordered closure of the Grand Canyon. (The shutdown was the result of a budget standoff between Congress and the president.) While Symington was publicly threatening to use force to keep the park open,[22] federal officials were quietly preparing to nationalize the guard. In the end, the deployment of fifty unarmed guardsmen to the gates of the national park was little more than a media spectacle. However, it accomplished the desired political result: the federal government negotiated an arrangement with the state that allowed the Grand Canyon to remain open.

Lawmaking Powers

The governor is not a member of the legislature. However, the constitution gives the governor three legislative powers that, if used shrewdly, can make the governor a significant player in the lawmaking process.

(1) The power to propose new legislation   The constitution specifically directs the governor to recommend new legislation at the start of every regular session.[23] A governor is particularly well suited to do this for several reasons. First, unlike individual legislators who come from small districts, the governor represents all the people in the state. Second, the governor also possesses superior information about the state's particular needs, because department heads regularly report to the governor.[24] Finally, the governor typically has more national and international contacts than other public officials in the state and is usually a leader in his or her party. All of these factors give the governor an ideal perspective for developing broad policy initiatives. Arizona governors make their annual recommendations in a speech to the legislature known as the "State of the State Address." However, activist governors do not

rely on this speech alone. Rather, publicly and behind the scenes, they propose new legislation all the time. The governor must find a sympathetic legislator to formally introduce a bill, but ordinarily this is not a problem. Although the governor's support does not guarantee that a particular bill will pass, it usually carries considerable weight.

(2) The power to call the legislature into special session   As noted in chapter 3, the constitution also gives the governor the authority to call the legislature into special session. This enables the governor to force lawmakers to meet and consider the particular issue specified in the governor's call. If the legislature is already in regular session, a special session serves to interrupt the legislature's regular business and divert its attention. Again, this does not guarantee that the legislature will take the action desired by the governor—or for that matter any action. (The legislature can adjourn as soon as it meets.) Nonetheless, the power to summon the legislature gives the governor the ability to set the legislature's agenda. In politically skillful hands, it can accomplish far more.

(3) The veto power   Clearly, the governor's most powerful legislative tool is the veto. Unless the legislature diverts a bill to the people using the statutory referendum (see chapter 4), the bill must go to the governor before it can become law. The governor ordinarily has five days to either accept the bill or veto it.[25] To veto the bill, the governor drafts a short statement containing objections. Technically, the veto does not completely kill the bill. Rather, the bill goes back to the legislature for a possible override vote. In actuality, however, vetoes are seldom overridden in Arizona for several reasons. First, an override requires a supermajority vote (see table 3.4), which is extremely hard to get. Second, the legislature often adjourns before an override vote can be taken. Finally, the legislature sometimes passes a bill with the expectation that it will be vetoed. (It does this to please constituents, allowing the governor to take the political heat.) For these and other reasons the governor's veto almost always sticks.

The governor's veto power, however, has limitations. Unless the bill involves appropriations (a special case discussed below), the governor has only two options: to accept the bill *exactly as written* or to veto the *entire* bill. That is, the governor cannot use the veto power to add new provisions, to rewrite objectionable language, or to strike parts of a bill while approving the remainder. Because the legislature knows this, it can force the governor's hand. For example, it might **piggyback** (combine) two bills, compelling the governor to accept something objectionable along with something that the governor badly wants. Conversely, opponents of a bill can sometimes engineer a veto by including objectionable language. Similar political strategies are widely utilized on the federal level where riders (unrelated pieces of legislation) are commonly tacked onto bills. However, as noted in chapter 3, the state constitution requires all bills to embrace a single subject.[26] This serves to reduce, but not entirely eliminate, such legislative tactics in Arizona.

The governor's veto power is much greater with respect to appropriation bills. Here, the governor possesses a true line item veto. That is, the governor can strike one or more items in the bill while approving the remainder. Even here, however, there are ways in which the legislature can outmaneuver the governor. For example, it can appropriate funds in a **lump sum** (nonitemized) fashion that deprives the governor of individual items to selectively veto. The downside is that this gives the governor greater discretion to determine how funds can be allocated—something that the legislature does not always wish to do.

Technically, the veto is only a negative, blocking tool. However, a governor with strong political skills can use it to achieve affirmative ends. For example, by threatening to veto legislation well in advance, the governor can pressure the legislature into rewriting the bill to the governor's liking. (No member of the legislature has equivalent clout.) Alternatively, the governor can threaten to veto *other* bills if the legislature does not pass the governor's legislation. Much like a game of poker, the governor's influence depends upon whether or not the legislature believes the governor is bluffing. Veto threats from governors who rarely veto are not likely to be taken seriously.

Governor Bruce Babbitt was the first modern governor to fully exploit the veto power (see figure 5.5). He vetoed a record 114 bills. Babbitt's aggressive use of the veto power enabled him to become a major player in the lawmaking process even when the legislature was controlled by a powerful speaker of the opposite party. Governor Fife Symington's equally forceful use of the veto power against his *own* party in 1996 surprised many observers. However, when the legislature returned the following year, it gave the governor's requests far more respect. Governor Hull, who later inherited the office from Symington, vetoed 21 bills in 1999. Many of the vetoes were unexpected and surprised observers because the bills had been sponsored by the leaders of her own party.

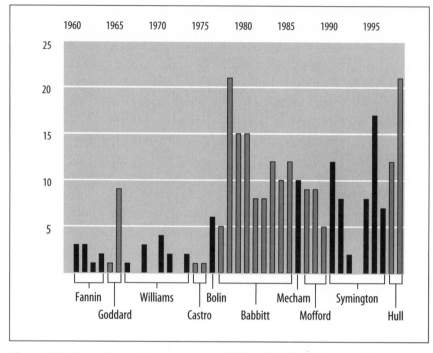

Figure 5.5 Vetoes by modern governors, 1961–1999. (Excludes special sessions.)

Playing hardball with the legislature has risks. If the governor goes too far, he or she can jeopardize the delicate relationships that are also needed for legislative success. In the end, the governor's influence over the lawmaking process depends upon a combination of factors including the governor's political skills, the partisan composition of the legislature, the caliber of legislative leadership, and the governor's overall popularity. However, if these factors are all favorably aligned, it is possible for a governor to dominate the lawmaking process, at least where major legislation is concerned.

Judicial Powers

The constitution also gives the governor limited judicial powers. They do not allow the governor to intrude significantly into the operation of the courts, which is a notoriously independent branch. However, they contribute to the system of checks and balances found in virtually all American governments.

The power to appoint judges   Since 1974, governors have appointed all of the state's appellate judges and most of its major trial court judges. As explained in chapter 6, this power is constrained by the fact that the governor must choose from a short list of names. However, the governor's choice is final— that is, unlike most gubernatorial appointments, it does not require senate approval. Of course, appointing someone to the bench does not guarantee particular outcomes. Moreover, Arizona judges do not serve for life. This makes the governor's appointment power less significant than the president's comparable power over federal judicial appointments. Nonetheless, it does allow the governor to exert some influence over the orientation and temperament of the state's judiciary.

Clemency powers   The constitution gives the governor three **clemency** powers.[27] The exercise of these powers invariably generates heated public debate. Clemency actually has a long history in Anglo-American jurisprudence. Punishments are supposed to be imposed in a uniform way. While most people regard this as "fair," there may be special circumstances that make a particular punishment "unjust." Clemency is intended to address this problem and prevent criminal laws from being applied too rigidly. It allows one person—the governor—to set aside or modify a punishment for any reason whatsoever. That is, the applicant appeals to the governor's conscience. (The president of the United States has comparable powers. However, because the president's powers extend only to violations of federal law, and most criminals are convicted under state law, governors actually possess the more significant authority.) Arizona governors can grant three different types of relief:

1. *Reprieve:* A **reprieve** simply delays the carrying out of a criminal sentence. For example, a governor could grant a reprieve to postpone a scheduled execution. Alternately, a reprieve might delay the start of a prison term for various humanitarian reasons.

2. *Commutation:* A **commutation** permits the governor to reduce the court's sentence. For example, a death sentence could be commuted to life imprisonment, a prison sentence could be shortened from ten years to five, or an offender could be released on probation, in lieu of imprisonment.

3. *Pardon:* A **pardon** completely releases the convicted person from all criminal penalties. It signifies official "forgiveness" by the state and is

therefore sometimes granted even after a person has fully served the original sentence.

There are some significant limitations on the governor's clemency powers. Clemency can be granted only after a person is convicted of a crime,[28] and it does not extend to treason or impeachment cases. Above all, the governor cannot act unless the **Board of Executive Clemency** recommends clemency first.[29] The board's approval is not a constitutional requirement; the constitution simply permits the legislature to add additional statutory limitations. The legislature adopted this requirement because of Governor Hunt's leniency in death penalty cases. The five-person board is intended to function as an independent check on the governor. Its members serve for staggered five-year terms and cannot be removed by the governor except for cause.[30] Today, when executions are scheduled, the board remains in close contact with the governor, ready to pass on any last-minute clemency recommendations. However, if a majority of the board does not approve clemency, the governor is powerless to act.

Clemency board members actually devote most of their attention to **parole** determinations, not clemency matters. (A parole enables an inmate to be released from prison before the end of the sentence, but it does not alter the sentence itself; the inmate can be returned for a parole violation.) Paroles generate public controversy too, but the governor has no formal role in their determination. Nonetheless, this has not stopped governors from periodically trying to influence board decisions.[31]

Finally, public opinion can serve as an equally potent check on the governor's clemency powers. The outcry that accompanied Governor Mofford's commutation of two life sentences caused the governor to attempt to rescind her grant of clemency.[32] Following the uproar, the legislature added a new limitation on the governor's clemency powers. Now, whenever executive clemency is granted, the governor is required to publish the reasons in the newspaper in "bold type."[33] The granting of clemency provokes as much political controversy today as it did when George Hunt exercised the powers as the state's first governor. For example, one of the two murderers involved in Governor Mofford's commutation was James Hamm. Hamm's postrelease efforts to earn a law degree, to teach at ASU, and to become a practicing member of the bar have spawned continuing public debate on the boundaries of clemency and rehabilitation.[34]

Informal Powers

All of the powers discussed above derive from the state constitution and statutes. However, the governor also possesses informal powers that can reinforce (or if exercised ineptly, dilute) the governor's formal authority. For example, like the president, the governor is the ceremonial "head of state." He or she delivers speeches on important public occasions, entertains visiting dignitaries, issues proclamations and awards, and is usually the most well known representative of the government. Indeed, a considerable portion of the governor's daily schedule is devoted to such public relations activity. Additionally, governors usually play a major leadership role within their respective political parties, although they often have competition from U.S. senators and others. Party leadership and ceremonial leadership can translate into real political power. Simply put, a popular governor is likely to have more clout with the legislature, the bureaucracy, and local officials.

Other Elected Officials

The Secretary of State

The secretary of state stands first in line of succession to the governor. As table 5.3 indicates, this position has become a fast track to the top office. Since 1977, three out of five elected secretaries of state acquired the governorship through this means. This has encouraged politically ambitious persons to trade more powerful positions for this office. For example, rumors of Governor Symington's legal troubles prompted the speaker of the house and the senate minority leader to run for secretary of state in 1994. The gamble paid off when Symington resigned following his federal criminal conviction.

The secretary of state's day-to-day responsibilities lie in two main areas: (1) record keeping and (2) elections. The office keeps the official records of the state, making it the best source for up-to-date editions of the constitution, laws, and administrative rules. It also maintains registries of trademarks, lobbyists, charities, and various other filings required by law. On the elections side, the secretary of state has multiple responsibilities. For example, the office officially certifies the results of all state elections. (In fact, the secretary of state's Web site is the place to be on election night—the results are posted as fast as they come in.) The office also prepares the ballot and voter information pamphlets, processes initiative and referendum petitions, and handles the many filings that candidates and officeholders are legally required to make (e.g., nominating petitions, campaign finance reports, and financial disclosures). Finally, the secretary of state is elected on the same four-year cycle as the governor (see figure 5.1) and must meet the identical age, citizenship, residency, and other requirements.

The Attorney General

The attorney general—colloquially known as the "AG"—is the state's top legal adviser. Although second in line of succession, the attorney general actually wields more real power than the secretary of state. The attorney general gives legal advice to other elected officials, the state's many agencies and boards, the courts, and occasionally school districts and local governments. Because the line between legal advice and policy advice is not always clear-cut, the attorney general can influence public policy through this means. Most of the attorney general's legal advice is rendered on an informal, ongoing basis by more than three hundred lawyers who work for the attorney general in the state's Department of Law. Occasionally, however, the attorney general is asked to formally opine on some important issue affecting the state. The office will then issue an attorney general opinion.[35] These formal, published opinions interpret ambiguous constitutional and statutory provisions. They are binding on state officials until a court rules to the contrary.

In addition to providing general legal advice, the attorney general's office serves as the lawyer for the state in most noncriminal litigation. It is also the primary enforcer of the state's antitrust, consumer fraud, racketeering, organized crime, and civil rights laws. The office prosecutes disciplinary actions against doctors, dentists, real estate agents, and others who hold occupational licenses. The attorney general also plays an important, but not exclusive, role in criminal law enforcement. In Arizona, most crimes are initially tried at the county level by prosecutors in the county attorney's office (see chapter 7). However, appeals of criminal convictions are handled by the attorney general's office. In addition, the attorney general has supervisory powers over county attorneys and can take over criminal prosecutions at the request of the governor or county. (This is often done when a county has a conflict of interest.) The attorney general is elected on the same four-year cycle as the governor (see figure 5.1) and must meet the same constitutional qualifications.

The State Treasurer

The state treasurer is the state's chief financial officer. The office receives all money belonging to the state and safeguards, invests, and disburses the funds in accordance with law. The treasurer also serves on various state boards that are involved with financial issues.[36] The treasurer is third in line for gubernatorial succession and must meet the same broad constitutional qualifications that apply to the other major executive branch offices. By the same token, this means that the treasurer does not have to possess any specific training, such as an accounting or financial background.[37] However, the Arizona Constitution has always singled out this office for special oversight. As noted previously, the treasurer can't leave the state without first giving notice, and the office has always been subject to term limits.

The Superintendent of Public Instruction

The superintendent of public instruction is the state's highest-ranking education official. However, the superintendent's authority is undercut by the astonishing number of other officials and boards that share power in this area.[38] The superintendent heads and manages the Arizona Department of Education. This large state agency certifies K–12 teachers, oversees statewide testing, approves textbooks, sets minimum pupil competencies, and apportions operating funds to public school districts and charter schools. The department's major policies are actually set by the State Board of Education. The superintendent is a member of this board, but the remaining eight members are appointed by the governor. This arrangement obviously dilutes the superintendent's power. Indeed, it is somewhat unusual to subject an elected official to the authority of an appointed board.

The superintendent's authority is further reduced by the five other state boards that control different aspects of public education.[39] In addition to these boards, the state legislature and the governor also play an active role in shaping the state's education policies through their power to enact education laws. In recent years the courts have also been heavily involved in school issues. Finally, this listing merely covers the participants at the *state* level. It omits the many local officials who also regulate schools (see chapter 7). In short, school governance in Arizona is exceedingly fragmented, and the superintendent of public instruction is just one of many players. However, the office provides a high-profile "bully pulpit" that allows the superintendent to direct public debate on education issues.

The superintendent of public instruction is elected on the same four-year cycle as the governor (see figure 5.1) and must meet the same general qualifications. Interestingly, this means that the superintendent does *not* have to have been an educator or school administrator. Finally, the superintendent is last in line for gubernatorial succession. (Despite this low ranking, in 1996 Superintendent Keegan briefly became the acting governor when the governor, secretary of state, attorney general, and treasurer all traveled to Pasadena to watch ASU take on Ohio State in the Rose Bowl.)

The State Mine Inspector

In addition to the major five offices discussed above, Arizona also elects a state mine inspector every four years. It is not unusual for a state with substantial mining interests to have such an inspector; mining is a dangerous activity. However, having the position as an elected, constitutional office is singular and anachronistic. (The state's many other health and safety inspectors are all appointed.) Arizona's unusual arrangement was a reaction to the mining industry's powerful—and often corrupt—influence over state government during the territorial period. The constitution's Progressive drafters reasoned that mineworkers would be better protected by an independently elected inspector than by one appointed by the governor.

The Corporation Commission

The Arizona Corporation Commission is one of the state's most powerful regulatory bodies. As its name indicates, the commission regulates corporations. That is, it certifies businesses that wish to incorporate under Arizona law and regulates the securities that they sell. It also registers out-of-state corporations that conduct business in Arizona. However, the real power of the commission centers on its authority over one particular type of corporation, namely **public service corporations**. These are private[40] utility companies that provide gas, electricity, water, sewage treatment, telephone, and similar types of services.[41] Because most of these businesses are legalized monopolies, the Arizona Corporation Commission determines the maximum rates they can charge. It also has sweeping control over what services these utilities offer and how the services are delivered. (In essence, government regulation serves as a substitute for the missing market competition.)

Accordingly, when a public service corporation requests a rate hike or wants to alter its services, the commission schedules a public, evidentiary hearing. The outcomes of these hearings, however, have not always been as proconsumer as the Progressives intended. In part, this is because the voters sometimes elect commissioners who have stronger ties to the regulated utilities (or their shareholders) than to consumers. In addition, the hearings have not always been evenly balanced. The superior expertise and resources of the utilities enabled them to present stronger cases to the commission than the disorganized consumers who objected. To rectify this problem, the legislature created the Residential Utility Consumer Office (RUCO) in 1983.[42] This office's mandate is to level the playing field. It intervenes in corporation commission hearings on the side of residential consumers and presents evidence and legal arguments to counter the utilities.

Arizona's Progressive framers created the corporation commission as a three-member elective body, with the members serving staggered six-year terms. They feared the influence of powerful corporations over government officials. Accordingly, they believed that the public interest would be better served with elected watchdogs than with appointed professionals. The commission's recent history, however, has been somewhat rocky. The small body has suffered from sharp divisions. In 1999, a newly elected commissioner was ousted from office for having a conflict of interest at the time of election.[43] On multiple occasions since statehood, the legislature has proposed constitutional amendments to overhaul the commission. For example, twice it proposed to make the commission an appointive body, following the practice of thirty-eight states.[44] Arizona voters rejected both proposals. At the 7 November 2000 election, voters will be asked to enlarge the commission to five members and reduce the terms to four years—proposals that failed in 1984.

Online Resources

Arizona Governor:
 www.governor.state.az.us/index.html

Arizona Secretary of State:
 www.sosaz.com/

Arizona Attorney General:
   www.ag.state.az.us./ (home page)
   www.ag.state.az.us./opinions/opinions_intro.html (Attorney General Opinions)

Arizona Treasurer:
   www.aztreasury.state.az.us/

Arizona Superintendent of Public Instruction:
   www.ade.state.az.us/administration/superintendent/

Arizona Corporation Commission:
   www.cc.state.az.us/

Complete listing of Arizona state departments and agencies:
   www.state.az.us/all.html

National Governors' Association:
   http://www.nga.org/

Western Governors' Association:
   http://www.westgov.org/

Council of State Governments:
   http://www.statesnews.org/

6 The Judicial Branch

The judicial branch is the least visible of Arizona's three branches of government. Judges actively promote anonymity by striving to remain "above politics." Nonetheless, the courts wield considerable power over public policy as well as the lives of private citizens. The Progressive drafters of Arizona's constitution were quite attuned to this fact. When they designed the state's judiciary they consciously deviated from the federal model. Once again, their main objective was to prevent the abuse of power by giving the citizens an enlarged role. Constitutional amendments have modernized the structure of the court system since statehood,[1] but the citizens still retain significant oversight powers over the judiciary.

The Power of the Judicial Branch

Courts resolve legal disputes. The dispute may involve a purely private matters, such as how a contract should be interpreted, or matters of wide social significance, such as how Arizona's public schools are funded. The cases may be **criminal**—that is, brought by government prosecutors to enforce specific penal statutes against accused wrongdoers—or they may be **civil** (everything else). The opposing parties can be private individuals, businesses, governments, public bodies, elected officials, or any combination of the above. Essentially, the courts provide a formal setting where disagreements can be resolved with fairness and finality. When the courts function properly, they prevent vigilante justice and social breakdown—things that Arizona did experience sporadically during its territorial period.

The full role of the judge is not well understood. Most people are familiar with the trial judge's role as a courtroom referee. We picture such jurists ruling on evidentiary objections, maintaining order, and instructing the jury as to how it should proceed. It is an undeniably important function. However, judicial power extends well beyond the disposition of individual cases. As explained below, judges actually make law. Judge-made law is called the common law, and it is just as authoritative as the statutes enacted by the legislature or the people. In addition, judges have an oversight power known as **judicial review**. It enables them to declare acts of other public officials, and even the voters, "unconstitutional." It is an equally significant power. The exercise of either of these powers can profoundly change the public policies of the state.

How Judges Make Law and Public Policy

In the American legal system, the judge's job is to apply the appropriate law to each case. This can be a fairly straightforward process, with the judge simply consulting the relevant statutes or constitutional provisions. However, in some civil cases—such as private injury cases—there are virtually no controlling statutes or constitutional provisions. In these circumstances, the trial judge looks to prior court rulings instead. More specifically, the judge turns to the published opinions of the state's appellate courts. When appellate courts review individual cases they do not merely determine who should win or lose. Rather, they explain their reasoning in published written opinions. The opinions set forth the legal principles that lower courts must follow in future cases. Arizona's common law currently fills over two hundred volumes and is as detailed as any statutory scheme.

The common law changes over time, but it evolves slowly. Appellate judges generally adhere to the principle of *stare decisis*, which literally means "let the decision stand." In plain English, courts strive to follow their prior rulings. Only on rare occasions will an appellate court completely abandon a common law principle in favor of an entirely new legal rule. The decision that does this is often described as a "landmark" decision. A striking example occurred in 1985, when the Arizona Supreme Court altered the state's employment law. Up to that time, private employers could fire most workers for any reason whatsoever (i.e., so long as it did not involve a civil rights violation.) This is because most Arizona workers are regarded as "at-will" employees. An at-will employee can quit at any time. However, the flip side is that the employer can summarily dismiss the worker as well. The landmark case, *Wagenseller v. Scottsdale Memorial Hospital*,[2] modified this principle. The lawsuit was brought by a nurse who claimed that she had been wrongfully fired for refusing to participate in a "mooning" skit that took place on a river rafting trip and later at the hospital. (The nurse's supervisor and coworkers had all participated.) Under the existing common law, it didn't matter *why* the nurse was fired; the hospital had a right to terminate an employee even for a bad reason. The Arizona Supreme Court, however, decided that a new rule was needed. It announced that employers couldn't fire workers for refusing to engage in immoral conduct or acts contrary to "public policy." In this narrow but significant way, the case changed employment law in the state. Of course, the legislature could have mandated the same—or even greater—protections for workers through the normal lawmaking process. But it had not done so. *Wagenseller* therefore stands as an example of public policy being made by judges.

Appellate courts also make law when they interpret existing statutes and constitutional provisions. This occurs whenever the meaning or scope of the law is unclear. The court must then fill in the gaps or resolve the ambiguities. When an appellate court does this, its interpretation becomes part of the law, as authoritative as the original language itself. For example, in another landmark case, the Arizona Supreme Court interpreted ambiguous statutory language to require the state and counties to provide substantially increased care to the state's chronically mentally ill.[3] Once again, the court issued this order after the more cost-conscious legislature had declined to act.

The courts' interpretative role is especially significant when constitutional provisions are called into question. Constitutional provisions are typically written in broad language. This gives the courts even more leeway. An activist judge can use a vague provision to expand the law in new directions. A good example involves Arizona's right to privacy, which is found in Article 2, section 8. The provision reads in its entirety:

§ 8. Right to privacy
No person shall be disturbed in his private affairs, or his home invaded, without authority of law.

Notably, the constitution does not define "private affairs," leaving this provision wide open to many different interpretations. For example, in 1985, the Arizona Supreme Court used section 8 to recognize a qualified right to die.

The decision grew out of a case in which a guardian went to court to "pull the plug" on a sixty-four-year-old woman in a chronic vegetative state. At the time, Arizona had no statute that permitted the termination of life support under these circumstances. The supreme court, however, decided that section 8, quoted above, covered the situation. More precisely, the court ruled that the right to privacy "encompass[es] an individual's right to refuse medical treatment."[4] The judges candidly acknowledged that the termination of life support raised complex philosophical, legal, religious, and scientific issues "to which no single person or profession has all the answers." Nonetheless, the supreme court preempted the legislature in a classic exercise of judicial lawmaking. In essence, the court created a new—and significant—constitutional right through the process of judicial interpretation.

The U.S. Supreme Court exercises this power as well. Moreover, when it interprets the national constitution, the ruling applies to the entire country, not just a single state. (Five years after Arizona's supreme court recognized a right to terminate life support, the U.S. Supreme Court did the same in an unrelated case.) Judicial lawmaking, although widely practiced, remains a controversial power. On one hand, some contend that it is undemocratic and that it usurps the authority that properly belongs to the legislature and voters. They favor a more restrained, "strict construction" of the constitution. On the other hand, Arizona Supreme Court Justice Stanley Feldman vigorously defends the practice, arguing that it gives Arizonans a "double security" in the protection of their rights.[5] And Arizona judges—unlike their federal counterparts—remain directly accountable to the voters through periodic **retention elections** and recall.

Judicial Review

Judges not only have the power to make new laws, they also have the power to strike down laws made by others. Courts can void statutes and constitutional provisions passed by the legislature or the people. And using their power of judicial review, they can also strike down any official act of the governor or other public official. This power, which was established by a landmark U.S. Supreme Court case in 1803,[6] gives the courts the last word on all questions of constitutional interpretation. Accordingly, whenever a statute, rule, ordinance, or governmental act is challenged on the ground that it conflicts with the state or federal constitution, the courts have the authority to declare the law or act "unconstitutional" (and therefore unenforceable). Theoretically, judges cannot void laws simply because they personally dislike them—that would usurp the power of the other branches. However, as suggested above, constitutional interpretation can be a fairly loose business. Judges are sometimes accused of crossing the line and engaging in improper policy making when they render controversial constitutional rulings.

The Arizona Supreme Court has not been shy about exercising the power of judicial review. For example, in 1994, the supreme court ruled that the state's method of funding public school improvements was unconstitutional.[7] More specifically, it concluded that Arizona's heavy reliance on local property taxes discriminated against poorer school districts. The governor and the legislature disagreed. However, the supreme court's ruling forced them to abolish the funding system that had been used since territorial days. And when the legislature initially stalled and failed to create a new system that satisfied the court, the court threatened to close the state's public schools!

The Arizona Supreme Court has also used the power of judicial review to resolve intergovernmental disputes. An interesting example occurred in 1992 when the senate got into a dispute with Governor Fife Symington. The governor refused to spend funds that had been appropriated for a program that he didn't like. The senate's president sued the governor to force him to spend the money and implement the program. In the end, the supreme court sided with the senate. It ruled that the governor could have initially blocked the appropriation by using his veto power; but since he failed to do this, he could not subsequently kill the program by impounding its funds.[8] More commonly, the supreme court adjudicates intergovernmental disputes between the state and its counties and cities.

Finally, citizen actions are not immune from judicial review either. For example, in 1998, the court struck down Official English, a constitutional initiative that had the strong support of the voters.[9] The court concluded that the provision—which required all public business to be conducted in English—violated the Free Speech Clause of the U.S. Constitution. (Although Official English still appears in the state constitution as Article 28, it no longer has legal effect due to the court's ruling.) The Arizona Supreme Court subsequently overturned all or part of *three* voter decisions from the 1998 election. It ousted a newly elected corporation commissioner on the ground that he lacked the legal qualifications to run.[10] It voided a voter-approved measure to change the legislature's per diem, on the ground that the matter was not properly on the ballot.[11] And it ruled that part of the Citizens Clean Elections Act was unconstitutional.[12] These decisions demonstrate that the courts' watchdog role should not be underestimated.

The Court System

Arizona's Major Courts

As indicated in figure 6.1, five major courts make up Arizona's judicial system.[13] Three handle the state's most serious cases and are known as "courts of record." The remaining two courts handle the less serious cases and are known as "limited jurisdiction" or "inferior" courts. Despite their name, no court in Arizona is unimportant. As outlined below, each performs a critical role in the overall administration of justice.[14]

Justice of the peace ("JP") court   Justice of the peace courts are located in every county. In the larger counties, they are situated in neighborhood precincts that bring them closer to the people they serve. Traffic violations and minor crimes (**misdemeanors** and **petty offenses**) make up most of the courts' caseload. However, JP courts also handle small, private lawsuits between citizens and conduct the **preliminary hearings** that precede felony trials. JP courts also issue search warrants and other types of judicial orders.

The cases in JP courts are processed in a streamlined manner that helps keep the litigation costs low. There is even a small claims division to handle the minor private disputes (i.e., those under $2,500) that arise between citizens. The proceedings in this division are conducted in a more informal, "People's Court" fashion. That is, the parties simply present their case to a hearing officer without the aid of lawyers. The hearing rarely lasts more than an hour, and a decision is rendered at the end.

Justice of the peace courts are actually remnants of Arizona's frontier past. Unlike the judges in the state's other courts, JPs are not required to have law degrees. Essentially, they need only be registered voters over the age of eighteen. JPs serve for four-year terms and are elected in contested elections that are often quite colorful and heated. Some argue that the qualifications are too low and that JP courts need to be modernized. Defenders insist that common sense is all that is required to adjudicate small cases. In any event, JP courts are an entrenched institution, and strong political opposition has blocked most reform attempts.

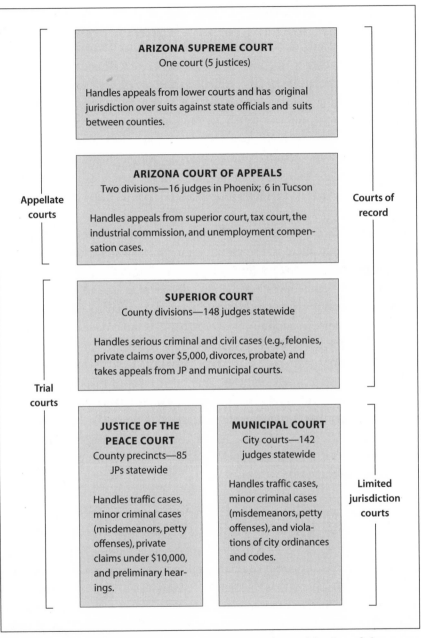

Figure 6.1 The Arizona court system (2000). Superior and justice of the peace courts now have concurrent jurisdiction over civil cases where the amount in controversy is between $5,000 and $10,000.

Municipal court   Most cities and towns operate their own court, which is variously called a "municipal," "city," or "magistrate" court. These courts chiefly handle traffic violations and minor crimes that occur within city limits. (Their jurisdiction in this respect overlaps with JP courts.) Municipal courts also try violations of city ordinances and codes. For example, a curfew violation, barking dog, or other nuisance would fall within this category. Finally, the courts authorize search warrants and issue injunctions in domestic violence and harassment cases. However, unlike JP courts, city courts do *not* handle private lawsuits between citizens. Although the jurisdiction of these courts is therefore fairly limited and mostly penal, as figure 6.2 indicates, municipal courts currently process more cases than any other court.

The Superior Court of Arizona   The superior court is the state's major trial court. Technically, there is a single superior court for the entire state. However, judges are assigned on a county basis according to a population formula, and the county units operate with some degree of independence. All **felony** trials—e.g., serious crimes such as murder, rape, armed robbery, etc.—take place in this court. In addition, the court handles the broadest range of civil cases. These include major personal injury lawsuits, contract disputes, domestic relations matters (e.g., divorce, adoption, child custody), evictions, disputes over real property and wills, and other types of cases. In contrast to JP court, the proceedings in superior court are quite formal, and it may take a year or more before a final judgment is rendered. A person without a lawyer is usually at a significant disadvantage in this court. Finally, superior court judges also perform a limited appellate function by reviewing cases from JP and municipal courts.

The Arizona Court of Appeals   As its name suggests, the court of appeals is an appellate court. This means that it handles cases that were originally tried elsewhere.[15] The court's task is to determine whether the lower court proceedings were fair and proper. It does not conduct any trials or new evidentiary hearings. If it concludes that a retrial is necessary, it will return the case to the lower court for further proceedings. Ordinarily, three judges are assigned to each appeal. They will review the record of the lower court proceedings, study written legal briefs submitted by the opposing parties, and conduct a short hearing where the parties can present oral arguments. (Normally, such hearings last less than an hour.) The three judges will then privately confer and reach a decision. They do not have to all agree. The concurrence of only two judges is needed for an official court ruling. When the court of appeals renders its decision, it normally issues a formal written opinion that becomes part of the common law of the state. Parties who are dissatisfied with the court's ruling can *try* to appeal to the state's supreme court. In reality, however, most Arizona appeals terminate with the court of appeals. As figure 6.2 indicates, the supreme court accepts relatively few cases each year.

The Arizona Supreme Court   The supreme court is the state's court of last resort. In contrast to the court of appeals, it chooses which appeals it accepts, and it is highly selective.[16] The court usually takes only the cases of greatest statewide importance. The one exception to the court's discretionary jurisdiction is death penalty cases; these automatically go to the supreme court for review (bypassing the court of appeals altogether). Five judges, called "justices," serve on this court, and normally all five participate in every case. The court's appellate procedures are similar to those of the court of appeals. Like the latter court, unanimity among the justices is not required; concurrence of

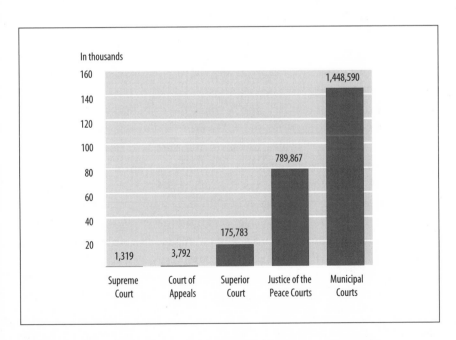

Figure 6.2 The number of cases annually filed in each court (FY 1999)

only three judges is necessary for an official ruling. Because it is primarily an appellate court, most of the supreme court's time is spent reviewing cases from lower courts. However, it also handles two special categories of lawsuits that actually can begin in this court: namely, cases between counties and cases against the governor or other state officials. The high status of the **defendants** is one reason for their special treatment.[17]

Finally, the supreme court also has important administrative responsibilities. It oversees the state's lower courts and approves the formal rules under which they operate. It has the authority to remove judges from office and to disbar the state's practicing attorneys. Additionally, the chief justice (who is chosen by the other justices for a five-year term) presides over impeachment trials.

The Relationship between State and Federal Courts

State courts handle the vast majority of litigation in this country, including more than 95 percent of all criminal cases. However, federal courts also have jurisdiction over Arizona and operate within the state's borders. The federal appellate courts have similar sounding names, which can cause confusion. For example, there is a U.S. Court of Appeals as well as a U.S. Supreme Court. Thus, when a reporter simply announces, "The court of appeals ruled today, . . ." it isn't always obvious whether the reporter is referring to the state or federal court.

The jurisdictional boundary line between the two court systems is also a source of confusion. In general, federal courts handle cases involving federal law, while state courts handle cases involving state law. However, it is a bit more complex than this. First, some cases can be brought in either court system at the option of the parties. For example, a case might raise both federal and state issues. The controversy over Official English provides a good illustration. Opponents of Arizona's state constitutional provision argued that it violated the federal constitution. Lawsuits were filed in both state and federal court by different parties, because both courts had jurisdiction. Ten years of litigation followed. In the end, the federal courts yielded to the state courts, and, as noted above, the Arizona Supreme Court struck down the state provision. Second, a losing party in state court can try to appeal the case to the U.S. Supreme Court. However, this is a longshot. The case must involve an important federal issue, and the U.S. Supreme Court is even more selective than the

MIRANDA

Decisions of the Arizona Supreme Court are usually the end of the line for criminal defendants. The *Miranda* case was a striking exception. It went all the way to the U.S. Supreme Court and changed police practices throughout the entire nation. Ernesto Miranda was arrested for kidnapping and rape by Phoenix police. He was twenty-three years old, had only a ninth-grade education, was poor, and possibly mentally ill. The eighteen-year-old victim had picked Miranda out of a police lineup. During the two-hour interrogation that followed, Miranda gave the police a handwritten confession. There was no evidence that he had been physically coerced or subjected to any psychological tricks. Miranda was convicted by a superior court jury and sentenced to prison. He appealed to the Arizona Supreme Court, contending that his confession should not have been admitted into evidence. The state's top court disagreed. It concluded that the confession was entirely voluntary and upheld the conviction. Miranda then appealed to the U.S. Supreme Court. Defying the odds, the court accepted the case. By a narrow 5 to 4 margin, it sided with Miranda. The nation's top court reasoned that even if the confession was technically voluntary, custodial police interrogations are inherently psychologically coercive. It concluded that the police should have first *told* Miranda (1) that he had a right to remain silent, (2) that his statements could be used against him, and (3) that he had a right to the assistance of counsel, even at government expense. The Supreme Court voided the state conviction and barred Arizona from using the confession in any subsequent retrial. Miranda did not particularly benefit from his own landmark ruling. He was convicted in the second trial because the state had ample evidence even without the tainted confession. Miranda was paroled from prison in 1973. Three years later, at age thirty-six, he was fatally stabbed during a poker game at a Phoenix bar. However, his case gave rise to the well-known Miranda warnings that have become standard operating procedure for police and "part of our national culture."[18]

state supreme court in accepting jurisdiction. Third, the federal courts will entertain purely state law disputes if the parties are residents of different states. (This falls under the U.S. Constitution's "diversity of citizenship" provision. Federal statutes, however, currently require a $50,000 jurisdictional minimum for these types of cases.)[19] Finally, and perhaps most controversially, criminal cases often bounce back and forth between state and federal courts long after direct appeals have been exhausted. The U.S. Constitution gives state prisoners the right to challenge their convictions in federal court by filing **habeas corpus petitions**.[20] These postconviction habeas proceedings are chiefly responsible for the long delays that occur in death penalty cases.

How Judges Are Chosen, Retained, and Removed

Judicial Selection and Retention

We have seen that judges wield considerable power. For this reason, the method of choosing them is important. Arizona's Progressive drafters deliberately rejected the federal approach where judges are nominated by the president and serve for life. They distrusted an appointed judiciary and wanted the judges to be more accountable to the voters. Instead, they opted to have all judges elected in contested, nonpartisan elections.[21] Supreme court justices were given unlimited six-year terms; superior court judges and JPs were given unlimited four-year terms.[22] This system operated in Arizona for over sixty years and is still the way that all JPs and superior court judges in the smaller counties are chosen.

In 1974, the system was significantly revamped as a result of mounting criticism of judicial elections. Some charged that the voters were simply not competent to choose the best judges. Others were disturbed by the unfairness of judicial campaigns. For example, challengers would run negative ads against sitting judges who were unable to defend their decisions due to judicial ethics rules. Candidates who lacked campaign skills, but possessed all the attributes of a good judge, were disadvantaged under the old system. And the rising cost of campaigns required most candidates to solicit funds. This raised concerns about the integrity of the judicial process, because the major contributors were big businesses and other entities frequently involved in litigation. For all of these reasons, the voters decided to adopt a new system known as **merit selection.** (In other parts of the country it is called "the Missouri Plan" because the system originated in that state.) Merit selection currently applies to all appellate judges and to the superior court judges in Maricopa and Pima counties. Its workings are described below.

Choosing judges under merit selection   Whenever there is a judicial vacancy, interested attorneys apply to a special judicial appointments commission.[23] The commission screens the applicants and sends the names of its top choices to the governor. Usually it recommends only three (the constitutional minimum), but it can recommend more. The governor then appoints a judge from the commission's short list—no senate approval is required. The newly appointed judge serves for either a two- or four-year term, depending upon the timing of the appointment in the state's election cycle. When merit selec-

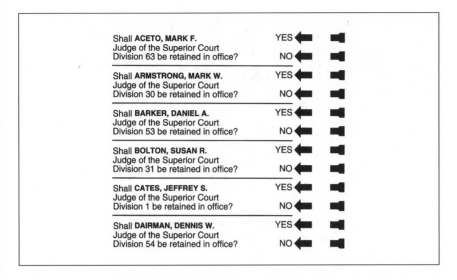

Figure 6.3 A judicial retention election ballot. (In Maricopa County, there may be more than forty judges on a single ballot.)

tion was first adopted, the nominating commissions were directed to make their selections solely on the basis of merit. However, the constitutional provision was amended in 1992. Merit still remains the primary criterion, but the commissions are also directed to consider diversity. Partisanship is *not* supposed to influence the selection process: the constitution specifically prohibits the nominees from all coming from the same party.[24]

Retaining judges under merit selection   A merit selection judge must survive a retention election at the end of each term in order to stay in office. In a retention election, the judge's name appears on the ballot, and the voters are simply asked to vote "yes" or "no" as to whether the judge should be given an additional term. This is quite different from a contested election; in a retention election the judge runs against his or her own record, not against an opponent (see figure 6.3). If more than half the voters vote "yes," the judge stays in office for another term. Because there are no term limits for judges, a judge can remain in office as long as the judge survives these periodic elections. If, however, the voters reject the judge at the polls, there is a new judicial vacancy. The merit selection process starts over, with the governor appointing a judge from the appointments commission's short list.

Figure 6.4 The Arizona Supreme Court (2000). (From left to right: Chief Justice Thomas A. Zlaket, Justice Stanley G. Feldman, Justice Frederick J. Martone, Justice Charles E. Jones, and Justice Ruth V. McGregor.)

Evaluating merit selection   In more than two decades of operation, merit selection has generated its share of criticism and praise. On one hand, supporters—which include most of the legal community—regard the system as a clear improvement over contested elections.[25] They argue that merit selection has increased the overall quality of judges; allowed younger, less affluent persons to serve; reduced the troubling dependence of judges upon fund raising; and eliminated the ugly media campaigns that eroded public confidence in the judiciary.

On the other hand, critics charge that merit selection has not lived up to its billing. They contend that politics still plays a major role in the judicial selection process. Governors *do* tend to favor members of their own party, although there are occasional exceptions. In addition to this partisan bias, considerable lobbying takes place behind the scenes. Accordingly, critics charge that merit selection has simply transferred the open politics of the electoral process to the manipulations of a narrower, less visible group. Another common complaint is that women and minorities are underrepresented on the bench. This criticism led to the 1992 constitutional amendment that added diversity to the selection criteria. The issue attracted attention in early 1998 when there was a vacancy on the supreme court, which was then all-male. (The state's sole female justice, Lorna Lockwood, had retired decades previously.) The nominating commission pointedly sent the governor five nominees, *four* of whom were female. In the end, Governor Hull appointed one of the four women, Ruth V. McGregor, to the supreme court. The appointment was noteworthy because the governor crossed party lines.

Finally, the retention phase of merit selection remains the most problematic. Voters have difficulty evaluating judges. This problem is compounded in

Maricopa County, where more than forty judges are up for retention at the same time. As a result, few judges get voted out of office even when there are compelling grounds. For example, in 1988, a superior court judge was arrested by U.S. Customs agents at a Houston airport when he returned from a Mexican vacation with marijuana and drug paraphernalia. He was subsequently convicted of criminal drug possession in a Texas court. The case attracted considerable public attention because the judge testified at his own trial and told a dubious story under oath. It just so happened that the Arizona judge was up for retention a few months later. However, with his name buried in the long list of judicial names, he managed to muster barely enough votes for another term. (The judge resigned three years later when he was convicted of a second drug offense and perjury.)

Efforts to assist voters in assessing judges have not proved particularly effective. The state constitution now requires judges to be formally evaluated and the results made public prior to judicial elections.[26] However, it is not clear that this information reaches the voters, let alone influences their decisions. The raw election returns suggest that many voters simply skip this portion of the ballot or arbitrarily vote "yes" or "no" across the board. However, supporters of merit selection contend that most judges are doing their jobs, that there are other ways of removing the few rotten apples, and that retention elections simply provide a backup that allows the public to have a say if the occasion warrants.

Removal

The constitution currently provides three ways to remove judges before the end of their terms. First, the legislature can impeach and remove a judge like any other state officer (see chapter 3). Second, the people of Arizona have the power to remove a judge through the recall process (see chapters 2 and 4). Despite the strong concerns of President Taft, only one judge has ever been removed through recall—and that was back in 1925. The third method for removing judges is a comparatively new administrative process. An eleven-member Commission on Judicial Conduct has the authority to investigate any type of conduct that "brings the judicial office into disrepute."[27] (This includes disabilities as well as incompetence and willful misconduct.) If the commission determines that a complaint against a judge has merit, it can impose private sanctions. More serious matters are referred to the state supreme court. The court then has the power to censure, suspend, or remove any judge. Currently, the commission investigates nearly three hundred complaints a year. Of course, not all of these have merit; many come from parties who are simply unhappy about losing their cases. Since the administrative process was created, two judges have been summarily removed by the supreme court and more have been suspended or censored.[28]

Judicial Procedures

Court procedures vary with the nature of the case. It should come as no surprise that divorce proceedings are not conducted the same way as murder trials. However, in the typical criminal or civil case there are three major stages: (1) pretrial, (2) trial, and (3) appeal. The appellate process (described previously) is essentially the same for criminal and civil cases. However, there are significant differences in the ways in which serious criminal and civil cases are initiated and tried. These differences can give rise to opposite outcomes even when the two types of cases arise from the identical facts. Most notably, this

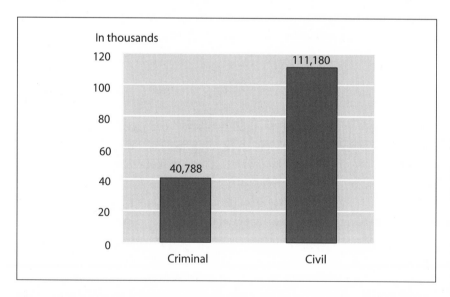

Figure 6.5 Civil and criminal cases filed in superior court (FY 1999). (Excludes 23,815 cases falling within neither category.) Source: Arizona Supreme Court,

occurred in the O. J. Simpson case. Simpson was **acquitted** in a murder case brought by the government of California but was ordered to pay the victims' families over $33 million in **damages** in a subsequent tort case. Similar discrepancies occur in parallel criminal and civil cases that are tried in Arizona. To appreciate why this can occur, we will contrast the procedures in a typical felony and tort case.

A Typical Felony Case

A felony is a serious crime. In Arizona, it is punishable by incarceration in a state prison or even death. The purpose of a felony case is to establish the accused's guilt and impose the appropriate punishment. It is an important governmental responsibility, and *only* the government has the power to bring a felony case. This is why such cases are always styled *State of Arizona vs. [named defendant]*. The state, of course, can't appear in court. It is represented by prosecutors, who are government lawyers. In Arizona, prosecutors in the county attorney's office[29] usually handle the case through trial; however, prosecutors in the state attorney general's office take over on appeal.

Pretrial proceedings in felony cases   One of the biggest differences between felony and tort cases involves how they are initiated. Felony cases are not easily commenced. The law recognizes that serious harm can result from simply being accused of a felony. For example, the defendant—although presumptively innocent—can be jailed until the trial is over. And even if the defendant is ultimately acquitted, a stigma attaches from having been formally accused. Accordingly, the state constitution does not permit prosecutors to begin felony trials whenever they or the police wish. Rather, the trial can commence only if it has first been authorized by (1) a **grand jury** *or* (2) a justice of the peace following a preliminary hearing.[30]

The grand jury is the older, more traditional way of initiating criminal cases in the United States. (It is still the only way that federal criminal cases can be begun.) Grand juries are made up of ordinary citizens who have been randomly summoned to serve. Unlike regular trial juries, grand juries can be impaneled for up to six months, and they typically review evidence in more than one case.[31] The prosecutor presents evidence to the grand jury in strictest secrecy. (The accused may not even know that he or she is under investigation.) If the grand jury concludes that there is sufficient evidence to justify a

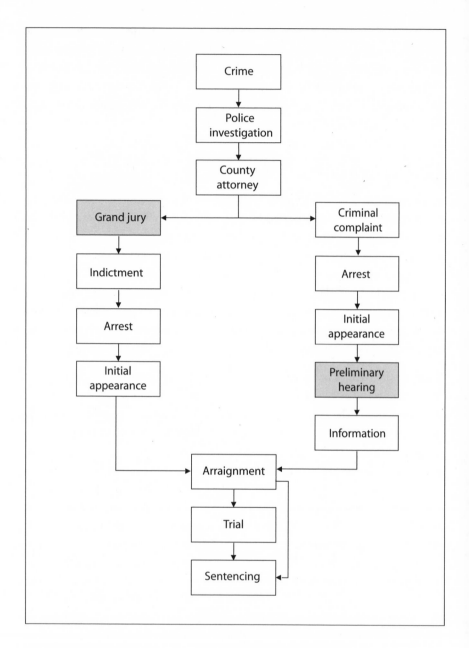

Figure 6.6 Alternative paths to conviction. A preliminary hearing or grand jury proceeding must always precede the trial. However, the arrest and initial appearance can take place before the case is referred to the county attorney.

criminal trial, it will sign an **indictment** (formal written charges) submitted by the prosecutor. The indictment formally initiates the criminal process, and an arrest warrant or summons is normally issued at this point (see figure 6.6).

The alternative, and more common, way of initiating felony trials in Arizona is through a preliminary hearing before a justice of the peace.[32] The JP performs a reviewing function similar to the grand jury's. At the preliminary hearing the prosecutor presents a small portion of the case to the JP. This often consists of the testimony of a single witness such as the investigating police officer. Unlike a grand jury proceeding, however, the preliminary hearing is conducted in public, and the accused's attorney has a limited right to participate. If the JP concludes that the state has sufficient grounds to proceed, the prosecutor files an **information** in superior court. This is a written document that accuses the defendant of specific criminal acts. It is equivalent to a grand jury indictment.

Preliminary hearings and grand jury proceedings have their respective advantages and disadvantages.[33] Prosecutors choose which route to take, and their choice is usually based upon strategic considerations that apply to the particular case.[34] Either way, a neutral third party—citizen grand jurors or a JP—serves as a check against the abuse of power by police or prosecutors. Finally, regardless of how the case is formally commenced, in a felony case two other short hearings precede the actual trial: an **initial appearance** (where the defendant is informed of the charges and advised of his or her constitutional rights)[35] and an **arraignment** (where the defendant enters a formal plea of "guilty," "not guilty," or "no contest"). If the defendant pleads not guilty, a trial date is set; otherwise the matter proceeds directly to sentencing, as shown in figure 6.6.

Felony trials   All felony trials take place in superior court. There are usually three major participants: the parties, the judge, and the jury. As outlined below, each performs a different function.

In the American system of justice, the opposing parties have the job of presenting evidence and proving the facts of the case. (This contrasts with many European systems in which the judge plays a more active, investigative role.) In felony cases the **burden of proof** always rests with the **plaintiff**—the party that initiates the case. This means that government prosecutors have the responsibility of bringing evidence into the courtroom. Prosecutors do this by summoning witnesses to testify under oath and by presenting physical evidence such as documents, photographs, weapons, or articles of clothing. The prosecutor, however, cannot force the defendant to take the witness stand, nor can the prosecutor comment on a defendant's refusal to testify. This is because the U.S. and state constitutions give criminal defendants a **privilege against self-incrimination.**[36] (No such privilege applies in civil cases.) The burden of proof in a criminal case is exceedingly high. The prosecution must introduce enough evidence to convince the jury that the defendant is guilty *beyond a reasonable doubt*. The defendant is not obligated to present any evidence whatsoever; a defendant can simply sit back and argue that the government did not prove the case.[37] However, this is a somewhat risky strategy. Most defendants do present evidence to tell their side of the story.

The trial judge has three major functions in a felony case. First, the judge ensures that the proceedings are conducted in a way that is fair to both sides. Ordinarily, this entails ruling on evidentiary objections that are raised by the parties. Second, the judge makes sure that the proper law is applied to the facts of the case. For example, the judge gives the jury detailed instructions regarding the applicable law before the jury retires to decide the verdict. Finally, if the defendant is found guilty, the judge conducts a sentencing hearing and imposes the actual sentence. Typically, the judge will order the court's probation department to prepare a detailed presentence report first.[38] There will also be a hearing where the victims have a right to testify.[39] In the past, judges had considerable discretion in determining the appropriate punishment. Today, however, statutes set highly specific punishment ranges for each offense, sharply reducing the judge's power.

The jury is the third major participant in felony trials. Arizona is deeply committed to the right to trial by jury. The Progressive framers of the constitution viewed the jury as an important citizen check on abuse of governmental power. The state constitution sweepingly declares that "the right of trial by jury shall remain inviolate."[40] This provision has been interpreted to guarantee jury trials in all criminal cases except for the most petty offenses. A defendant can always waive the right to a jury trial; in this circumstance the judge assumes the jury's role. It is the jury's job to resolve *factual* issues that are in dispute (e.g., is the witness telling the truth?). The judge instructs the jury as to the relevant *law* to be applied to the facts of the case. The Arizona Constitution jealously guards the jury's role and warns judges not to encroach upon it. It states: "Judges shall not charge juries with respect to matters of fact, nor comment thereon, but shall declare the law."[41]

Juries are made up of ordinary citizens over the age of eighteen who are randomly summoned to appear in court.[42] (Names of potential jurors are obtained from drivers' license, voter registration, and other lists.) In Arizona, the size of a jury varies. The most serious felony cases (crimes punishable by death or by more than thirty years' imprisonment) use twelve-member juries. Other felony cases use eight-member juries.[43] Irrespective of the jury's size, the verdict must always be unanimous in criminal cases.[44] If all the members on the jury cannot agree, the jury is said to be "hung" and the trial has no legal effect. Prosecutors will normally retry the case before a new jury. (Obviously, this is an undesirable outcome. It delays the administration of justice; subjects the witnesses, victims and defendants to a second ordeal; ties up the courts; and is quite costly.)

In felony cases the jury must choose between two verdicts: "guilty" or "not guilty." Contrary to popular perception, a "not guilty" verdict does not establish the defendant's innocence. Rather, it simply signifies that the state did not present enough evidence to establish the defendant's guilt to the high level of certainty required by the constitution. If the jury finds the defendant not guilty, the proceedings are completely over. Government prosecutors cannot appeal the acquittal because the state and federal constitutions protect criminal defendants from **double jeopardy**.[45] Alternatively, if the defendant is found guilty, the judge dismisses the jury and sets a date for sentencing. A defendant can appeal both the conviction and the sentence.

A Typical Tort Case

In contrast to criminal cases, tort cases are usually brought by private parties to recover damages (money) for injuries. The injury can be of a personal nature (physical or emotional harm); it can involve damage to the plaintiff's reputation; or it can involve financial or property loss. The wrongful conduct giving rise to the tort case may be intentional, negligent, or neither. When the defendant intentionally inflicts harm, the conduct usually constitutes a crime as well as a tort. Thus, the crimes of murder, assault, theft, and fraud all give rise to parallel torts. There is a need for separate criminal and civil cases because they serve different purposes. The criminal prosecution is brought by the government to protect society as a whole. Although it may give the victim some emotional satisfaction, punishing the defendant does not pay the victim's bills. This is the purpose of the private tort action.

Most tort cases, however, do not involve intentional misconduct by the defendant. Rather, they fall into the category of negligence. In these cases the plaintiff argues that the defendant failed to exercise "reasonable care" under the circumstances. Simple negligence cases rarely have parallel criminal actions. For example, when a grocery store fails to warn patrons of a wet floor it is not committing a crime. Nonetheless, an injured shopper can sue the store and recover damages for the injuries incurred. Automobile accident, malpractice, and "slip and fall" cases make up the bulk of negligence cases.

Finally, a defendant can be held liable under tort law even when there is no real moral culpability. For example, manufacturers of defective products are sometimes held responsible on **strict liability** theories even when they exercised all possible care. The rationale of these cases is that it is better to shift the burden of unforeseeable harms to the manufacturer (who can distribute the burden by raising prices) than to leave the unlucky purchaser without legal redress.

In Arizona, minor tort cases—in which the claimed damages are less than $5,000—are handled by JP courts in a fairly streamlined fashion. If the claim is between $5,000 and $10,000, the case can go to either JP or superior court. Serious tort cases (above the $10,000 cutoff) are handled exclusively by superior courts. As with felony cases, the proceedings are quite formal. However, there are some important differences, as explained below.

Pretrial proceedings in tort cases   In sharp contrast to criminal cases, there are no screening processes like grand juries or preliminary hearings to determine whether a tort case has sufficient merit to proceed. The plaintiff unilaterally commences the case by paying a court fee and filing a written complaint with the clerk of the superior court. Once a copy of the complaint is served on the defendant, the defendant has a short period of time (usually twenty days) to file a formal answer that either admits to or denies the allegations in the complaint.

When the complaint and answer have been filed, the case enters an investigative stage known as pretrial **discovery**. Court rules compel the parties to exchange information with each other. Sometimes the litigants demand information through formal written questionnaires known as **interrogatories**. They also orally question each other, as well as potential witnesses, in proceedings known as **depositions**. Depositions normally take place in private settings such as lawyers' offices. However, the witnesses are under oath, a court reporter transcribes the deposition word for word, and potentially the transcript can be used at trial. Judges supervise but do not directly participate in pretrial discovery.

Fortunately, the majority of tort cases do *not* go to trial; Arizona's court system could not sustain such a burden. Instead, after the discovery phase is over, most cases either are settled by mutual agreement of the parties or are resolved by the judge on legal grounds. For example, if a case is frivolous on its face, the defendant can file a motion with the court to have the case dismissed. Alternatively, either side can file a motion for **summary judgment**. This motion argues that there is no need for a trial because the relevant facts are not in dispute. The judge is asked to enter judgment by applying the law to the undisputed facts. If the court grants either of these two motions, the case terminates at this juncture and the losing party can appeal.

Tort trials   Tort trials resemble felony trials in most respects. Indeed, an observer who walked into the courtroom would be hard-pressed to know which type of proceeding was under way. The same three participants—the parties, the judge, and the jury—are usually present. The parties play the same role as they do in felony trials. That is, it is their job to present the facts of the case in the form of live testimony and physical evidence. Similarly, the plaintiff (the injured party) has the burden of proof. However, it is a much lower burden than in felony cases. In order to prevail, the plaintiff must merely prove the case by a *preponderance of the evidence*. In plain English, this means that the jury must simply believe that it is "more likely than not" that the defendant is responsible for the injury; the jury does *not* have to be convinced to a virtual certainty as in felony cases.

There are other important procedural differences between civil and criminal trials. Tort defendants have fewer constitutional rights than their criminal counterparts. For example, a tort defendant *can* be called to the witness stand and interrogated by the plaintiff. If the defendant refuses to answer questions on Fifth Amendment grounds,[46] the refusal will be in front of the jury and prejudicial. Additionally, tort defendants are not entitled to have a lawyer at public expense.

As in felony cases, the judge maintains order in the courtroom and rules on procedural objections to ensure the fairness of the proceedings. However, because few statutes apply to tort cases, the judge has an expanded role. As explained previously, the judge must apply the common law to the facts of the case. This is an interpretative activity that allows the judge some latitude. Much of the action in tort cases takes place behind the scenes. Significant issues are often resolved in legal motions argued by the lawyers in the judge's chambers, outside the presence of the jury.

The parties in tort cases have a right to trial by jury. However, the size of the jury is smaller than in felony cases, and unanimity is not necessary. Agreement of six out of eight jurors is all that is required to render a verdict.[47] Two judgments are possible in tort cases: the defendant can be found "liable" or "not liable." (The term "guilt" applies only to criminal proceedings.) If the defendant is found liable, the jury determines the appropriate level of damages. Some types of damages—such as medical expenses, lost wages, and property damage—can be easily quantified. However, Arizona common law also allows the plaintiff to recover money for more speculative losses such as pain, suffering, loss of enjoyment, and loss of companionship. All of these types of damages, whether speculative or not, are called "actual damages."

When the defendant's conduct is particularly egregious (intentional, reckless, or grossly negligent) the plaintiff may be able to recover **punitive damages** as well. This is an additional windfall amount that is awarded to punish the defendant and deter a repetition of the wrongful conduct. Although juries do not always award punitive damages, such awards can be sizeable—they usually exceed the actual damages by a substantial amount. Large punitive damage awards have become quite controversial; some critics contend that juries can be too easily swayed by emotional arguments and that such awards raise insurance and other costs for everyone.

Arizona's constitution jealously guards the jury's role in determining the amount of damages. For example, Article 2, section 31 states in unambiguous language:

§ 31. Damages for death or personal injuries
No law shall be enacted in this state limiting the amount of damages to be recovered for causing the death or injury of any person.[48]

A related constitutional provision prohibits a case from being dismissed by the judge in advance of trial even when the plaintiff is mostly at fault. For example, automobile accidents often have more than one cause. Should a driver be allowed to sue the state for a poorly lit roadway if the driver's own drunkenness was 95 percent responsible for the accident? Alternatively, should an injured passenger be allowed to sue the state if the passenger voluntarily got in the car knowing the driver was drunk? The Arizona Constitution answers "yes" to both of these questions.[49] Although the jury is not obligated to award damages to plaintiffs under either circumstance, the constitution requires the decision to be left to the jury.[50]

As explained in chapter 2, organized labor pushed for the adoption of these provisions when the constitution was written. It feared the state's most powerful industries—the mines and railroads—would procure legislation that limited their liability to injured workers. In recent years these constitutional provisions have been at the center of a public debate over tort reform. Critics of the present system argue that frivolous cases and excessive jury verdicts raise costs for everyone, clog the court system, subject defendants to unpredictable liability, and unfairly burden defendants with legal costs even when they are ultimately exonerated. In some states, these arguments have carried the day. That is, legislatures have passed laws that cap jury awards or require the early dismissal of frivolous cases. Arizona's constitutional provisions, however, prevent similar laws from being enacted. The Progressive drafters put the provisions in the state constitution because they did not trust the legislature or judges to draw lines. Instead, they chose to trust the common sense of ordinary citizens "to render individualized justice under the facts of each case."[51] The insurance industry has vigorously lobbied for the removal of these barriers. Proposed constitutional amendments to eliminate them were on the ballot in 1986, 1990, and 1994. Each time, the voters said no. The debate over tort reform, however, is not over.

Online Resources

Arizona Judicial Department:
    www.supreme.state.az.us/
    www.supreme.state.az.us/info/pubinfo.htm (publications)
    www.supreme.state.az.us/info/guide/gtc.htm (*Guide to Arizona Courts*)

Arizona Supreme Court:
    www.supreme.state.az.us/azsupreme (home page)
    www.supreme.state.az.us/opin/default.htm (recent decisions)

Arizona Court of Appeals, Division 1:
    www.state.az.us/co/ (home page)
    www.state.az.us/co/opidx.htm (recent decisions)

Arizona Court of Appeals, Division 2:
www.apltwo.ct.state.az.us/ (home page)
www.apltwo.ct.state.az.us/decis.html (recent decisions)

Superior Court of Maricopa County:
www.superiorcourt.maricopa.gov/default.html

Superior Court of Pima County:
www.sc.co.pima.az.us/

Arizona Commission on Judicial Conduct:
www.supreme.state.az.us/cjc/

Arizona Commission on Judicial Performance Review:
www.supreme.state.az.us/jpr/

U.S. Supreme Court Opinions:
supct.law.cornell.edu/supct/

National Center for State Courts:
www.ncsc.dni.us/

Legal Information Institute (state law):
wwwsecure.law.cornell.edu/states/listing.html

7 Local Government

Our focus so far has been on state government. However, roughly 1,700 local governments also operate within Arizona's borders. These include 15 county governments, 87 municipal governments (cities and towns), and over 1,600 district governments (school districts, community college districts, and special taxing districts). It is difficult to give a precise count, because special taxing districts come and go. Moreover, our list does not include *all* the governments that operate within Arizona's borders. It deliberately omits Arizona's twenty-one reservation governments because they are not part of the state. Tribal governments derive their authority from the national government. Although Arizona's Indian communities interact with state and local governments, they are largely beyond the state's control.[1]

Local governments have their own officials, and they can levy taxes, borrow money, and make rules. However, they differ from the state government in an important legal respect. They are not sovereign governments. Rather, they are called "creatures of the state" because their very right to exist and most of their power derive from the state's constitution and statutes.[2] Despite this subordinate status, local governments perform critical public functions. For example, they provide police and fire protection, run public schools, operate the trial courts and jails, protect public health, and directly or indirectly furnish residents with water, sanitation, and other vital utilities. In ordinary times, this is the American government that most people would miss first.

Why We Have Local Governments

Few countries have as many local governments as the United States. Certainly, there are downsides to this situation. It complicates things when there is a need for a coordinated response to problems like pollution, crime, and transportation that cross jurisdictional lines. Official accountability is also reduced when separate governments can point the finger of blame at each other. Uneven conditions are intensified and perpetuated with multiple jurisdictions. Local governments are periodically associated with scandals such as bid-rigging, kickbacks, nepotism, and misuse of public property. Small governments can be inefficient. Finally, having multiple governments increases the burden on voters. For example, in the 1998 general election, Phoenix residents were asked to choose officials for *seven* different governments. Needless to say, this resulted in a very long ballot.[3]

Despite these downsides, most Americans strongly favor the concept of local governments. There are numerous reasons why. From ancient times onward, citizens have resented being governed by distant public officials who are unfamiliar with local circumstances. Arizona's diverse geographic, demographic, economic, and other conditions make a "one size fits all" governing approach problematic. It is also doubtful that a single, central government could efficiently deliver all the services demanded by today's citizens. Local governments foster participatory democracy. They enable citizens to directly influence public decisions that affect their own community. They also provide more opportunities for holding public office—and therefore serve as a valuable training ground for those seeking political careers. Local governments permit greater policy experimentation by allowing individual communities to pioneer their own solutions to social problems. Effective solutions can be copied by others; conversely, the impact of mistakes is reduced. Local governments tend to be more responsive to citizens. Officials know that dissatisfied residents and businesses can "vote with their feet"—that is, relocate to a community that better serves their needs. In short, for practical, historical, and even emotional reasons, local governments are deeply entrenched in the Arizona political landscape.

Counties

Arizona's fifteen counties are shown in figure 7.1. They are products of Arizona's past. Except for La Paz (which was created when Yuma County was

Figure 7.1 Arizona counties

split in 1982), all of the state's counties were established during the territorial period, when towns were relatively small and far flung. It would have been impractical back then for every small community to operate its own courthouse and jails, collect taxes, build and maintain roads, etc. Accordingly, counties were established to provide these services on a more efficient regional basis. Until recently, county governments were the most important units of local government, and the **county seat** was the center of both political and cultural life. This still holds true in many of Arizona's rural counties. However, in urban Maricopa and Pima counties, large city governments now compete for power and influence.

In a technical sense, Arizona's county governments are all alike. Because counties do not enjoy **home rule** as cities do (see discussion below), county

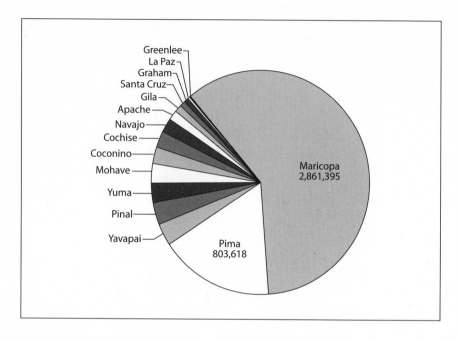

Figure 7.2 Population distribution by county (1999 estimate). Source: U.S. Bureau of the Census <http://www.census.gov/population/estimates/county/co-99-1/99C1_04.txt>.

governments are structured in very similar ways. Essentially, they must follow the generic design prescribed by the state constitution and statutes. However, the actual conditions in each county vary enormously. For example, Maricopa County is home to nearly 60 percent of the state's residents.[4] Within its boundaries are twenty-four separate municipalities and two Indian communities. With over 2.8 million people, it is the fifth largest county in the entire nation, and it has more people than twenty states. At the opposite end of the scale is Greenlee County, with a mere 9,300 people.[5] Obviously, these size differences present the two counties with profoundly different governing challenges.

There are other differences that impact county governance. In Gila County 96 percent of the land is publicly owned.[6] This makes raising revenues difficult, because public lands cannot be taxed. The presence of Indian reservations within counties is another differentiating factor. Seventy-eight percent of the residents in Apache County are Native Americans, and the county is home to large portions of both the Navajo and Apache reservations. These circumstances produced a political crisis in the early 1980s when Native Americans gained a majority on the county board of supervisors and approved bond sales that raised taxes for non-Indian property owners.[7] (Reservation land could not be taxed.) The legislature's solution—to isolate the reservation by splitting the county in two—was vetoed by Governor Bruce Babbitt. Tensions, however, remain to this day in Apache and other counties with high reservation populations. In short, as we generalize about Arizona's county governments, it is important to keep in mind that these governments confront very different problems and are necessarily shaped by the unique contexts in which they operate.

What Counties Do

County governments perform services that fall within two broad categories. First, they function as "administrative arms of the state." That means that

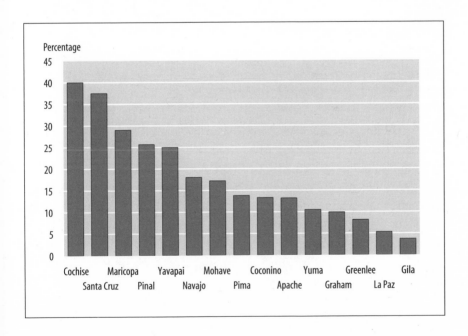

Figure 7.3 Privately owned land by county. Source: adapted from Arizona Department of Commerce, *County Profiles*.

Table 7.1 Major County Functions

State-Type Functions	City-Type Functions[a]
Assesses and collects property taxes	Furnishes utilities (water, sewage, garbage collection, electricity, gas, irrigation, landfill services, etc.)
Conducts elections and maintains voter registration records	
Operates jails	Provides law enforcement
Prosecutes state crimes	Provides fire protection
Operates superior and JP courts	Provides public housing
Administers welfare and social service programs	Makes and enforces zoning, subdivision, and other land-use regulations
Operates county hospitals and provides indigent health care	Regulates traffic, public nuisances, building safety
Administers public health programs and inspections	
Administers air pollution and environmental programs	
Records deeds and mortgages	
Builds and maintains bridges and roads	
Operates county fairs, parks, libraries, agricultural extension services	

[a] Counties may contract to have all or some of these services provided by private companies. Alternatively, they may be provided by special taxing districts.

they carry out *state*-mandated services on a more efficient, regional basis. Counties have little discretion when performing these state functions; typically, the legislature calls the shots. And the services falling within this category (see table 7.1) are generally available to all the residents of the county, including those who reside within cities and towns. Second, counties provide "city-type services" for those who do not live within municipal boundaries. For example, persons living in unincorporated areas look to the county sheriff for police protection. Other functions in this increasingly important category are summarized in table 7.1.

How Counties Are Governed

Arizona's counties follow the oldest governmental pattern, the "traditional county commission" form.[8] In this design, power is divided between an elected governing body and numerous separately elected officials (see figure 7.4). The governing body is called the **board of supervisors,** and its size varies. Large counties are required to have five-member boards; smaller counties can choose three-member boards instead. The supervisors are elected from separate districts within the county. The remaining officials are elected on a countywide basis. They include a sheriff, a county attorney, a recorder, a treasurer, a tax assessor, a superintendent of schools, and a superior court clerk. The primary responsibilities of each office are summarized in table 7.2. Except for the county attorney (who must be a lawyer) and the school superintendent (who must have a teaching certificate), the qualifications for holding an elective county office are minimal. Officials must merely be eighteen years old, English proficient, registered voters, and residents of the county.[9] County officials are elected in partisan elections. Since 1964, they have had four-year terms that coincide with the presidential election cycle. Other important county officers are appointed by the board of supervisors.[10] Finally, the coun-

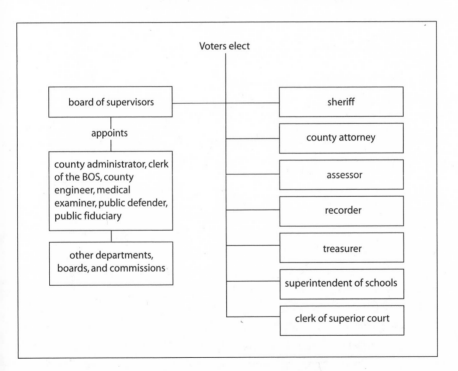

Figure 7.4 County government. (The separately elected officials also oversee large departments, such as sheriff's and county attorney's offices.)

ties employ a workforce that varies in size from over 12,000 full-time employees in Maricopa County to approximately 130 employees in Greenlee County.

The Debate over County Reform

In the early 1990s, Maricopa County was branded one of the worst governments in the entire nation.[11] The county teetered on the brink of bankruptcy. Its elected officials had overspent their budgets for years, ignoring a rising county deficit and the pleas of the board of supervisors. The county assessor was so far behind in appraising properties that the county was estimated to have lost as much as $100 million in uncollected taxes. The sheriff was suing the board, demanding more funds. Wall Street was losing confidence in the county's bonds. Ultimately, Maricopa County required massive layoffs and a $9 million bailout from the state in order to stay afloat. Maricopa County's troubles could be attributed to a variety of causes, including a poor economy. However, it was not the only county that was struggling. Many blamed the troubles on the counties' traditional form of government. The debate continues to this day.

The argument for reform   Critics charge that Arizona's counties are "headless." That is, there is no single county leader comparable to a president, governor, mayor, or strong city manager. The independently elected county officials have little incentive to function as team players. Rather, they often run their departments like independent fiefdoms, banking on their personal popularity with the voters. For example, at the height of Maricopa County's budget crisis, the sheriff reflected the attitude of many when he declared, "I don't report to the Board of Supervisors. I serve the people only."[12]

A second common complaint is that the counties lack sufficient governing authority. Counties can exercise only those powers expressly delegated by the state legislature and constitution.[13] These delegations were designed for a nineteenth-century world and have not kept pace with the counties' expanding, modern responsibilities. Counties also complain that the state's part-time legislature fails to address their needs in a timely fashion. They also resent the fact that legislators from other areas are deciding local county affairs.

Third, Arizona counties face chronic fiscal problems. Historically, property taxes have been the primary source of county revenues. However, ever since

Table 7.2 Major Responsibilities of County Officials

Office	Responsibilities
Board of supervisors	Determines the county's annual budget, sets the county's tax rates, enacts ordinances and codes, hires and oversees other county employees, and adjudicates zoning matters and other appeals.
Sheriff	Operates the jails and enforces the law in all unincorporated areas.
County attorney	Prosecutes major state crimes and provides legal advice for the county and school districts.
County recorder	Conducts state and local elections; maintains voting, real estate, and other local records.
County treasurer	Manages the county's financial assets, collects property taxes, and disburses funds to other jurisdictions (e.g., special taxing districts) within the county.
County assessor	Determines the current value of all taxable property within the county.
County superintendent of schools	Serves as an administrative liaison between the state and local school districts, disburses funds to individual school districts, and fills school board vacancies.
Clerk of the superior court	Maintains all court records, collects court fees, manages court finances, and disburses child support payments.

the voters put strict limits on the tax in 1980 (see chapter 3), the counties have struggled to find alternative funding sources.[14] At the same time they have been burdened with some of the most costly—and least popular—governmental responsibilities, such as running the jails and providing indigent health care. Although the state provides more supplemental funding than most states, the counties contend that it is insufficient.

Finally, reformers criticize county government for having elected sheriffs, assessors, recorders, and other department heads instead of appointed professionals with the requisite training and experience. They argue that the counties' modern responsibilities are too complex to be left to officials whose tenure in office may rest upon personal popularity and name recognition, rather than professional competence.

The home rule defeat   The legislature responded to these criticisms by proposing a constitutional amendment that permitted the state's two largest
counties to adopt home rule. It was approved by the voters in 1992.[15] It meant
that the counties could adopt their own **charter** (a county constitution) with
their own desired form of government. Home rule would also allow the
county to manage its affairs with greater independence from the state legislature. Reformers advocate such autonomy; in fact, roughly three-quarters of
the nation's counties currently enjoy home rule. Maricopa and Pima counties
embarked on the lengthy process to convert to home rule in the mid-1990s.
New governments were proposed for each county that emphasized management principles over electoral politics.[16] However, the proposed charters were
vigorously opposed by most of the counties' elected officials. They argued
that the citizens' role would be reduced and that professional managers would
be less accountable than elected officials. The new governments were also
attacked as being too big and costly. Finally, charter opponents feared that
greater county independence would result in higher taxes and fees.[17] The timing for the home rule debate was especially poor. Maricopa County voters
were upset over a controversial stadium tax that had been levied by county
supervisors to build the Bank One Ballpark.[18] In the end, the opposition pre-
vailed. Maricopa County voters rejected the proposed charter in 1996; Pima
County voters followed suit in a low-turnout election the following year. At
least for the present, county home rule in Arizona is dead.

Cities and Towns

The vast majority of Arizona residents live in cities and towns. Contrary to
popular perception, the state has always been predominately urban. From the
beginning, scarce water, Indian threats, and other frontier hazards necessi-
tated close group living for survival. Until fairly recently, however, Arizona's
towns were relatively small and slow-growing. Indeed, the state's many ghost
towns provide striking reminders of the precarious existence of early settlements. We have seen how chronically low population delayed Arizona's
admission as a state (chapter 2).

Today, the story could not be more different. Arizona's growth began to
take off after World War II (see figure 7.5). The establishment of military bases
was the key catalyst. New businesses were also attracted to the state's mild
winter climate, nonunion labor market, and progrowth public policies.[19]

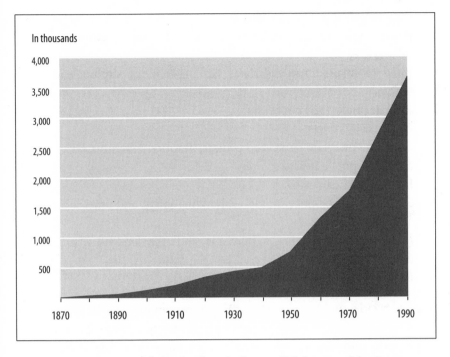

Figure 7.5 Arizona's population by decade. Source: U.S. Bureau of the Census

During the 1980s and 1990s, Arizona's growth skyrocketed. Phoenix—a relatively young city founded in 1870—became the seventh largest city in the United States. Smaller rural communities like Chandler and Gilbert grew at even faster rates.[20] For example, between 1990 and 1998, Chandler grew by 78 percent, and Gilbert grew by an astounding 205 percent.[21] New communities began incorporating. Strikingly, one-third of Arizona's present-day municipalities didn't legally exist prior to 1960.[22] An *Arizona Republic* series reported that the state's open spaces were disappearing at the rate of "an acre an hour." Urban sprawl became a hot issue as municipalities wrestled with building moratoriums, developers' impact fees, and various antigrowth initiatives.

What Cities and Towns Do

Cities and towns are Arizona's "bread and butter" governments. They furnish a wide range of indispensable services. For example, larger cities

1. Provide police and fire protection;
2. Furnish water, sewage treatment, garbage collection, irrigation, and land-fill services;
3. Build and maintain streets, roads, parking facilities, airports, and cemeteries;
4. Provide public transportation;
5. Operate city courts;
6. Build and maintain parks, golf courses, libraries, museums, civic centers, and other public facilities;
7. Provide public housing;
8. Regulate traffic, public nuisances, building safety, and other local health and safety matters;
9. Make and enforce zoning, subdivision, and other land-use planning regulations;
10. Promote tourism and economic development.

In smaller cities and towns, some of the above services may be provided by special districts (discussed below) or by private corporations regulated by the corporation commission. And some municipalities furnish services to their residents that are not on the above list, such as providing gas and electricity.

Although the list of municipal services is a long one, it is important to emphasize what Arizona cities and towns do *not* do. Notably, they do not have authority over public schools. Elementary and secondary schools in Arizona are operated by school districts, which are independent governments (discussed below). This arrangement has caused real difficulties for communities that have experienced sudden population growth. For example, between 1990 and 1998, school enrollment in the town of Gilbert nearly doubled.[23] New school construction simply could not keep pace with new home construction. After existing schools were strained to the breaking point, frantic school officials persuaded city officials to impose a controversial one-year moratorium on new residential development. (The city did this by refusing to issue new building permits.) Cities and school districts in other communities are similarly struggling to coordinate their responses to the challenge of rapid growth.

How Cities and Towns Are Governed

Cities and towns are **municipal corporations**. Like private business corporations, they derive their right to exist from state law. The principal difference between cities and towns is size and complexity of government. Towns are smaller and have simpler governing structures. To incorporate (become an officially recognized, self-governing municipality) a community must have a minimum population of 3,000 for city status and only 1,500 for town status.[24] Currently, Arizona has forty-four cities and forty-three towns. It should be noted that many well-known Arizona communities, such as Sun City, are neither cities nor towns. Despite their names, these are simply unincorporated areas. They do not have the authority to govern themselves; instead, the county serves as their local government.

Arizona's Progressive founders valued local autonomy, so they put constitutional limits on the legislature's ability to interfere with cities and towns. For example, the legislature is expressly prohibited from enacting "local or special" laws that treat communities individually.[25] Even more importantly, the Progressives encouraged municipal home rule. In contrast to the counties, from the very beginning, cities with populations of at least 3,500 could design their own forms of government by adopting a charter.[26] Today, Arizona has twenty **charter cities** that enjoy individualized forms of government.[27] The remaining sixty-seven municipalities are called **general law cities** (or towns) because they must follow the governing structure laid down by state statutes (which permit minor variation). In short, there is no single governing structure for Arizona cities and towns as there is for counties. There are, however, some significant, common patterns.

Arizona's council-manager governments   As explained previously, Arizona counties follow a traditional governing structure that emphasizes electoral politics over professional management. The situation is the exact opposite with the state's cities and towns. With one exception (Nogales), Arizona's municipalities use the **council-manager form of government**. This is the design favored by most urban experts. It originated in the early twentieth century as a Progressive reform, and the city of Phoenix (see box) was one of the first cities in the nation to embrace it.

The council-manager structure was intended to replace the traditional, mayor-centered government that is still found in the nation's largest cities. The Progressives associated elected mayors with **patronage**, corruption, conflict, and inefficiency. They reasoned that problems at the local level are primarily *technical* in nature: e.g., how to deliver utilities in the most efficient manner, how to engineer good roads, etc. The reformers concluded that residents would be better served by city governments that emphasized technical expertise over electoral politics. The council-manager innovation was essentially an attempt to take the politics out of urban governance.

Arizona's council-manager governments vary slightly from city to city. In general, power is divided between an elected city council (usually consisting of seven members)[28] and a powerful, professional city manager appointed by the council. The council's responsibility is to set broad policies, while the city manager actually runs the city. That is, the manager hires and supervises the other city personnel, prepares the budget, and recommends actions to the council.

Today, most city managers have degrees in public administration or political science. They typically work their way up through the ranks of city government. However, once they become city managers, their tenure can be as precarious as that of managers of professional sports teams. They must walk a fine line between management and political issues, taking care not to step on the toes of their elected bosses, the members of the city council. In the absence of a charter provision to the contrary, city managers can be summarily dismissed upon a simple majority vote of the council.[29] (Phoenix, Tucson, and a few other charter cities require a supermajority vote for removal.) Not surprisingly, the most successful city managers maintain a very low profile. For example, few Phoenix residents could name their city manager even though he runs a city that is larger than most major business corporations. In fact, Frank Fairbanks has smoothly managed Phoenix for nearly a decade and won national awards in the process.

Although Arizona's council-manager governments have mayors, the mayor's role is greatly reduced. Apart from ceremonial functions, the mayor is typically a member of the city council with no greater voting power than any other council member. In some cities, the mayor is chosen by the members of the council themselves. Increasingly, however, Arizona cities have chosen to have mayors directly elected by the voters. (In these cities, the mayor's higher public profile can translate into greater political power, even though the mayor still has only a single vote.)

Nonpartisan elections   Nearly all city council and mayoral elections in Arizona are **nonpartisan**. Only Tucson and South Tucson deviate from this pattern. Nonpartisan elections are another Progressive reform. As with the council-manager design, the rationale was to eliminate "politics" from local governance. Reformers believed that having nonpartisan elections would

PHOENIX: THE CITY OF URBAN REFORM

Like its mythological namesake, Phoenix has risen from the ashes of scandal to successful urban government.[30] It took some time to accomplish. Actually, Phoenix never experienced the big-time corruption associated with the nation's older cities. Nonetheless, in 1913, it became one of the first cities to enthusiastically embrace urban reform. The city did away with ward elections and hired a manager who was expected to run the city in a professional (i.e., nonpolitical) manner.[31] Unfortunately, it didn't work. The manager got into continual conflicts with city council members and was fired within a year. In fact, he set a precedent. In the next thirty-five years, Phoenix had thirty-one city managers!

By the 1940s, the city's government was widely perceived as inept. Phoenix developed a reputation for tolerating gambling, prostitution, venereal disease, cronyism, and corruption. At the low point, Luke Field declared the city off-limits to military personnel. Fearing that the city's unsavory reputation was hindering growth, a business elite calling itself the Charter Government Committee (CGC) took over. In 1948, it succeeded in converting the city to a true council-manager form of government.[32] When that failed to cure things, the CGC decided to run its own, hand-picked candidates for every office. Barry Goldwater was one of its first picks. He and the other CGC candidates swept the 1949 election. The CGC maintained an iron grip on the city's government for the next twenty-five years, losing only 2 out of 90 races. The CGC reign brought undeniable stability. For the first time, a city manager enjoyed an eleven-year run, the government was largely free of scandal, and the city grew and prospered. However, there was a price. City elections became mere formalities. Few opposition candidates were willing to take on the powerful CGC or the major newspapers that supported it. Eventually, Phoenicians resented the CGC's elitist control. The election of a non-CGC mayor and loss of four council seats in 1975 ended the CGC's long run.

In the early 1980s, Phoenix lawyer Terry Goddard advocated more traditional city government. He argued that the council-manager system gave too much power to developers and neglected the needs of minority and low-income neighborhoods. Goddard led a successful grassroots campaign to restore district elections. Although he also strengthened the mayor's office during his own tenure, Goddard later came to respect the city manager's role. And while mayors came and went from 1980 to 2000, two successive city managers, Marvin Andrews and Frank Fairbanks, quietly and effectively ran the city.

Today, Phoenix is widely cited as a model city government. It has won national and international recognition.[33] For nearly fifty years, the city has stressed professional management over electoral politics. Whether it can maintain its successful governing formula as it grows is an interesting question. Big cities tend to develop social cleavages that city managers are ill-suited to resolve. Regardless, Phoenix's history is a story of continual adaptation and commitment to reform.

focus attention on local issues; put emphasis on the qualifications of the candidates; lessen the influence of irrelevant, national politics; diminish community conflict; and reduce corruption and graft.

To some degree, nonpartisan elections have fulfilled these expectations. However, like most political choices, they have downsides as well. Voter turnout is significantly reduced in nonpartisan elections—indeed, less than 20 percent of the registered voters typically bother to vote in Arizona city elections. Low-income, less-educated voters tend to skip these elections altogether. Lack of party labels deprives voters of information about the ideological orientation of the candidates—a problem compounded when candidates run bland, low-content campaigns designed to avoid giving offense. Nonpartisan elections also give incumbents an advantage because a familiar name may be the only information that some voters possess. As a result, council members are rarely voted out of office. Finally, nonpartisan elections may be nonpartisan in name only. Political parties often operate behind the scenes. For example, in a hotly contested 1997 Phoenix city council election, the Republican party quietly sent a mailer to its members urging them to reject a frontrunner who was not a member of the party.

At-large versus district elections   In most Arizona cities, the mayor and council members are elected on an **at-large** (citywide) basis. Again, this represents a Progressive reform. At the turn of the century, reformers criticized the traditional "ward system" in which council members were elected from separate districts. They believed that it led to infighting on city councils, facilitated corruption, and fostered NIMBY ("not in my backyard") attitudes, which sacrificed the city's overall needs to narrow, neighborhood interests. However, in recent years, Phoenix and other larger cities have abandoned the Progressives' thinking and returned to the traditional ward system. District proponents claim that at-large elections unfairly favor candidates from more affluent parts of the city and lead to the neglect of minority and lower-income neighborhoods. They also contend that at-large elections reduce voter turnout and exaggerate the influence of special interests. Phoenix made the switch to district elections in 1982 (see box). Today, Mesa, Glendale, and several other communities have converted as well.

Recall   Arizona mayors and council members are subject to recall by the voters under the same constitutional procedures that apply to state officials (see chapter 4). However, recall is much more common on the city level.

Because voter turnout is so low in local elections, the 25 percent petition threshold is easier to achieve. Some contend that it is too easy. For example, in 1997, two Phoenix council members were the targets of recall elections (both survived). Since then, elected officials in Mesa, Chandler, Buckeye, Peoria, Litchfield Park, and many other communities have been targeted. Oftentimes, a single, unpopular council vote can trigger a recall effort. Critics charge that recalls are disruptive and costly, that they put unreasonable pressure on public officials, and that they discourage competent people from running for office. Defenders, echoing the Progressive view, contend that recalls keep elected officials in line, provide a defense against too much special interest influence, permit citizens to participate in the governing process, and provide an important safety valve for disgruntled citizens.

Districts

Arizona's 1,600-plus districts constitute a third form of local government. Unlike counties and municipalities, they exist to perform a single or limited function for the residents and businesses within their jurisdictional boundaries. These boundaries can be large or small, and they can cross city and county lines. District governments have their own elected or appointed officials. They typically have the power to tax, spend money, and borrow funds through the sale of bonds. However, like all local governments within Arizona, they must operate within the limitations imposed by the state constitution and state statutes.

School Districts

Arizona currently has 226 public school districts. These include primary school districts, secondary school districts, and unified districts that combine both types of schools. Each district is governed by a three- or five-member board consisting of unpaid citizen volunteers. The board members are chosen in nonpartisan elections. They serve for staggered, four-year terms and can be recalled like all other elected officials. The actual day-to-day management of the school district rests with a full-time superintendent. The superintendent is appointed by the school board and serves at its pleasure. The superintendent hires principals, teachers, and other school personnel subject to board approval. Finally, each school within the district also has a site council consisting of parents, teachers, school administrators, and community representatives. Its role is to address curriculum and other issues assigned by the board. With input from the superintendent and site council, the school board sets school policies, manages school property, establishes a budget, levies taxes, and borrows money.

In public opinion polls, Arizonans invariably identify education as one of their top concerns. However, as outlined below, many controversies surround the governance of the state's public schools:

The debate over state versus local control   The most fundamental debate centers on who should run the state's public schools. We have already seen that numerous state officials and boards play a major regulatory role (chapter 5). This is in addition to county and local officials mentioned here. Having so many officials setting educational policy inevitably leads to conflicts, inefficiency, and reduced accountability. Unfortunately, Arizona remains deeply divided over the appropriate solution. For example, former governor Fife Symington—a vigorous supporter of local autonomy—called for the total elimination of the state's department of education, state teacher certification, and most other state-mandated requirements.[34] Although his proposals were not implemented, the legislature's creation of site-based councils in 1994 was intended to advance the decentralization cause.[35] On the opposite side, school superintendent Lisa Graham Keegan, along with most of the state's educational establishment, favors uniform state standards and professional school management. The superintendent has publicly criticized site-based councils[36] and argued that decentralization accentuates the economic and academic disparities that exist in the state's public schools. The debate over state versus local control is an old one, and it is not likely to be resolved any time soon.

School board conflicts   At the local level, political conflicts are fairly commonplace. School board members are frequent targets of recall efforts. These can be triggered by a single unpopular decision. Often, however, they are the result of longstanding cleavages within the district itself. Whatever the catalyst, the low voter turnout in school elections makes it relatively easy to achieve the 25 percent petition threshold. Not all recall efforts are successful. However, the mere threat of recall tends to be disruptive. It also contributes to the difficulty many districts face in attracting school board candidates.[37]

The Dysart school district provides a dramatic illustration of some of the conflicts that can arise. Seventy-five percent of the district's student population consists of low-income minorities. However, the district boundaries also include retirees from Sun City West extension areas. In 1995, the retirees formed a group called Citizens for Tax Equity that successfully defeated school bond and budget override elections over the next few years. In the aftermath of the election defeats, the district eliminated physical education, art, music, and other programs.[38] By 1998, the retirees had taken over the school board itself by winning all five seats in successive regular, special, and recall elections. Their initial objective was to have the retirement communities removed from the school district altogether. When that failed, they focused on implementing more efficient, cost-effective school management. The superintendent was forced to resign, and several Hispanic principals, teachers, and staff voluntarily left the district. Today, tensions still run high within the district. Parents, students, and Hispanic groups protest that the board is unrepresentative and unresponsive, but they have not been able to organize as effectively as the retirees.[39] While the demographic and economic cleavages in the Dysart school district are admittedly extreme, few school districts are completely immune to internal strife.

School funding   School funding is another pervasive source of controversy. Historically, costly capital improvements (new schools, remodeling, and equipment) were primarily funded by each local school district through the sale of bonds. Bonds are financed by local property taxes. This system produced glaring inequities, because property values vary from district to district. Poor districts often had higher tax rates than their wealthier neighbors but still couldn't raise sufficient funds to adequately maintain their schools. Residential districts that lacked businesses and industries were also disadvantaged. In 1994, the Arizona Supreme Court declared the funding system unconstitutional and ordered the legislature to come up with a new way to finance school facilities.[40] After rejecting two of the legislature's subsequent proposals, the court finally approved a sweeping new approach in 1998, known as Students First.[41] A new state board was created to set minimum standards for public schools and evaluate the funding requests of individual districts. The state then provides the funding needed to bring all schools to this level. Individual school districts can still exceed the minimum standards through local bond and override elections; and the new system does not apply to maintenance and operation costs of running schools.[42] The new approach, although barely under way, has not been free of controversy. The state underestimated the money needed to bring the schools up to standard, and debates continue over how the required funds should be raised.

The charter school debate   Charter schools constitute a new source of controversy. Technically, charter schools are public schools that receive public funds on a per-pupil basis like other state schools. However, they can be run by private persons and organizations, and they are exempt from most of the state's school laws, including teacher certification requirements.[43] Charter schools are a recent educational innovation. They are designed to provide more flexible educational opportunities and parental choice. Although thirty-six states now have laws permitting charter schools, Arizona currently leads the nation with roughly 350 charter schools.[44] Critics of charter schools contend that these schools undermine the public school system, siphoning off students and funds. They also charge that charter schools are inadequately regulated and financially unstable. Because the experiment is so new, the verdict is still out.

Community College Districts

Arizona's community college districts represent yet another type of local government. The state's community college system was created by legislative enactment in 1960. Today, there are ten separate community college districts. The boundaries of each district coincide with county lines except for Yuma and La Paz, which have a combined district, and four smaller counties that are served by the other districts. Not surprisingly, Maricopa Community College District—with ten separate colleges and a student enrollment in excess of 200,000—is the largest district in the state system. It holds the national record as well.

Each local community college district is governed by a five-person board. Board members are elected in nonpartisan elections from individual precincts within the district (i.e., generally the county). They have six-year terms and are also subject to recall elections like other Arizona officials. As with K–12 schools, community college governance is split between state and local levels. The State Board of Directors for Community Colleges exercises overall governing authority.[45] For example, it enacts rules for all the colleges, prescribes admission standards, sets tuition and fees, approves courses and curricula, certifies faculty, authorizes district bond elections, and determines the location of new college campuses. Within these constraints, the local district governing boards actually run the colleges within their jurisdiction. That is, the districts set their own annual budgets, levy property taxes, hire and remove all college personnel, award degrees, etc.

Special Taxing Districts

Special taxing districts are the most numerous local governments in Arizona, and their numbers are steadily increasing. These districts are organized for a variety of different—but always limited—purposes. For example, there are fire districts, irrigation districts, water conservation districts, sanitary districts, flood control districts, electrical districts, pest control districts, hospital districts, road improvement districts, regional transportation districts, lighting districts, special road districts, jail districts, library districts, and—most controversially—stadium districts.

Special districts are found in both rural and urban areas. The boundaries of these districts vary. Some districts encompass only a small neighborhood within a city or town; other districts coincide with county boundaries; and there are regional districts that cross county lines. It is equally difficult to generalize about the governing structures of special districts. Many of the state's special taxing districts have small, elected boards made up of unpaid citizen volunteers. This is the structure used by fire districts, for example. While it is democratic in theory, in actual practice few citizens know much about the candidates who run for these small boards. Other districts, however, are governed by the county board of supervisors, wearing a second hat. (This is how the Maricopa County stadium district, owner of the Bank One Ballpark, is governed.) Most special districts set their own budgets and raise revenues through property tax levies, bond sales, and user fees. In rare cases revenues come from sales taxes instead. Legally, special taxing districts are "subdivisions of the state" with privileges and immunities comparable to those enjoyed by cities and towns.[46]

There are several reasons why special districts have become so popular in recent years. The growth of population in unincorporated areas is one explanation. When there is no city to supply water, fire, and other essential services, residents often turn to special districts. Many property owners believe that these districts provide basic services more cheaply than cities and therefore reject the option of incorporating. Second, even in urban areas, special districts can efficiently address a localized need. For example, one neighborhood may be located in a floodplain, or another may require street lighting. The special district structure allows the affected homeowners and businesses to tax themselves for the necessary improvements, without burdening other taxpayers. Second, it gives district residents a greater measure of control over the expenditures. Third, because the special district can cross city and county lines, it permits regional problems to be more effectively addressed. Finally, special districts are exempt from the constitutional debt limitations that apply to counties and municipalities.[47] A cash-starved county, therefore, can more effectively perform certain functions by reconstituting itself as a special district.

Despite their "bread and butter" nature, special districts are not immune to political conflict either. The very creation of a district can arouse controversy. For example, many Maricopa County residents were upset when the board of supervisors created a special district in 1991 to build a major league baseball stadium. A countywide quarter-cent sales tax was levied to pay for the project. (Although the tax has now expired, the public funding of the stadium still generates controversy.) Even well-established districts have disputes over major capital expenditures. For example, citizens are often divided over whether a fire district needs a new fire station or truck, because such costly expenditures will usually result in increased property taxes. Recall attempts often emanate from such controversies. In short, like all governments, special districts must make tough policy choices and weather the political conflict that usually accompanies them.

Online Resources

Arizona Department of Commerce, Community Profiles:
  www.azcommerce.com/publications/county_profiles.htm (counties)
  www.azcommerce.com/publications/community_profile_index.htm (cities, towns, and places)

Arizona Association of Counties:
  www.azcounties.org/ (home page)
  www.azcounties.org/AACo/memcou.html (links to counties)

Maricopa County:
  www.maricopa.gov/

Maricopa Association of Governments (MAG):
www.mag.maricopa.gov/

Pima County:
www.co.pima.az.us/

Pima Association of Governments:
www.pagnet.org/

Northern Arizona Council of Governments:
www.infomagic.com/%7Enacog/

Phoenix:
www.ci.phoenix.az.us/

Tucson:
iwtucson.com/

League of Arizona Cities and Towns:
www.azleague.org/ (home page)
www.azleague.org/links_city_town.htm (links to Arizona cities and towns)

National Association of Counties:
www.naco.org/

National League of Cities:
www.nlc.org/

Arizona State Department of Education:
www.ade.state.az.us/ (home page)
www.ade.state.az.us/schools/directory/Default.htm (educational directory)
www.ade.state.az.us/schools/schools/ (links to Arizona school districts)
www.ade.state.az.us/charterschools/info/ (charter school information)

State Board of Directors for Community Colleges:
www.stbd.cc.az.us/ (home page)
www.stbd.cc.az.us/azccdists.htm (links to community college districts)

Maricopa Community College District:
www.maricopa.edu/

Pima Community College:
www.pima.edu/

Appendix

Taft's Veto of Arizona Statehood

To the House of Representatives: I return herewith, without my approval, House joint resolution No. 14, "To admit the territories of New Mexico and Arizona as States into the Union on an equal footing with the original States."

Congress, by an enabling act approved June 20, 1910, provided for the calling of a constitutional convention in each of these Territories, the submission of the constitution proposed by the convention to the electors of the Territory, the approval of the constitution by the President and Congress, the proclamation of the fact by the President, and the election of State officers. Both in Arizona and New Mexico conventions have been held, constitutions adopted and ratified by the people and submitted to the President and Congress. I have approved the constitution of New Mexico, and so did the House of Representatives of the Sixty-first Congress. The Senate, however, failed to take action upon it. I have not approved the Arizona constitution, nor have the two Houses of Congress, except as they have done so by the joint resolution under consideration. The resolution admits both Territories to statehood with their constitutions, on condition that at the time of the election of State officers New Mexico shall submit to its electors an amendment to its new constitution altering and modifying its provision for future amendments, and on the further condition that Arizona shall submit to its electors, at the time of the election of its State officers, a proposed amendment to its constitution by which judicial officers shall be excepted from the section permitting a recall of all elective officers.

If I sign this joint resolution, I do not see how I can escape responsibility for the judicial recall of the Arizona constitution. The joint resolution admits Arizona with the judicial recall, but requires the submission of the question of its wisdom to the voters. In other words, the resolution approves the admission of Arizona with the judicial recall, unless the voters themselves repudiate it. Under the Arizona constitution all elective officers, and this includes county and State judges, six months after their election, are subject to the recall. It is initiated by a petition signed by electors equal to 25 per cent of the total number of votes cast for all the candidates for the office at the previous general election. Within five days after the petition is filed the officer may resign. Whether he does or not, an election ensues in which his name, if he does not resign, is placed on the ballot with that of all other candidates. The petitioners may print on the official ballot 200 words showing their reasons for recalling the officer, and he is permitted to make defense in the same place in 200 words. If the incumbent receives the highest number of the votes, he continues in his office; if not, he is removed from office and is succeeded by the candidate who does receive the highest number.

This provision of the Arizona constitution, in its application to county and State judges, seems to me so pernicious in its effect, so destructive of independence in the judiciary, so likely to subject the rights of the individual to the possible tyranny of a popular majority, and, therefore, to be so injurious to the cause of free government, that I must disapprove a constitution containing it. I am not now engaged in performing the office given me in the enabling act already referred to, approved June 20, 1910, which was that of approving the constitutions ratified by the peoples of the Territories. It may be argued from the text of that act that in giving or withholding the approval under the act my only duty is to examine the proposed constitution, and if I find nothing in it inconsistent with the Federal Constitution, the principles of the Declaration of Independence, or the enabling act, to register my approval. But now I am discharging my constitutional function in respect to the enactment of laws, and my discretion is equal to that of the Houses of Congress. I must therefore withhold my approval from this resolution if in fact I do not approve it as a matter of governmental policy. Of course, a mere difference of opinion as to the wisdom of details in a State constitution ought not to lead me to set up my opinion against that of the people of the Territory. It is to be their government, and while the power of Congress to withhold or grant statehood is absolute, the people about to constitute a State should generally know better the kind of government and constitution suited to their needs than Congress or the Executive. But when such a constitution contains something so destructive of free government as the judicial recall, it should be disapproved.

A government is for the benefit of all the people. We believe that this benefit is best accomplished by popular government, because in the long run each class of individuals is apt to secure better provision for themselves through their own voice in government than through the altruistic interest of others, however intelligent or philanthropic. The wisdom of ages has taught that no government can exist except in accordance with laws and unless the people under it either obey the laws voluntarily or are made to obey them. In a popular government the laws are made by the people—not by all the people—but by those supposed and declared to be competent for the purpose, as males over twenty-one years of age, and not by all of these—but by a majority of them only. Now, as the government is for all the people, and is not solely for a majority of them, the majority in exercising control either directly or through its agents is bound to exercise the power for the benefit of the minority as well as the majority. But all have recognized that the majority of a people, unrestrained by law, when aroused and without the sobering effect of deliberation and discussion, may do injustice to the minority or to the individual when the selfish interest of the majority prompts. Hence arises the necessity for a constitution by which the will of the majority shall be permitted to guide the course of the government only under the controlling checks that experience has shown to be necessary to secure for the minority its share of the benefit to the whole people that a popular government is established to bestow. A popular government is not a government of a majority, by a majority, for a majority of the people. It is a government of the whole people by a majority of the whole people under such rules and checks as will secure a wise, just, and beneficent government for all the people. It is said you can always trust the people to do justice. If that means all the people and they all agree, you can. But ordinarily they do not all agree, and the maxim is interpreted to mean that you can always trust a majority of the people. This is not invariably true; and every limitation imposed by the people upon the power of the majority in their constitutions is an admission that it is not always true. No honest, clear-headed man, however great a lover of popular government, can deny that the unbridled expression of the majority of a community converted hastily into law or action would sometimes make a government tyrannical and cruel. Constitutions are checks upon the hasty action of the majority. They are the self-imposed restraints of a whole people upon a majority of them to secure sober action and a respect for the rights of the minority, and of the individual in his relation to other individuals, and in his relation to the whole people in their character as a state or government.

The Constitution distributes the functions of government into three branches—the legislative, to make the laws; the executive, to execute them; and the judicial, to decide in cases arising before it, the rights of the individual as between him and others and as between him and the Government. This division of government into three separate branches has always been regarded as a great security for the maintenance of free institutions, and the security is only firm and assured when the judicial branch is independent and impartial. The executive and legislative branches are representative of the majority of the people which elected them in guiding the course of the Government within the limits of the Constitution. They must act for the whole people, of course; but they may properly follow, and usually ought to follow, the views of the majority which elected them in respect to the governmental policy best adapted to secure the welfare of the whole people. But the judicial branch of the Government is not representative of a majority of the people in any such sense, even if the mode of selecting judges is by popular election. In a proper sense, judges are servants of the people; that is, they are doing work which must be done for the Government and in the interest of all the people, but it is not work in the doing of which they are to follow the will of the majority except as that is embodied in statutes lawfully enacted according to constitutional limitations. They are not popular representatives. On the contrary, to fill their office properly they must be independent. They must decide every question which comes before them according to the law and justice. If this question is between individuals, they will follow the statute, or the unwritten law if no statute applies, and they take the unwritten law growing out of tradition and custom from previous judicial decisions. If a statute or ordinance affecting a cause before them is not lawfully enacted, because it violates the constitution adopted by the people, then they must ignore the statute and decide the question as if the statute had never been passed. This power is a judicial power imposed by the people on the judges by the written constitution. In early days some argued that the obligations of the Constitution operated directly on the conscience of the legislature, and only in that manner, and that it was to be conclusively presumed that whatever was done by the legislature was constitutional. But such a view did not obtain with our hard-headed, courageous, and far-sighted statesmen and judges, and it was soon settled that it was the duty of judges in cases properly arising before them to apply the law and so to declare what was the law, and that if what purported to be statutory law was at variance with the fundamental law, i.e., the Constitution, the seeming statute was not law at all, was not binding on the courts, the individuals, or any branch of the Government, and that it was the duty of the judges so to decide. This power conferred on the judiciary in our form of government is unique in the history of governments, and its operation has attracted and deserved the admiration and commendation of the world. It gives to our judiciary a position higher, stronger, and more responsible than that of the judiciary of any other country, and more effectively secures the adherence to the fundamental will of the people.

What I have said has been to little purpose if it has not shown that judges to fulfill their functions properly in our popular Government must be more independent than in any other form of government, and that need of independence is greatest where the individual is one litigant and the state, guided by the successful and governing majority, is the other. In order to maintain the rights of the minority and the individual and to preserve our constitutional balance, we must have judges with courage to decide against the majority when justice and law require.

By the recall in the Arizona constitution, it is proposed to give to the majority power to remove arbitrarily, and without delay, any judge who may have the courage to render an unpopular decision. By the recall it is proposed to enable a minority of 25 per cent of the voters of the district or State, for no prescribed cause, after the judge has been in office six months, to submit the question of his retention to the electorate. The petitioning minority must say on the ballot what they can against him in 200 words, and he must defend as best he can in the same space. Other candidates are permitted to present themselves and have their names printed on the ballot so that the recall is not based solely on the record or the acts of the judge, but also on the question whether some other and more popular candidate has been found to unseat him. Could there be a system more ingeniously devised to subject judges to momentary gusts of popular passion than this? We can not be blind to the fact that often an intelligent and respectable electorate may be so roused upon an issue that it will visit with condemnation the decision of a just judge, though exactly in accord with the law governing the case, merely because it affects unfavorably their contest. Controversies over elections, labor troubles, racial or religious issues, issues as to the construction or constitutionality of liquor laws, criminal trials of popular or unpopular defendants, the removal of county seats, suits by individuals to maintain their constitutional rights in obstruction of some popular improvement—these and many other cases could be cited in which a majority of a district electorate would be tempted by hasty anger to recall a conscientious judge if the opportunity were open all the time. No period of delay is interposed for the abatement of popular feeling. The recall is devised to encourage quick action and to lead the people to strike while the iron is hot. The judge is treated as the instrument and servant of a majority of the people and subject to their momentary will, not after a long term in which his qualities as a judge and his character as a man have been subjected to a test of all the varieties of judicial work and duty so as to furnish a proper means of measuring his fitness for continuance in another term. On the instant of an unpopular ruling, while the spirit of protest has not had time to cool, and even while an appeal may be pending from his ruling, in which he may be sustained, he is to be haled before the electorate as a tribunal, with no judicial hearing, evidence, or defense, and thrown out of office and disgraced for life because he has failed, in a single decision, it may be, to satisfy the popular demand. Think of the opportunity such a system would give to unscrupulous political bosses in control, as they have been in control not only of conventions but elections! Think of the enormous power for evil given to the sensational, muckraking portion of the press in rousing prejudice against a just judge by false charges and insinuations, the effect of which in the short period of an election by recall it would be impossible for him to meet and offset! Supporters of such a system seem to think that it will work only in the interest of the poor, the humble, the weak and the oppressed; that it will strike down only the judge who is supposed to favor corporations and be affected by the corrupting influence of the rich. Nothing could be further from the ultimate result. The motive it would offer to unscrupulous combinations to seek to control politics in order to control the judges is clear. Those would profit by the recall who have the best opportunity of rousing the majority of the people to action on a sudden impulse. Are they likely to be the wisest or the best people in a community? Do they not include those who have money enough to employ the firebrands and slanderers in a community and the stirrers-up of social hate? Would not self-respecting men well hesitate to accept judicial office with such a sword of Damocles hanging over them? What kind of judgments might those on the unpopular side expect from courts whose judges must make their decisions under such legalized terrorism? The character of the judges would deteriorate to that of trimmers and timeservers, and independent judicial action would be a thing of the past. As the possibilities of such a system pass in review, is it too much to characterize it as one which will destroy the judiciary, its standing, and its usefulness?

The argument has been made to justify the judicial recall that it is only carrying out the principle of the election of the judges by the people. The appointment by the executive is by the representative of the majority, and so far as future bias is concerned there is no great difference between the appointment and election of judges. The independence of the judiciary is secured rather by a fixed term and fixed and irreducible salary. It is true that when the term of judges is for a limited number of years and reelection is necessary, it has been thought and charged sometimes that shortly before election, in cases in which popular interest is excited, judges have leaned in their decisions toward the popular side.

As already pointed out, however, in the election of judges for a long and fixed term of years, the fear of popular prejudice as a motive for unjust decisions is minimized by the tenure on the one hand, while the opportunity which the people have calmly to consider the work of a judge for a full term of years in deciding as to his reelection generally insures from them a fair and reasonable consideration of his qualities as a judge. While, therefore, there have been elected judges who have bowed before unjust popular prejudice, or who have yielded to the power of political bosses in their decisions, I am convinced that these are exceptional, and that, on the whole, elected judges have made a great American judiciary. But the success of an elective judiciary certainly furnishes no reason for so changing the system as to take away the very safeguards which have made it successful.

Attempt is made to defend the principle of judicial recall by reference to States in which judges are said to have shown themselves to be under corrupt corporate influence and in which it is claimed that nothing but a desperate remedy will suffice. If the political control in such States is sufficiently wrested from corrupting corporations to permit the enactment of a radical constitutional amendment like that of judicial recall, it would seem possible to make provision in its stead for an effective remedy by impeachment in which the cumbrous features of the present remedy might be avoided, but the opportunity for judicial hearing and defense before an impartial tribunal might be retained. Real reforms are not to be effected by patent shortcuts or by abolishing those requirements which the experience of ages has shown to be essential in dealing justly with everyone. Such innovations are certain in the long run to plague the inventor or first user and will come readily to the hand of the enemies and corrupters of society after the passing of the just popular indignation that prompted their adoption.

Again, judicial recall is advocated on the ground that it will bring the judges more into sympathy with the popular will and the progress of ideas among the people. It is said that now judges are out of touch with the movement toward a wider democracy and a greater control of governmental agencies in the interest and for the benefit of the people. The righteous and just course for a judge to pursue is ordinarily fixed by statute or clear principles of law, and the cases in which his judgment may be affected by his political, economic, or social views are infrequent. But even in such cases judges are not removed from the people's influence. Surround the judiciary with all the safeguards possible, create judges by appointment, make their tenure for life, forbid diminution of salary during their term, and still it is impossible to prevent the influence of popular opinion from coloring judgments in the long run. Judges are men, intelligent, sympathetic men, patriotic men, and in those fields of the law in which the personal equation unavoidably plays a part, there will be found a response to sober popular opinion as it changes to meet the exigency of social, political, and economic changes. Indeed, this should be so. Individual instances of a hidebound and retrograde conservatism on the part of courts in decisions which turn on the individual economic or sociological views of the judges may be pointed out; but they are not many, and do not call for radical action. In treating of courts we are dealing with a human machine, liable, like all the inventions of man, to err, but we are dealing with a human institution that likens itself to a divine institution, because it seeks and preserves justice. It has been the corner stone of our gloriously free Government, in which the rights of the individual and of the minority have been preserved, while governmental action of the majority has lost nothing of beneficent progress, efficacy, and directness. This balance was planned in the Constitution by its framers, and has been maintained by our independent judiciary.

Precedents are cited from State constitutions said to be equivalent to a popular recall. In some, judges are removable by a vote of both houses of the legislature. This is a mere adoption of the English address of Parliament to the Crown for the removal of judges. It is similar to impeachment in that a form of hearing is always granted. Such a provision forms no precedent for a popular recall without adequate hearing and defense, and with new candidates to contest the election.

It is said the recall will be rarely used. If so, it will be rarely needed. Then why adopt a system so full of danger? But it is a mistake to suppose that such a powerful lever for influencing judicial decisions and such an opportunity for vengeance because of adverse ones will be allowed to remain unused.

But it is said that the people of Arizona are to become an independent State when created, and even if we strike out judicial recall now, they can reincorporate it in their constitution after statehood.

To this I would answer that in dealing with the courts, which are the corner stone of good government, and in which not only the voters, but the nonvoters and nonresidents, have a deep interest as a security for their rights of life, liberty, and property, no matter what the future action of the State may be, it is necessary for the authority which is primarily responsible for its creation to assert in no doubtful tones the necessity for an independent and untrammeled judiciary.

WM. H. TAFT

THE WHITE HOUSE, *August 15, 1911*

Glossary

Acquitted: Found not guilty by a jury or judge in a **criminal case**.

Administrative rules: Detailed rules adopted by executive branch officials and bodies to make the implementation of the laws more uniform, fair, and efficient. (Also called "regulations.")

Appellate courts: Courts that review the decisions of lower courts for legal mistakes.

Appropriation: A formal legislative authorization for the spending of public money.

Arraignment: A pretrial hearing where the defendant appears in court and enters a formal plea of guilty, not guilty, or no contest to criminal charges.

At-large elections: A system in which the members of a multimember body are elected by the entire community as opposed to individual districts or wards within the community.

Bicameral: A body made up of two separate chambers, such as the Arizona legislature and the U.S. Congress.

Bill: A proposed law that has been introduced in either house of the legislature. A bill creates new law or amends or repeals existing law.

Bipartisan: Cooperation on a matter between the members of the two major parties.

Board of Executive Clemency: A five-member board that determines **parole** eligibility and screens **clemency** applications for the governor.

Board of supervisors: Elected body that serves as the general governing authority for the county.

Burden of proof: The responsibility to prove the facts in a case. (The plaintiff usually bears the burden of proof, but plaintiffs in **criminal cases** have a higher burden than in **civil cases**.)

Bureaucracy: The employees of the executive branch who carry out the state's laws and policies.

Carpetbagger: An opportunistic politician who moves to a new state or district to run for office.

Caucus: An informal meeting typically confined to members of the same political party, to consider legislature, policies, or other group actions.

Charter: A document that serves as a constitution for cities or counties; it establishes the basic structure and powers of the government.

Charter cities: Cities that have their own charters and operate with greater independence from the state. Also known as "home rule" cities.

Citizen legislature: A part-time legislature, such as Arizona's, composed of members who typically have private employment on the side.

Civil case: A noncriminal case.

Codes: Rules enacted by local governments for the protection of public health and safety (e.g., city building codes). The term is sometimes also applied to a compilation of statutes or codes (e.g., the "criminal code" and the "administrative code").

Clemency: The governor's discretionary power to grant **pardons, reprieves,** and **commutations** to convicted offenders.

Committee of the Whole: A meeting of the entire membership of the house or senate, sitting as a committee, to debate legislation and adopt amendments. (Also called "cow.")

Common law: Judge-made law principally derived from **appellate court** opinions, as distinguished from statutory law.

Community property: Joint ownership of property by a husband and wife.

Commutation: A reduction in a criminal sentence granted by the governor as an act of **clemency.**

Conference committee: A legislative committee composed of members from both chambers, appointed to resolve differences between house and senate versions of the same measure.

Conflict of interest: A situation in which a public official's position on an issue would benefit or harm the official's private financial interests.

Constituent: A citizen who resides in the district of a legislator or other elected representative.

Constitutionalism: A political doctrine that requires lawful governmental power to be defined and limited by a constitution.

Corporation commission: The elected body that regulates Arizona's public utilities.

Council-manager form of government: A city government in which power is divided between an elected city council and a powerful, appointed city manager.

County seat: The headquarters of county government.

Criminal case: A case brought by government prosecutors to enforce specific penal statutes against an accused wrongdoer.

Damages: A monetary award in a **tort** action to compensate the **plaintiff** for personal injuries or other losses.

Declaration of Rights: Portion of the Arizona Constitution that sets forth fundamental rights (art. 2).

Defendant: The party sued in a **civil case** or accused of a crime in a **criminal case**.

Deposition: Oral interrogation of potential witnesses or opposing parties. Depositions are a typical part of the pretrial **discovery** process in civil cases.

Direct democracy: A system of government in which the people directly govern themselves. In Arizona, direct democracy also refers to the **initiative, referendum,** and **recall** processes. (Also called "participatory democracy" or "pure democracy.")

Direct primary: A popular election to choose the candidates of a political party.

Discovery: A process that enables a party to examine the evidence that the other side possesses in advance of trial.

Double jeopardy: Trial or punishment by the same government for the same criminal offense; prohibited by both the U.S. and Arizona constitutions.

Dracula Clause: Potential **impeachment** penalty that disqualifies officials from holding future public office.

Emergency clause: A provision in a **bill** declaring that public health or safety requires the immediate enactment of the measure. An emergency clause can be attached to any bill with a two-thirds vote of the legislature.

Enabling Act (1910): Federal law that established the terms under which Arizona and New Mexico could become states.

Federal system: A system of government, such as that in the United States, in which power is shared by the national government and the states. Both levels of government exercise direct authority over citizens and operate with substantial independence.

Felony: A serious crime punishable by imprisonment in a state prison or death.

Fracturing: Gerrymandering practice in which districts are broken up to dilute the voting strength of the opposing political party. (Also called "splintering.")

Gadsden Purchase: Purchase of narrow strip of land from Mexico in 1853 that established Arizona's present-day southern border.

General appropriation bill: A comprehensive spending **bill** that appropriates money to all of the state's departments and institutions.

General election: A statewide election that is held on the first Tuesday after the first Monday in November of every even-numbered year.

General law cities and towns: Cities and towns that do not have **home rule**.

Gerrymandering: The creative drawing of district boundaries to give an electoral advantage to a particular party, group, or individual.

Grand jury: A group of citizens that is impaneled to investigate criminal activity and issue an **indictment** when there is sufficient evidence to justify a criminal trial.

Gubernatorial: Pertaining to the governor.

Habeas corpus petition: A petition filed in federal court by a prisoner to review the legality of the imprisonment. The U.S. Constitution guarantees the right to file such petitions.

Home rule: A local government that has its own **charter**, an individualized form of government, and greater autonomy. (In Arizona, cities that have home rule are called **charter cities**, to distinguish them from **general law cities**.)

Impeachment: The formal process of bringing charges of misconduct against a public official by the house of representatives. (The official is removed from office if convicted by the senate following an evidentiary trial.)

Incumbent: A person who currently holds office.

Indictment: Formal written charges issued by a **grand jury** accusing a person of specific criminal acts.

Information: Formal criminal charges against a defendant filed by a prosecutor following a **preliminary hearing**.

Initial appearance: The first appearance by a criminal defendant before a judicial officer where the accused is formally advised of important constitutional rights.

Initiative: A **direct democracy** process that allows citizens to draft and enact changes to the state's constitution or statutes.

Interest group: An organized group that tries to influence government policy. Interest groups may be based upon economic, professional, ideological, demographic, or other shared interests.

Interim committee: A legislative committee that meets when the legislature is not in **regular session** to study the need for new legislation.

Interrogatories: Written questions directed to an opposing party prior to the start of a civil trial. Interrogatories are a typical part of the **discovery** process in **civil cases**.

Joint Legislative Budget Committee (JLBC): A permanent legislative committee established by statute, responsible for fiscal oversight and the preparation of the state budget.

Judicial review: The power of the courts to authoritatively interpret the constitution. This power enables judges to nullify laws, executive actions, and citizen measures on the ground that they are "unconstitutional."

Line item veto: The power of the governor to **veto** one or more items in an **appropriation bill** while approving the remainder. (Sometimes called an "item veto.")

Lobbyist: A person who represents a corporation, **interest group**, or other organization and attempts to influence government policy by communicating with public officials.

Log rolling: Vote-trading among legislators.

Lump sum appropriation: A consolidated **appropriation** that does not contain itemized breakdowns for specific programs.

Majority party: The party in each chamber of the legislature that has the most seats.

Majority-minority district: A district that has been gerrymandered to make a racial or ethnic minority a voting majority within the district.

Manifest Destiny: The belief, held by many Americans in the nineteenth century, that the United States was destined to occupy the continent from the Atlantic to the Pacific.

Merit selection: System for selecting and retaining judges that combines **gubernatorial** appointments with **retention elections**. (Also called the "Missouri Plan.")

Minority party: The political party in each chamber of the legislature that has the second most seats.

Misdemeanor: A crime that is less serious than a **felony**, and more serious than a **petty offense**. Misdemeanors are punishable by fines, probation, or imprisonment in jail for up to a year.

Municipal corporations: Legally incorporated cities or towns.

Negligence: A category of **tort** cases that accuses the defendant of failing to exercise "reasonable care" (e.g., automobile accident, malpractice, slip and fall cases).

Nonpartisan: Not ascribing a party label to a candidate or position.

Ordinance: A local law enacted and enforced by counties, cities, and towns.

Organic Act (1863): Federal law that established Arizona as a separate territory.

Override: The power of the legislature to nullify the governor's **veto** by repassing the legislation by a **supermajority**—two-thirds or three-fourths—vote.

Packing: Gerrymandering practice in which opponents are consolidated into a few, super-strong districts that "waste" their votes and remove them from surrounding districts, thus giving the gerrymanderer an overall advantage.

Pardon: The power of the governor to set aside all criminal penalties imposed on a convicted offender as an act of **clemency**.

Parole: Conditional release of a convicted offender from prison before the sentence is completed.

Partisan: Identifying with a political party.

Patronage: Giving jobs, contracts, or other favors to persons who support the winning party.

Per diem: A daily allowance of money to reimburse officials for housing, meal, and transportation costs while they are performing government business away from home.

Petty offense: A minor infraction of the law, usually punishable by a fine.

Piggyback: The practice of attaching a measure to a more popular **bill** in order to get it passed.

Plaintiff: The party that brings the lawsuit or legal action to court. In a **criminal case**, the plaintiff is always the government.

Plural executive branch: An executive branch, like Arizona's, that is composed of many separately elected offices and independent boards.

Populist: A national political movement of the 1880s and 1890s that attacked the banks, railroads, and other established powers, and influenced the **Progressive** movement that followed.

Preliminary hearing: A proceeding that typically takes place before a Justice of the Peace to determine whether there is enough evidence against an accused person to justify a **felony** trial.

President (Arizona legislature): The presiding officer of the senate; formally elected by the entire chamber but actually chosen by the **majority party**.

Privilege against self-incrimination: A constitutional privilege that prevents the government from compelling criminal defendants to testify against themselves. The privilege is guaranteed by both the U.S. and Arizona constitutions.

Progressive: A **bipartisan** reform movement of the early 1900s that advocated direct democracy and other political reforms to combat corruption and the influence of monopolies and big business.

Proposition: An issue that appears on the ballot for voter approval or rejection.

Public service corporation: A public utility, such as a power company, that is subject to extensive regulation by the **corporation commission**.

Punitive damages: An extra sum of money that a **tort defendant** can be ordered to pay the injured party as punishment for gross **negligence** or intentional misconduct.

Recall: A **direct democracy** process that enables the voters to remove elected officials from office before the end of their terms.

Redistricting: The redrawing of district boundaries to ensure that an equal number of persons live in each voting district. U.S. Supreme Court cases require the states to redistrict after every decennial census. (Also called "reapportionment.")

Referendum: A **direct democracy** process that enables the voters to accept or reject changes to the constitution or statutes that are proposed by the legislature. A referendum can be triggered by citizen petition or by the legislature on its own volition.

Regular session: The annual meeting of the legislature when lawmaking and other official legislative business is conducted. Regular sessions in Arizona begin on the second Monday in January of each year and typically last no more than one hundred days.

Representative democracy: A political system, such as that in the United States, in which citizens choose accountable representatives to govern on their behalf. (Also called "a republican form of government.")

Reprieve: A delay in the carrying out of a criminal sentence that is granted by the governor as an act of **clemency**.

Retention election: An uncontested election in which the voters, by voting "yes" or "no," decide whether an officeholder should be allowed an additional term. In Arizona, retention elections are part of the **merit selection** process.

Rider: A measure, unlikely to pass on its own, that is tacked on to a more popular **bill** to secure passage.

Right-to-work: A provision that prohibits workers from being forced to join unions as a condition of employment. (Found in Article 25 of the Arizona Constitution.)

Rules committee: A **standing committee** in each legislative chamber that studies bills to determine whether they are constitutional and in proper form.

Secret ballot: The citizens' right, guaranteed by the Arizona Constitution, to have their votes remain secret.

Simple majority: One more than half.

Speaker (Arizona legislature): Presiding officer of the house of representatives; formally elected by the entire chamber but actually chosen by the **majority party**.

Special session: Extra session of the legislature, in addition to the annual **regular session**, that can be initiated by the governor or the legislature whenever needed.

Sponsor: The legislator or group of legislators who formally introduce a bill or measure.

Standing committee: A semipermanent legislative committee that studies bills prior to consideration by the entire chamber.

Statute: A state law enacted by the legislature or the people.

Strict liability: A category of **tort** cases that holds the **defendant** liable irrespective of fault. Such liability is sometimes imposed on manufacturers and sellers of products that cause injuries.

Suffrage: The right to vote.

Summary judgment: A legal ruling by a judge that ends a **civil case** without a trial. A summary judgment can be granted only when the relevant facts are not in dispute.

Sunset review: The automatic termination of a state agency or program after a fixed period of time unless the legislature votes to renew it.

Supermajority: More than a **simple majority**; usually a vote that requires the concurrence of two-thirds or three-fourths.

Supremacy Clause: Provision in the U.S. Constitution (Article 6) that makes the federal constitution, duly enacted federal laws, and treaties superior to conflicting state and local laws.

Term limits: A constitutional limitation on the number of terms that an officeholder can serve. (In Arizona the limitations apply only to consecutive terms.)

Tort: A wrongful act (other than breach of contract) that causes injury to another and gives rise to a **civil** lawsuit for damages.

Treaty of Guadalupe Hidalgo (1848): The treaty between the United States and Mexico that ended the Mexican-American War and transferred most of Arizona and the Southwest to the United States.

Veto: The formal rejection of a bill by the president or governor. A veto kills the bill unless both houses of the legislature **override** the veto by a **supermajority** vote. See also **line item veto**.

Voter turnout: Alternatively refers to the proportion of registered voters that actually votes, or the proportion of the voting age population (VAP) that actually votes.

Notes

1 The Arizona Constitution

1. The U.S. Constitution was written in 1787. Massachusetts' constitution was adopted in 1780 and New Hampshire's in 1784.
2. Arizona's privacy right is found in Article 2, section 8. *Rasmussen ex rel. Mitchell v. Fleming*, 154 Ariz. 207, 741 P.2d 674 (1987), held that life support could be terminated for a patient in a chronic, vegetative state. The U.S. Supreme Court's parallel ruling was based upon the Due Process Clause of the Fourteenth Amendment. See *Cruzan v. Director, Missouri Department of Health*, 497 U.S. 261 (1990).
3. Arizona Constitution, art. 2, sec. 2.1.
4. For example, the Arizona Constitution specifically prohibits public expenditures for religious purposes (art. 2, sec. 12) and expressly protects nonbelief (art. 20, first ordinance). This contrasts with the more general language found in the Establishment and Free Exercise clauses of the U.S. Constitution (amend. 1). Similarly, the state's right to bear arms refers to self-defense—a factor not mentioned in the U.S. Constitution. Compare Arizona Constitution, art. 2, sec. 26 with U.S. Constitution, amend. 2. Finally, Article 2, section 6 declares: "Every person may freely speak, write, and publish on all subjects, being responsible for the abuse of that right." This contrasts with the terse, negative phrasing of the U.S. Constitution's Free Speech Clause (amend. 1).
5. The Arizona Supreme Court has declared that it will not "blindly" follow federal precedent. *Pool v. Superior Court*, 139 Ariz. 98, 677 P.2d 261 (1984). In *State v. Ault*, 150 Ariz. 459, 724 P.2d 545 (1986), the court excluded key evidence against an accused child molester on the ground that the police had violated the defendant's search and seizure rights. It dismissed federal precedent, holding that Arizona's constitution provided greater privacy protections. And in *Mountain States Telephone & Telegraph Co. v. Arizona Corporation Commission*, 160 Ariz. 350, 773 P.2d 455 (1989), the court declared that the state's regulation of "900" telephone numbers violated the more liberal free speech protections in the state's constitution. For a general discussion of the courts' power in this area, see William J. Brennan Jr., "State Constitutionalism and the Protections of Individual Rights," *Harvard Law Review* 90 (January 1977): 489–504; John Kincaid, "State Constitutions in a Federal System," *Annals of the American Academy of Political and Social Science* 496 (March 1988): 12–22; Stanley G. Feldman and David L. Abney, "The Double Security of Federalism: Protecting Individual Liberty under the Arizona Constitution," *Arizona State Law Journal* 20 (spring 1988): 115–50; and Jodi A. Jerich, "Considerations of the Arizona Legislature: The Effects of State Constitutionalism," *Arizona Attorney* (December 1998): 30–35. For criticism of this state power, see Steven J. Twist and Len L. Munsil, "The Double Threat of Judicial

Activism: Inventing New 'Rights' in State Constitutions," *Arizona State Law Journal* 21 (winter 1989): 1005–1065.

6. See chapter 6 for a discussion of this issue.

7. Arizona Revised Statutes, sec. 41-171. The provision was in effect when Arizona became a separate territory in 1863 (Howell Code, ch. 17, sec. 1). In a similar vein, the constitution originally imposed term limits *only* for the state treasurer. Arizona Constitution, art. 5, sec. 10 (1910). Term limits for other officials weren't added until 1992.

8. See Arizona Revised Statutes, secs. 41-853 to 41-859.

9. Arizona Session Laws 1982, ch. 1. For the adoption of the original song, see Arizona Session Laws 1919, ch. 28.

10. The U.S. Supreme Court upheld the federal government's right to do this in *South Dakota v. Dole*, 483 U.S. 203 (1987).

11. *The Book of the States*, 1998–99 ed. (Lexington: Council of State Governments, 1998), 368.

12. U.S. Constitution, art. 6.

13. *Ruiz v. Hull*, 191 Ariz. 441, 957 P.2d 984 (1998).

14. In a similar vein, for nearly thirty years the Arizona Constitution has misleadingly stated that a person must be at least *twenty-one* years old in order to vote (art. 7, sec. 2). Although originally valid, the provision had no legal effect once the U.S. Constitution lowered the voting age to eighteen in 1971 (U.S. Const., amend. 26). At the 7 November 2000 election, Arizona voters will be asked to belatedly correct their constitution to bring its voting age language into conformity with the federal law.

15. Arizona Constitution, art. 9, sec. 13(2).

16. However, the constitution itself contributes to this state of affairs, because Article 9, section 2 prohibits the legislature from granting tax exemptions that are not constitutionally authorized.

17. U.S. constitutional amendments can also be proposed through a constitutional convention called by two-thirds of the states, although this method has never been used. See U.S. Constitution, art. 5.

2 Constitutional Origins

1. Modern-day Hopis and other pueblo peoples are likely descendants of the Anasazi and Mogollon cultures, which lasted into the 1500s. However, there is debate as to whether the Hohokam culture left any modern-day descendants. Several Indian communities (e.g., the Gila River, Salt River Pima-Maricopa, Tohono O'odham, and Ak-Chin) claim lineage. This has become more than an academic question since passage of the Native American Graves Protection and Reparation Act. *U.S. Code*, vol. 25, sec. 3001, et seq. (1990). The federal law allows descendant tribes to claim remains and other sacred burial objects found on federal land.

2. He was accompanied by Estéban, a slave of likely Moorish descent, who is generally credited with being the first non-Indian to enter Arizona. Estéban was a survivor of a previous expedition led by Alvar de Vaca. It is uncertain whether the slave crossed into the southeastern corner of Arizona on that earlier expedition in 1536. See generally Jay J. Wagoner, *Early Arizona: Prehistory to Civil War* (Tucson: University of Arizona Press, 1989), 47–49.

3. Neither expedition apparently encountered any Athabaskan-speaking peoples (Navajos and Apaches), leading to speculation that these tribes may have entered Arizona after the Spanish.

4. The formal governing structure of the region underwent multiple changes from 1776 to

1821, prompted in part by the longstanding neglect of the region by Mexico City. In 1776, the six northern provinces of New Spain (which included southern Arizona) were united in a single jurisdiction known as the Interior Provinces. These provinces reported to a representative of the king rather than to Mexico City. In 1787, however, the northern provinces were split and made subject to Mexico City once again. Finally, in 1792, King Carlos IV reconsolidated the northern provinces and restored their former autonomy from New Spain. See generally James E. Officer, *Hispanic Arizona, 1536–1856* (Tucson: University of Arizona Press, 1987), 53–70 and Wagoner, *Early Arizona,* 133–34.

5. Officer, *Hispanic Arizona,* 214–15.
6. Although the Apaches were a significant barrier to Hispanic and Anglo settlement, they were not alone. Pima and Hopi uprisings took place in the early years; Yuman-speaking tribes controlled the lower Colorado River area until the 1850s; and the Navajos engaged in sporadic raids that led to warfare and defeat in 1865. See generally Thomas E. Sheridan, *Arizona: A History* (Tucson: University of Arizona Press, 1995); Wagoner, *Early Arizona;* and Officer, *Hispanic Arizona.*
7. Joseph F. Park, "Spanish Indian Policy in Northern Mexico, 1765–1810," in *New Spain's Far Northern Frontier: Essays on Spain in the American West, 1540–1821,* ed. David J. Weber (Dallas: Southern Methodist University Press, 1979), 219–34; Wagoner, *Early Arizona,* 149–51.
8. Occidente Constitution, sec. 2, arts. 7 and 8. Odie B. Faulk, ed., *The Constitution of Occidente* (Tucson: Arizona Pioneers' Historical Society, 1967).
9. Ibid., sec. 2, art. 6.
10. Provisions of the Occidente Constitution were incorporated into the Sonoran constitutions of 1831 and 1848. Ibid., 1–4.
11. Officer, *Hispanic Arizona,* 2.
12. Ibid., 17.
13. The most costly proposal, at $50 million, would have given the United States Baja California as well as a large swath of Mexican territory reaching all the way to the Gulf of Mexico. See Henry P. Walker and Don Bufkin, *Historical Atlas of Arizona,* 2d ed. (Norman: University of Oklahoma Press, 1986) and Wagoner, *Early Arizona,* 281–97.
14. Quoted in Wagoner, *Early Arizona,* 294. See also Odie B. Faulk, *Too Far North . . . Too Far South* (Los Angeles: Westernlore Press, 1967) for a lengthier treatment of the events surrounding the Gadsden Purchase.
15. A final major change in Arizona's boundaries occurred in 1867 when the northwestern corner of the territory—which includes the present site of Las Vegas—was transferred to the state of Nevada.
16. See Thomas E. Sheridan, *Los Tucsonenses: The Mexican Community in Tucson, 1854–1941* (Tucson: University of Arizona Press, 1997), 26–31. U.S. troops promised superior military protection against the Indians, the country had better economic prospects, and Tucson was experiencing internal political strife.
17. Annual Message to Congress (19 December 1859), *A Compilation of the Messages and Papers of the Presidents* (New York: Bureau of National Literature, 1897–1917), 7: 3099–3100.
18. See generally B. Sacks, *Be It Enacted: The Creation of the Territory of Arizona* (Phoenix: Arizona Historical Foundation, 1964), 35–42. (The self-proclaimed territory included portions of southern New Mexico, as well as Arizona.)
19. Proclamation of 1 August 1861, reproduced in Sacks, *Be It Enacted,* 64.
20. See Wagoner, *Early Arizona,* 443–79 for a discussion of the military maneuvers in Arizona during the Civil War period.
21. U.S. Senate, *Federal Census—Territory of New Mexico and Territory of Arizona,* 89th Cong.,

1st sess., 1965. S. Doc. No. 13, 1. (This special reprint extracted the Arizona portion of the territorial census.) By 1870, the territory's non-Indian population had grown to 9,627 with 907 dwellings in Tucson and 151 in Prescott. Ibid., 162, 207.

22. Arizona Constitution, art. 20, ninth ordinance. However, a similar provision in the Oklahoma enabling act was later struck down as an unconstitutional interference in state affairs. *Coyle v. Smith,* 221 U.S. 449 (1911).

23. Lincoln initially appointed Goodwin to be chief justice of Arizona. Goodwin was promoted to governor when Lincoln's first choice, former Ohio congressman John Addison Gurley, died. For general background on Arizona's territorial governors see John Jay Wagoner, *Arizona Territory, 1863–1912: A Political History* (Tucson: University of Arizona Press, 1970) and John S. Goff, *Arizona Territorial Officials: The Governors* (Cave Creek: Black Mountain Press, 1978).

24. Actually, Goodwin initially went east as Arizona's nonvoting delegate to Congress. However, when his term ended 4 March 1867, he ended his official connection with Arizona.

25. Howard Roberts Lamar observes, "The roster of Arizona governors from 1869 to 1900 demonstrates . . . that the real function of government on the frontier was business development." *The Far Southwest, 1846–1912: A Territorial History* (New Haven: Yale University Press, 1966), 476.

26. Safford's wife had published flyers alleging that the governor had been unfaithful and had contracted venereal disease. Goff suggests that the governor's self-granted divorce may be unique in gubernatorial annals. *Arizona Territorial Officials,* 51. However, Wagoner notes that the legislature had previously annulled a legislator's marriage. *Arizona Territory,* 58. In fact, six years later, the Tenth Legislature passed an "Omnibus Divorce Bill" that terminated the marriage of 15 couples, including the territory's secretary and acting governor. Ibid., 60.

27. Wagoner, *Arizona Territory,* 224–26; Goff, *Arizona Territorial Officials,* 96–97. Goff views these governors somewhat more sympathetically, observing that as a whole, they "were no better and no worse than those subsequently elected by the voters of the state." Ibid., 12.

28. Wagoner, *Arizona Territory,* 219–20.

29. Amazingly, a successor, Governor Franklin, similarly returned the excess portion of a bribe to a mining company. Both episodes are recounted in Wagoner, *Arizona Territory,* 256–67, 330.

30. Angelo Patane, "Old-Fashioned Justice: Law and (Dis)Order on the Arizona Frontier," *Arizona Attorney* 34, no. 6 (February 1998): 28–29.

31. See generally Charles S. Peterson, *Take Up Your Mission: Mormon Colonizing along the Little Colorado River, 1870–1900* (Tucson: University of Arizona Press, 1973), 170–71.

32. U.S. Constitution, art. 4, sec. 3.

33. Senate Committee on Territories, *New Statehood Bill,* 57th Cong., 2d sess., 1902, S. Rept. 2206, pt. 1, 15.

34. Ibid., 16–20.

35. In 1870, 60.1 percent of Arizona's population was foreign born. By 1910, the number had declined to 23.9 percent—although this was still above the national average. U.S. Bureau of the Census, *Historical Statistics on the Foreign-born Population of the United States: 1850–1990,* prepared by Campbell J. Gibson and Emily Lennon (Washington, D.C., February 1999), Table 13.9. March 1999. <http://www.census.gov/population/www/documentation/twps0029/twps0029.htmltwps0029.html>.

36. *New Statehood Bill,* 16.

37. John D. Leshy, "The Making of the Arizona Constitution," *Arizona State Law Journal* 20 (spring 1988): 11.

38. *New Statehood Bill*, 15–16.
39. Beveridge exclaimed:

    And what a glorious State this new Arizona would be. . . . Arizona, second in size and eminent in wealth among the States of the greatest nation; Arizona, standing midway between California and Texas, three giant Commonwealths guarding the Republic's southwestern border. . . . not Arizona the little, but Arizona the great; not Arizona the provincial, but Arizona the national; not Arizona the creature of a politician's device, but Arizona the child of the nation's wisdom! How its people and the people of the Republic will glory in such an Arizona!

    Congressional Record, 58th Cong., 3d sess. (6 February 1905), 39, pt. 2: 1931.
40. Wagoner, *Arizona Territory*, 412.
41. Ethnic bigotry was part of Arizona's intense opposition to jointure. Hispanics represented a larger proportion of New Mexico's population and had political power. During the Senate debate over jointure, pejorative comparisons were often made between the makeup of the two territory's populations. Senator Beveridge attempted to downplay the differences, declaring at one point that it was "not true you are loading upon a pure American strain of Arizona the Spanish stock of New Mexico." *Congressional Record*, 59th Cong., 1st sess. (8 March 1906), 40, pt. 4: 3522. Previously he had argued that the Arizona's "American" population would combine with the American minority in New Mexico, "Americanizing within a few brief years every drop of the blood of Spain." *Congressional Record*, 58th Cong., 3d sess. (6 February 1905), 39, pt.2: 1929. See also David R. Berman, *Reformers, Corporations, and the Electorate: An Analysis of Arizona's Age of Reform* (Niwot: University Press of Colorado, 1992), 50–52.
42. U.S. Bureau of the Census, *The Population of States and Counties of the United States: 1790–1990*. 21 July 1999. <http://www.census.gov/population/censusdata/table-16.pdf>.
43. Senator Beveridge, the prime mover behind the land restrictions, was also upset that the territory of New Mexico had sold land granted in 1898 for unreasonably low prices. See discussion in *Lassen v. Arizona Highway Department*, 385 U.S. 458 (1967).
44. The Enabling Act required Arizona to include a provision in the state constitution agreeing to abide by the federal land restrictions "in every respect and particular." (See Arizona Constitution, art. 20, twelfth ordinance.) Other Enabling Act mandates are incorporated in Article 10.
45. *Lassen v. Arizona Highway Department*, 385 U.S. 458 (1967).
46. The state legislature asked the voters to give the state the power to swap land in 1990, 1992, and 1994. The constitutional referenda were defeated on all three occasions.
47. Arizona Constitution, art. 10, sec. 3 and *Fain Land & Cattle Company v. Hassell*, 163 Ariz. 587, 790 P.2d 242 (1990).
48. Sally K. Fairfax, Jon A. Souder, and Gretta Goldenman, "The School Trust Lands: A Fresh Look at Conventional Wisdom," *Environmental Law* 22 (1992): 883.
49. On the national level, the Progressives also successfully campaigned for the adoption of the Seventeenth Amendment to the U.S. Constitution, which provided for the direct election of U.S. senators. (Prior to the adoption of that amendment in 1913, senators were chosen by state legislatures.)
50. For example, in 1910, the average wage for Mexican mineworkers was $2.00 a day. This did not buy much because most workers lived in company towns where the goods were sold at inflated prices. Moreover, many workers were paid in company scrip, rather than in cash. See generally Sheridan, *Arizona: A History*, 168–73.
51. On 12 July 1917, Bisbee's sheriff rounded up 2,000 striking mineworkers from their homes at gunpoint and imprisoned them overnight in a ballpark. The 1,186 who refused to aban-

don the strike were jammed into railroad boxcars guarded by armed vigilantes, transported to a remote location in the New Mexico desert, and abandoned without food or water. The episode shocked the country, and the federal government ultimately came to the workers' rescue. Although the sheriff and twenty prominent Bisbee residents were subsequently indicted for their roles in the kidnapping, they were acquitted in state trials. See generally Sheridan, *Arizona: A History*, 181–86 and Berman, *Reformers, Corporations, and the Electorate*, 146–48.

52. Arizona Constitution, art. 25 (this provision outlaws union shops).
53. Arizona's constitution called for a popular, "advisory" vote for U.S. senators, slightly predating the Seventeenth Amendment to the U.S. Constitution (which became effective in 1913). Arizona Constitution, art. 7, sec. 9 (1910).
54. Ibid., art. 14, sec. 15.
55. John S. Goff, *George W. P. Hunt* (Cave Creek: Black Mountain Press, 1987), 13.
56. See, e.g., Arizona Constitution, art. 2, sec. 31 and art. 18, secs. 4–6. These provisions, which are discussed more fully in chapter 6, have become controversial in recent years, and proponents of tort reform have sought to modify or eliminate them.
57. Ibid., art. 20, seventh and eighth ordinances. However, it should be noted that the delegates to the constitutional convention refused to add an English literacy voter qualification that would have disenfranchised Hispanic pioneers. Several of the delegates passionately defended the contributions of Arizona's Hispanic settlers and their qualification to vote. See *The Records of the Arizona Constitutional Convention of 1910*, ed. John S. Goff (Phoenix: Supreme Court of Arizona, 1991), 865, 872–75, and 930–31. Admittedly, there were political considerations as well: Fred Ingraham, a Democrat from Yuma County candidly noted that one-third of the voters in his county were Spanish-American, and if they were disenfranchised "the Democratic party [would] receive a hard blow." Ibid., 872. There were also concerns that a literacy test might jeopardize congressional approval of the constitution. (Senator Beveridge opposed the test not because of the impact on Hispanic voters, but because he feared it could be corruptly administered for political advantage.)
58. Arizona Constitution, art. 17, sec. 1.
59. See, e.g., *Maricopa County Municipal Water Conservation District No. 1 v. Southwest Cotton Company*, 39 Ariz. 65, 4 P.2d 369 (1931), which discusses the Spanish legal legacy. Water law in Arizona is quite complex, and it evolved flexibly and pragmatically even under Spanish/Mexican control. See, e.g., Michael C. Meyer, *Water in the Hispanic Southwest: A Social and Legal History, 1550–1850* (Tucson: University of Arizona Press, 1984).
60. Louisiana, which was originally part of France, also recognized the Roman community property law.
61. *Records of the Constitutional Convention*, 537–38. A law passed over the governor's veto in 1909 permitted individual school districts to establish racially segregated schools. Arizona Laws 1909, ch. 67, sec. 1. The law was upheld by the Arizona Supreme Court in *Dameron v. Bayless*, 14 Ariz. 180, 126 P. 273 (1912).
62. Although antimiscegenation laws are commonly associated with the South, they were actually quite popular in the western states. See Peggy Pasco, "Race Gender and the Privileges of Property: On the Significance of Miscegenation Laws in the U.S. West," in *Over the Edge: Remapping the American West*, ed. Valerie J. Matsumoto and Blake Allmendinger (Berkeley: University of California Press, 1999), 215–30. Arizona's ban on interracial marriage was first enacted by the territorial legislature in 1865 (Howell Code ch. 30, sec. 3), and the ban remained in effect until 1962. Arizona Session Laws 1962, ch. 14, sec. 1. At various times, the law banned Caucasians from marrying "negroes," "mulattoes," "Indians," "Mongolians," "Malays," and "Hindus."

63. Arizona Constitution, art. 18, sec. 10. However, a provision rejected by the delegates was enacted by the voters using the statutory initiative in 1914. It barred employers from hiring noncitizens in excess of 20 percent of their workforce. The U.S. Supreme Court declared the Arizona law unconstitutional the following year. *Truax v. Raich*, 239 U.S. 33 (1915).

64. Arizona Constitution, art. 20, fourth and fifth ordinances establish federal control over Indian lands and prohibit state taxation of reservation property. These provisions were mandated by the Enabling Act and cannot be repealed without the permission of Congress.

65. See generally *American Indian Relationships in a Modern Arizona Economy: Sixty-fifth Arizona Town Hall, October 30–November 2, 1994*, background report prepared by the University of Arizona (Phoenix: Arizona Town Hall, 1994). Not all the tension is between Arizona and the tribes; federal land management decisions are also the source of continuing controversy. For example, Arizona officials were miffed when President Clinton established two new national monuments in Arizona without consulting with state officials. The legislature and governor enacted a formal resolution "denouncing" the federal action. See House Joint Resolution 2001, 44th Leg., 2d reg. sess. (2000).

66. Arizona Constitution, art. 4, part 2, sec. 23.

67. Ibid., art. 5, sec. 6. This includes the power to appoint, veto, or even pardon. When Republican governor Fife Symington traveled outside Arizona during 1991–94, gubernatorial power nominally shifted to the Democratic secretary of state, Richard Mahoney. The latter often joked about vetoing the governor's pet bills.

68. Ibid., art. 2, pt. 2, sec. 19.

69. Ibid., art. 22, sec. 20.

70. The territory had more than one seal. One became known as the "baking powder seal" because it bore a suspicious resemblance to the label of a popular commercial product. *The Records of the Arizona Constitutional Convention*, 650–51.

71. Ibid., 994–98, 1002.

72. In 1914, the Arizona Constitution was amended to make alcohol illegal. Although this was the first general election in which women were allowed to vote, women were not the only supporters of prohibition. See Berman, *Reformers, Corporations, and the Electorate*, 119–21.

73. *Arizona Highways Album: The Road to Statehood*, ed. Dean Smith (Phoenix: Arizona Department of Transportation, 1987), 138–43.

74. See Arizona Constitution, art. 8, pt. 1, sec. 1, which, as a result of that election, now states: "*Every* public officer in the state of Arizona, holding an elective office . . . is subject to recall from such office" (emphasis added).

3 The Legislative Branch

1. A constitutional initiative to abolish the senate and make the legislature unicameral was decisively rejected by Arizona voters in 1916.

2. U.S. Constitution, art. 4, sec. 4.

3. The Arizona Constitution has always had term limits for the state treasurer. See Arizona Constitution, art. 5, sec. 10 (1910). The 1992 amendment added term limits for the governor, secretary of state, attorney general, and superintendent of public instruction. Ibid., art. 5, sec. 1.

4. Twenty-two of the state's ninety legislators began their final term in January 1999.

5. The initiative was approved by 74.2 percent of the voters.

6. However, during this period house members often moved to the senate—a practice facilitated by Arizona's coterminous election cycle.

7. In the beginning, the five most populous counties got two senators, while the remaining nine counties got one apiece. After 1953, all counties were given two senators apiece. The house always had some system of apportionment by population. Initially, the constitution prescribed the number of representatives that each county would receive, varying from one to seven. However, a 1918 amendment apportioned representatives to each county on the basis of votes cast for governor in the prior election. Counties entitled to more than one representative were required to create legislative districts of equal population that were "compact" and "contiguous." Subsequent amendments in 1932 and 1953 altered the apportionment formula but kept the same basic approach.

8. See, e.g., *Baker v. Carr*, 369 U.S. 186 (1962) (requiring the reapportionment of Tennessee's lower house) and *Reynolds v. Sims*, 377 U.S. 533 (1964) (requiring both houses of the Alabama state legislature to be apportioned on the basis of population).

9. The history of Arizona's "long and fitful attempt to devise a constitutionally valid reapportionment scheme" is partially chronicled by the U.S. Supreme Court in *Ely v. Klahr*, 403 U.S. 108 (1971). The three-judge district court case that actually designed Arizona's historic reapportionment is *Klahr v. Goddard*, 250 F. Supp. 537 (D. Ariz. 1966).

10. Arizona Constitution, art. 4, pt. 2, sec. 1.

11. Democrats regained control of the senate on three subsequent occasions; however, the party has not controlled the house of representatives since reapportionment in 1966.

12. Prior to the court's reapportionment ruling in 1966, the board of supervisors in each county drew the house districts. A citizen initiative was launched in September 1999 to take the responsibility away from the legislature and give it to an independent commission. Fair Districts, Fair Elections Initiative, 2-c-2000.

13. *Klahr v. Williams*, 339 F. Supp. 922, 927 (D. Ariz. 1972).

14. *Goddard v. Babbitt*, 536 F. Supp. 538 (D. Ariz. 1982).

15. The U.S. Justice Department got involved pursuant to the Voting Rights Act of 1965, as amended. Arizona is required to "pre-clear" all election changes with the federal justice department under this law. The state is subject to the Act because of its past history of legalized racial discrimination. *U.S. Code*, ch. 42, sec. 1973b.

16. See *Miller v. Johnson*, 515 U.S. 900 (1995); *Shaw v. Hunt*, 517 U.S. 899 (1996); and *Bush v. Vera*, 517 U.S. 952 (1996), which struck down such gerrymandered districts.

17. Arizona Secretary of State, *State of Arizona Registration Reports*.

18. The 1990s map was not actually implemented until the 1994 election. At that time, 44.8 percent of the state's registered voters were Republicans and 42.5 percent were Democrats. (The remainder identified with no party at all or with small third parties.) Ibid., January 1994.

19. Citizen legislatures are, however, fairly common on the state level. Other than California, New York, and a few other large states, most have low-paid, part-time legislatures like Arizona's. *The Book of the States*, 1998–99 ed. (Lexington: Council of State Governments, 1998), 80–81.

20. Arizona's age requirement for the lower house is among the nation's highest. Only three other states require representatives to be 25 years old. Ibid., 71–72.

21. Arizona Constitution, art. 4, pt. 2, sec. 2; art. 7, sec. 15; and art. 20, eighth ordinance. The English requirement was imposed by the federal government in the Enabling Act as a condition of statehood (see chapter 2).

22. Current house and senate rules, for example, require adjournment on the Saturday of the week in which the one hundredth day falls. The speaker or president can unilaterally

authorize a seven-day extension; thereafter, extensions require a majority vote of the chamber. Arizona Senate, *Rules*, 44th Leg. (1999–2000), rule 27; and Arizona House of Representatives, *Rules*, 44th Leg. (1999–2000), rule 2.

23. Their per diem allowance dramatically shrinks after the 120th day, providing added incentive to adjourn. Arizona Revised Statutes, sec. 41-1104.

24. Arizona Constitution, art. 4, pt. 2, secs. 1 and 3. (The legislature calls itself into session through a petition supported by two-thirds of the members.)

25. Another reason for calling the session at this time is that it advances the date on which the legislation becomes effective. (An emergency clause does this too, but it requires a two-thirds vote.)

26. Arizona Constitution, art. 4, sec. 22 (1910).

27. The history of legislative compensation in Arizona is rather complex, with salary and per diem issues intermingled. As originally worded, the constitution expressly permitted the legislature to enact an overriding salary law. Ibid. In fact, the Eighth Legislature did so in 1928, increasing its salary to $15 per day. Arizona Session Laws, ch. 2 (1928). However, from 1932 onward, the constitution eliminated the legislature's discretion to set its own salary. Instead, the constitution set specific dollar amounts. Arizona Constitution, art. 4, pt. 2, sec. 1 (1932) and amendments in 1958 and 1968. The legislature began awarding itself a per diem (in addition to its annual salary) beginning in 1947. See Arizona Session Laws, ch. 16, sec. 1 (1947). The 1958 and 1968 constitutional amendments to art. 4, pt. 2, sec. 1 expressly authorized a per diem, and the latter amendment gave the legislature complete discretion as to its rate and terms. The current constitutional provision controlling legislative salaries, art. 5, sec. 12, makes no reference to per diem, and the Arizona Supreme Court has left per diem rates in the hands of the legislature. *Randolph v. Groscost*, 195 Ariz. 423, 989 P.2d 751 (1999).

28. Compared to other states, Arizona's legislative salary is about average; it is even on the high side for western states. Arizona Department of Administration, *1999 Report to the Commission on Salaries for Elective Officers*, 2, 27–28. However, straight salary comparisons are somewhat misleading because per diem and other benefits vary from state to state.

29. Only legislative salaries go to the voters. The salary commission's recommendations for other elected officials go to the governor and legislature for approval. Arizona Constitution, art. 5, sec. 12 and Arizona Revised Statutes, sec. 41-1904.

30. Arizona Revised Statutes, sec. 41-1104. (The per diem drops to a lower rate after 120 days.)

31. In 1998, two senators received in excess of $23,000 as per diem and mileage. The senate president and house speaker—who both resided in Maricopa County—received $8,635 and $10,643, respectively. See Chris Moeser, "Legislators' Stealth Pay: Special Deal Let Ex-Speaker Cash In," *Arizona Republic*, 24 January 1999, sec. A, p. 3 and Chris Moeser, "Per Diems Can Double a Paycheck," *Arizona Republic*, 24 January 1999, sec. A, p. 1.

32. *Randolph v. Groscost*, 195 Ariz. 423, 989 P.2d 751 (1999). The salary commission had recommended that legislators be subject to the statutory per diem that applied to all other state workers. They coupled this with their salary recommendation and sent the combined measure to the voters for approval. The Arizona Supreme Court ruled that the commission lacked the authority to address matters other than annual salary.

33. One study found that the average Florida legislator tripled his or her net worth over ten years. Cited in Thomas R. Dye, *Politics in States and Communities*, 10th ed. (Englewood Cliffs: Prentice Hall, 2000), 158–59.

34. See, e.g., Dennis Wagner and Kathleen Ingley, "Disregard of Voters in Vogue: Elected Officials Go Their Own Way," *Arizona Republic*, 23 February 1997, sec. A, p. 1.

35. Arizona Constitution, art. 4, pt. 2, sec. 8 and Arizona Revised Statutes, sec. 41-1102.

36. Kris Mayes, "Speaker Tosses Reporter," *Arizona Republic*, 14 February 1997, sec. B, p. 1 and Hal Mattern and Chris Moeser, "Locked-In Legislators Still Fail on Budget," *Arizona Republic*, 2 April 1999, sec. A, p. 1.
37. Arizona Revised Statutes, sec. 41-1271. Other joint committees include the Joint Committee on Capital Review (sec. 41-1251) and the Joint Legislative Audit Committee (sec. 41-1279).
38. Arizona Constitution, art. 4, pt. 2, sec. 15.
39. Ibid., sec. 19 lists twenty categories of prohibited special laws. The legislature sometimes evades this requirement by passing laws that appear to be of general application but in fact have limited applicability. For example, a statute that generally applies to "any city with a population over 500,000" is actually a law targeted at Tucson and Phoenix.
40. Ibid., art. 4, pt. 2, sec. 13. An exception is made for the state's general appropriation bill. Ibid., sec. 20. Not surprisingly, the single subject and proper title requirements have generated a fair amount of litigation. See generally John D. Leshy, *The Arizona Constitution: A Reference Guide* (Westport: Greenwood Press, 1993), 113–14.
41. Arizona Constitution, art. 4, pt. 2, sec. 20.
42. It may be more accurate to describe the bill as "severely wounded," borrowing Senator Gnant's phrase. That is, there are various procedural devices that can be used to resurrect bills, including discharge petitions and "strike all" amendments. See Randall Gnant, *The Legislative Process in the Arizona Senate*, 2d ed. (Phoenix, 1996). <http://www.azleg.state.az.us/bill3law.htm>.
43. Arizona Legislative Council, *Arizona Legislative Manual*, 1998 ed. <http://www.azleg.state.az.us/council/legman.pdf>. This is sometimes called "pigeonholing."
44. The legislature has the option of sending a measure to the voters instead of the governor, using the statutory referendum (see chapter 4).
45. Although the legislature can function as long as a quorum is present, the constitution makes it plain that passage of bills requires "a majority of *all members elected* to each house" (emphasis added). Arizona Constitution, art. 4, pt. 2, sec. 15.
46. Outside of lawmaking, there are other situations for which supermajority votes are required. For example, it takes a two-thirds vote to expel a legislator or to remove another public official from office through the impeachment process. Ibid., art. 4, pt. 2, sec. 11 and art. 8, pt. 2, sec. 2. In contrast, when the *voters* enact laws or constitutional changes through the initiative and referendum processes, only a simple majority is required for passage. Arizona Constitution, art. 4, pt. 1, sec. 1(5). A proposed constitutional amendment would require a two-thirds majority for any initiatives that restrict hunting. SCR 1006, 44th Leg., 2d sess. (2000).
47. Ibid., art. 4, pt. 1, sec. 1 (3).
48. Ibid., art. 9, sec. 22.
49. Ibid., art. 4, pt. 1, sec. 6 (C).
50. Ibid., art. 5, sec. 7 and art. 4, pt. 1, sec. 1 (3).
51. "Bill Naming Arizona Dinosaurs Gets Stomped into History," *Arizona Republic*, 24 August 1998, sec. B, p. 1.
52. For example, there are controversial "strikers" that allow presumptively dead bills to be dramatically revived in the waning hours of the session. See, e.g., Robbie Sherwood, "'Strike-all' Tool Puts Dead Bills Back on Table," *Arizona Republic*, 7 April 2000, sec. A, p. 1. More in-depth accounts of the lawmaking process are available at the legislature's official web site (see the online resources listed at the end of this chapter).
53. Through log rolling, they can sometimes leverage the power to kill bills into the power to pass bills. In addition, the power to kill bills also permits them to shape legislation to their liking.

54. "America's Billion Dollar Governments," *Governing*. 1998. <http://governing.com/bilin-tro.htm>. Arizona ranks 27th among all state and local governments. In the same billion-dollar ranking, Maricopa County ranks 86th and the city of Phoenix ranks 96th.

55. U.S. Senate, Senator Albert Beveridge speaking on the jointure proposal, 59th Cong., 1st sess., *Congressional Record* (8 March 1906), 40, pt. 4: 3535.

56. See, e.g., Arizona Constitution, art. 9, sec. 2, prohibiting the legislature from granting exemptions not authorized by the constitution itself, and art. 4, pt. 2, sec. 19(9), prohibit-ing "special" tax and valuation laws for the benefit of particular taxpayers.

57. Ibid, art. 9, secs. 18 and 19. In California, the tax revolt was accomplished through the ini-tiative process. Although Arizona's legislature referred the matter to the people, it passed by a margin of over 5 to 1. Essentially, the constitutional provisions limit residential prop-erty tax to 1 percent of the full cash value of the property; it also caps the rate at which the valuation of the property can increase in any given year. Because there are some exceptions, Arizona has developed a complex system that recognizes "primary" taxes (which are sub-ject to the limits) and "secondary" taxes (which are not). See generally, Arizona News Ser-vice, *An Explanation of Arizona Property Taxes*. 1998. <www.arizonatax.org/images/proptaxbook.pdf>.

58. See generally Dan A. Cothran, "The Arizona Budget in an Age of Taxpayer Revolt," in *Pol-itics and Public Policy in Arizona*, 2d ed., ed. Zachary A. Smith (Westport: Praeger, 1996), 173–90.

59. Arizona Constitution, art. 9, sec. 22.

60. In 1998, it ranked 8th among the states in reliance on sales tax. U.S. Bureau of the Census, *State Government Tax Collections 1998*. 29 April 1999. <http://www.census.gov/govs/statetax/98tax.txt>.

61. For this reason, some experts advocate greater reliance on income taxes, which are typi-cally graduated and therefore progressive. See, e.g., Cothran, "The Arizona Budget in an Age of Taxpayer Revolt," 182. The Arizona Constitution, art. 9, sec. 12 expressly authorizes graduated income and inheritance taxes, to avoid arguments that such taxes violate the uniformity requirement in sec. 1.

62. Ibid., art. 9, sec. 5.

63. See generally Donald W. Jansen, "Arizona's Constitutional Restraints on the Legislative Powers to Tax and Spend," *Arizona State Law Journal* 20 (spring 1988): 181–208 and Leshy, *The Arizona Constitution: A Reference Guide*, 209–11.

64. Arizona Joint Legislative Budget Committee, *Fiscal Year 2000 Appropriations Report*. <http://www.azleg.state.az.us/jlbc/lease.pdf>.

65. Arizona Constitution, art. 9, sec. 5.

66. As with other types of legislation, supplemental appropriation bills can embrace "but one subject." Ibid., art. 4, pt. 2, sec. 20.

67. Arizona Revised Statutes, sec. 35-111. The biennial schedule is new. The budget was previ-ously adopted on an annual basis that put a strain on the legislature's one-hundred-day session.

68. Ibid., sec. 41-1272.

69. Arizona Constitution, art. 9, sec. 3.

70. Ibid., art. 9, sec. 17.

71. Ibid., art. 9, sec. 14.

72. That is, except to pay limited administrative costs. Arizona Revised Statutes, sec. 36-771.C

73. Arizona Constitution, art. 8, pt. 2, sec. 1

74. Ibid., sec. 2.

75. U.S. Constitution, art. 2, sec. 4.

76. *Mecham v. Arizona House of Representatives*, 162 Ariz. 267, 782 P.2d 1160 (1989).
77. Arizona Constitution, art. 5, sec. 6.
78. Ibid., art. 8, pt. 2, sec. 2.
79. Ibid.
80. He was convicted of obstruction of justice and misuse of public funds. The senate decided not to address the allegation relating to campaign finance violations, because that allegation was the subject of a pending criminal proceeding. (Mecham was acquitted by a jury in the criminal case after he had already been removed from office.)
81. Arizona Constitution, art. 5, sec. 6.
82. Some voters challenged Mecham's right to run in the courts. They argued that the senate had wrongly interpreted the constitution and that Mecham was automatically disqualified from holding future office by virtue of the conviction vote. The supreme court acknowledged that the passage could be interpreted either way. However, it opted to defer to the senate's judgment. *Ingram v. Shumway*, 164 Ariz. 514, 794 P.2d 147 (1990).
83. Arizona Constitution, art. 4, pt. 2, sec. 11.
84. Arizona Revised Statutes, sec. 41-1155.
85. See ch. 3, n. 12 .
86. U.S. Constitution, art. 5. The U.S. Constitution also provides for ratification through people's conventions in each state, but this alternative method has been used only on a single occasion in U.S. history.

4 Direct Democracy

1. Most states refer constitutional amendments to the voters. However, only five states (California, Michigan, Nevada, North Dakota, and Oregon) have Arizona's full range of initiatives, referenda, and recall. *Book of the States,* 1998–99 ed. (Lexington: Council of State Governments, 1998), 210, 222–23.
2. "Citizens" did not include all the adults living in Athens. Although the definition was quite liberal for the times, more than half the people—including women, slaves, and those of foreign ancestry—were excluded.
3. Madison writes in *Federalist No. 10:*

   [A] pure democracy, by which I mean a society consisting of a small number of citizens, who assemble and administer the government in person, can admit of no cure for the mischiefs of faction. . . . Hence it is that such democracies have ever been spectacles of turbulence and contention; have ever been found incompatible with personal security of the rights of property; and have in general been as short in their lives as they have been violent in their deaths.

   Similar criticisms of democracy can be found throughout the *Federalist Papers.* See especially *Nos. 6, 9, 14, 49,* and *58.*
4. This is the term that the U.S. Constitution uses (see art. 4, sec. 4); the term "democracy" does not appear anywhere in the document.
5. *Federalist Paper No. 10.* See also *Nos. 9* (Hamilton), *14* (Madison), and *51* (Madison).
6. Direct democracy actually has earlier roots in American political life than this brief history suggests. Village government in New England was highly participatory from the 1640s; some states required constitutional changes or select issues to be referred to the people; and recall was even debated at the Constitutional Convention of 1787. For a fuller history see Thomas E. Cronin, *Direct Democracy: The Politics of Initiative, Referendum, and Recall* (Cambridge: Harvard University Press, 1989).

7. New Mexico became a state under the same enabling act as Arizona, but its constitution was more conservative and contained only the less controversial referendum.

8. *Pacific States Telephone & Telegraph Company v. Oregon,* 223 U.S. 118 (1912). A delegate at Arizona's constitutional convention referred to the pending case and urged his fellow delegates not to include the direct democracy procedures because of their likely unconstitutionality. *The Records of the Arizona Constitutional Convention of 1910,* ed. John S. Goff (Phoenix: Supreme Court of Arizona, 1991), 740.

9. See Arizona Revised Statutes, sec. 19-101 et seq. for the procedural details of Arizona's direct democracy procedures.

10. The secretary of state delegates much of the task to county recorders, who check individual signatures against their voter registration lists. Ordinarily, they check only a random sample. Arizona Revised Statutes, sec. 19-121.01. However, if the number of signatures is between 95 and 105 percent of the constitutional minimum, every signature must be checked. Ibid., sec. 19-121.03.

11. As of this writing, there is a proposed constitutional amendment that would require a higher, two-thirds vote to pass any initiative that restricts hunting. If it is approved by the voters at the 7 November 2000 general election, it would amend the simple majority requirement in art. 4, pt. 1, sec. 1(5). The measure was referred to the ballot by the legislature, but it was pushed by a hunting lobby unhappy over the passage of animal rights initiatives in 1994 and 1998. See SCR 1006, 44th Leg., 2d sess. (2000).

12. As noted previously, this provision was declared unconstitutional by the Arizona Supreme Court in 1998.

13. *The Book of the States,* 210.

14. Arizona Constitution, art. 22, sec. 14 reads:

    Any law which may be enacted by the legislature under this constitution may be enacted by the people under the initiative. Any law which may not be enacted by the legislature under this constitution shall not be enacted by the people.

15. The 1914 amendment stated that "the power of the Legislature, to repeal or amend, shall not extend to initiative or referendum measures approved by a majority vote of the qualified electors." Ibid., art. 4, pt. 1, sec. 1(6) (1914). The Arizona Supreme Court ruled that this language barred legislative alteration of voter-approved measures only when the measures had been approved by a majority of all *registered* voters—a situation that has never occurred due to low voter turnout. See *Adams v. Bolin,* 74 Ariz. 269, 247 P.2d 617 (1952).

16. Arizona Constitution, art. 4, pt. 1, sec. 1(6)(A)–(D).

17. For a full account of this episode, see Bob Jacobsen, "An ASU Victory Like No Other," *ASU Vision* (fall 1998): 9.

18. This was subsequently declared unconstitutional by the U.S. Supreme Court. See chapter 2, n. 63.

19. Arizona Constitution, art. 4, pt. 2, sec. 1(6)(A).

20. Ibid., sec. 1(3).

21. Ibid.

22. Ibid., art. 9, sec. 22(A).

23. Mecham reported that he was relying upon a recent legal opinion by Arizona's attorney general. *State of the State Address of Governor Evan Mecham to the 38th Legislature,* 12 January 1987. That opinion concluded that the governor lacked the power to create a paid holiday for state workers. *Arizona Attorney General Opinions,* No. I86-062 (1986).

24. The Arizona Constitution does anticipate this possibility. Article 4, pt. 1, sec. 1(12) states that when two conflicting measures are both passed by the voters, the one that receives the most votes prevails.

25. David R. Berman, *Arizona Politics and Government: The Quest for Autonomy, Democracy, and Development* (Lincoln: University of Nebraska Press, 1998), 86.

26. For the influence of money on ballot propositions, see generally Cronin, *Direct Democracy,* 99–116 and David S. Broder, *Democracy Derailed: Initiative Campaigns and the Power of Money* (New York: Harcourt, 2000), 163–97.

27. Phoenix businessman John Sperling was joined by New York financier George Soros and Ohio businessman Peter B. Lewis. See Broder, *Democracy Derailed,* 191–97, for an account of their successful undertaking. As of this writing, the three have each contributed $155,000 to a third drug initiative, "The People Have Spoken," 9-1-2000.

28. Berman, *Arizona Politics and Government,* 85.

29. These claims, while intuitive, are difficult to prove. Even the evidence as to whether initiatives increase voter turnout is somewhat mixed. Cronin, *Direct Democracy,* 226–28.

30. Arizona Constitution, art. 8, pt. 1, sec. 2.

31. Article 5, sec. 6 lists the normal succession order as follows: secretary of state, attorney general, state treasurer, and superintendent of public instruction. In order to assume the office, however, the official must have been *elected* to his or her post.

32. In 1972, Cesar Chavez and the United Farm Workers led a recall effort against Governor Jack Williams. Although they collected sufficient signatures to trigger an election, the secretary of state voided many of the collected signatures on technical grounds. By the time this ruling was overturned by a court, the governor's term had expired, making the recall effort moot.

33. *Green v. Osborne,* 157 Ariz. 363, 758 P.2d 138 (1988).

5 The Executive Branch

1. A proposal to expand the corporation commission from three members to five will appear on the ballot for voter approval for the third time at the 7 November 2000 general election.

2. *Hull v. Albrecht,* 192 Ariz. 34, 960 P.2d 634 (1998).

3. Arizona Revised Statutes, sec. 32-1402.

4. A major exception is the corporation commission; its members are elected.

5. As noted in chapter 4, a controversial law that would have given the governor the power to fire appointed board members triggered a referendum in 1996 and was subsequently repealed by the legislature before the people could vote.

6. *The Records of the Arizona Constitutional Convention of 1910,* ed. John S. Goff (Phoenix: Supreme Court of Arizona, 1991), 370.

7. In 1992, the state mine inspector's term was lengthened to four years, with a four consecutive term limit. Corporation commission members have always had six-year terms. At the 7 November 2000 general election, voters will be asked to reduce the commissioners' terms to four years.

8. David Berman argues that this is partially explained by Arizona's high percentage of Hispanics and new arrivals—two groups with traditionally lower participation rates. *Arizona Politics and Government: The Quest for Autonomy, Democracy, and Development* (Lincoln: University of Nebraska Press, 1998), 78–80.

9. Arizona Constitution, art. 5, sec. 1. The state mine inspector can serve for four consecutive four-year terms. Ibid., art. 19. As of this writing, Arizona's three corporation commissioners serve for a single six-year term. Ibid., art. 15, sec. 1. The legislature has proposed a constitutional amendment that would expand the commission to five members and reduce the

term to four years with a two-term limit. This proposal will go to the voters at the 7 November 2000 election.

10. Ibid., art. 5, sec. 2; art. 7, sec. 15; and art. 20, eighth ordinance.

11. *The Book of the States*, 1998–99 ed. (Lexington: Council of State Governments, 1998), 19.

12. Arizona Constitution, art. 7, sec. 2 (1912).

13. Arizona Constitution, art. 5, sec. 12.

14. Ibid., and art. 4, pt. 2, sec. 17.

15. The salary commission recommended that the governor's salary be increased from $95,000 to $145,000; it also recommended sizeable raises for other elected officials. Letter of Martha Thomas, Chairman of the Commission on Salaries for Elective State Officers to Jane Dee Hull (10 December 1999). The governor decided to send only the recommendations for judges and corporation commissioners to the legislature, and she reduced those recommendations. *The Executive Mid-Biennium Update for Fiscal Years 2000 and 2001* (January 2000), 39. <http://www.governor.state.az.us/pdffiles/ExecBudget.pdf>.

16. In fact, of the six highest paid state employees, four are head coaches. (Doctors at the state's medical school and university deans and administrators are also among the highest paid.) David Parish, "Government's Richest Jobs in College Sports. Coaches Grab 4 of Top 6 Spots on State Payroll," *Arizona Republic*, 20 June 1999, sec. A, p. 1.

17. Arizona Constitution, art. 5, sec. 6.

18. When Governor Wesley Bolin died in office in 1978, Attorney General Bruce Babbitt became governor because the secretary of state, Rose Mofford, had not been elected to her office. Mofford had been appointed to fill the vacancy created when Secretary of State Bolin became governor upon Raul Castro's resignation.

19. John S. Goff, *George W. P. Hunt* (Cave Creek: Black Mountain Press, 1987), 21–22.

20. The troops took over a ferryboat, which was dubbed Arizona's "navy" in bemused news accounts. See Thomas Sheridan, *Arizona: A History* (Tucson: University of Arizona Press, 1995), 224.

21. Berman, *Arizona Politics and Government*, 119–20.

22. Pat Flannery, Clint Williams, and Jeff Barker, "U.S. Feared Symington Coup to Keep Grand Canyon Open," *Arizona Republic*, 12 February 1996, sec. A, p. 6.

23. Arizona Constitution, art. 5, sec. 4.

24. Like the president, the governor has the power to demand formal written reports from all executive officials. Ibid., art. 5, sec. 4.

25. The legislature enacts many bills en masse at the very end of the session and then adjourns. Under these circumstances, the governor has ten days to approve or veto the bills and the legislature loses its override power. Ibid., art. 5, sec. 7.

26. Ibid., art. 4, pt. 2, sec. 13.

27. Ibid., art. 5, sec. 5.

28. Ibid. This contrasts with the comparable clemency provision in the U.S. Constitution (art. 2, sec. 2).

29. Arizona Revised Statutes, sec. 31-402.

30. Ibid., sec. 31-401.

31. Governor Symington once pressured the board to reverse a controversial parole decision by demoting its chairperson and refusing to reappoint another board member. Governor Hull's staff has contacted the board on high-profile cases and has also been accused of attempting to influence board decisions. See, e.g., Mike McCloy, "Parole Board Chairman Resigns; Critic Says Decision Tied to Governor's Interference," *Arizona Republic*, 14 December 1999, sec. B, p. 1.

32. A superior court judge later ruled that the rescission was not legal.
33. Arizona Revised Statutes, sec. 31-445.
34. Governors Symington and Hull interjected themselves into the Hamm controversy as well. Symington condemned Hamm's admission to a state law school and, along with prominent legislators, threatened funding cuts. See, e.g., Karen McCowan, "Admitting Killer May Imperil Law School's Funding," *Arizona Republic,* 25 August 1993, sec. A, p. 1; and Karina Bland, "Lawmaker Targets Law School Budget; Irate at Killer's Admission, He Wants to Send $11,000 Message," *Phoenix Gazette,* 15 March 1994, sec. B, p. 1. Governor Hull sent a staffer to the 1999 parole board meeting that voted against Hamm's release from parole. Mike McCloy, "Parole Board Chairman Resigns; Critic Says Decision Tied to Governor's Interference."
35. Arizona Revised Statutes, sec. 41-193.A.7.
36. E.g., the Debt Oversight Commission, the Greater Arizona Development Authority, and the Water Infrastructure Finance Authority.
37. The Arizona Supreme Court has ruled that the constitutional qualifications are exclusive and that the legislature cannot add additional qualifications. See *Campbell v. Hunt,* 18 Ariz. 442, 162 P. 882 (1917) and *State ex rel. Sawyer v. LaSota,* 119 Ariz. 253, 580 P.2d 714 (1978).
38. The Arizona Constitution gives some hint of this when it states:

    The general conduct and supervision of the public school system shall be vested in a state board of education, a state superintendent of public instruction, county school superintendents, and such governing boards for the state institutions as may be provided by law.

    Art. 11, sec. 2.
39. These include the Arizona Board of Regents (which governs the state's universities), the State Board of Directors for Community Colleges, the State Board for Vocational and Technological Education (which regulates vocational schools), the State Board for Charter Schools (which regulates privately operated public schools), and the recently formed School Facilities Board (which disburses state funds to bring school facilities up to standards). The superintendent is a voting member of some, but not all, of these boards.
40. In Arizona, some cities provide water, sewage, garbage, or electrical service to residents. These are not subject to the corporation commission's regulatory jurisdiction.
41. The constitution's definition of a public service corporation is somewhat murky and has spawned numerous court cases as to whether a particular business falls within this classification. For example, to the dismay of some consumers, an appellate court declared in 1983 that cable television companies are not public service corporations. *American Cable Television, Inc. v. Arizona Public Service Company,* 143 Ariz. 273, 693 P.2d 928 (App. 1983).
42. Arizona Revised Statutes, secs. 40-461 to 40-464.
43. *Jennings v. Woods,* 194 Ariz. 314, 982 P.2d 274 (1999).
44. *The Book of the States,* 376.

6   The Judicial Branch

1. Since 1912, there have been three major structural changes to the judicial branch: in 1960, the Modern Courts Amendment enlarged the Arizona Supreme Court from three to five justices, gave the supreme court administrative powers over all courts, and authorized the creation of an intermediate appellate court. (The legislature did not actually establish the court of appeals until 1965.) In 1970, a Commission on Judicial Qualifications (later

enlarged and called the Commission on Judicial Conduct) was established to oversee judicial discipline. And in 1974, merit selection of judges was added to the constitution.

2.   147 Ariz. 370, 219 P.2d 1025 (1985).

3.   *Arnold v. Department of Health Services,* 160 Ariz. 593, 775 P.2d 521 (1989).

4.   *Rasmussen ex rel. Mitchell v. Fleming,* 154 Ariz. 207, 741 P.2d 674 (1987).

5.   For an interesting debate on this issue, compare Stanley G. Feldman and David L. Abney, "The Double Security of Federalism: Protecting Individual Liberty under the Arizona Constitution," *Arizona State Law Journal* 20 (spring 1988): 115–50 with Steven J. Twist and Len L. Munsil, "The Double Threat of Judicial Activism: Inventing New 'Rights' in State Constitutions," *Arizona State Law Journal* 21 (winter 1989): 1005–1064.

6.   *Marbury v. Madison,* 1 Cranch 137 (1803).

7.   *Roosevelt Elementary School District No. 66 v. Bishop,* 179 Ariz. 233, 877 P.2d 806 (1994).

8.   *Rios v. Symington,* 172 Ariz. 3, 833 P.2d 20 (1992).

9.   *Ruiz v. Hull,* 191 Ariz. 441, 957 P.2d 984 (1998).

10.   *Jennings v. Woods,* 194 Ariz. 314, 982 P.2d 274 (1999).

11.   *Randolph v. Groscost,* 195 Ariz. 423, 989 P.2d 751 (1999).

12.   *Citizens Clean Elections Commission v. Myers,* No. CIV-00-0054-SA (Ariz., 16 June 2000).

13.   The larger counties assign one or more superior court judges to a separate juvenile court. In addition, the state has had a tax court since 1988. Although this is technically a department of the Maricopa County Superior Court, it handles tax disputes throughout the state.

14.   For a more complete description see Arizona Supreme Court, *Guide to Arizona Courts.* <http://www.supreme.state.az.us/info/guide/gtc5.htm>.

15.   It also takes appeals from the Industrial Commission of Arizona, the Arizona Department of Economic Security (worker compensation rulings), and the tax court.

16.   Most of the supreme court's cases come from the court of appeals. On occasion, however, the court accepts an appeal directly from superior court.

17.   In the case of lawsuits between counties, there is the additional issue of finding a neutral forum, because superior courts operate on a county basis.

18.   *Dickerson v. United States,* No. 99-5525, slip op. at 14 (U.S., 26 June 2000) reaffirming *Miranda v. Arizona,* 384 U.S. 436 (1966).

19.   U.S. Constitution, art. 3, sec. 2 and *U.S. Code,* ch. 28, sec. 1332.

20.   This is a fundamental right guaranteed by the U.S. Constitution. See art. 1, sec. 9.

21.   Technically, the elections were "nonpartisan" because no party labels accompanied the names on the general election ballot. However, the candidates were initially chosen in partisan primary elections. Accordingly, it was not difficult to learn the candidate's party affiliation. (The system still operates this way in the counties that elect judges.)

22.   The court of appeals did not exist back then. (Judges on this appellate court have six-year terms like those of the supreme court.) Municipal courts are under the authority of cities, and the method of selecting judges is therefore up to the individual municipality. Most municipal judges are appointed.

23.   There are actually three separate commissions: one for Pima County Superior Court, one for Maricopa County Superior Court, and one for the state's two appellate courts. Each commission consists of sixteen members, including the chief justice of the supreme court. The remaining members are attorneys and private citizens appointed by the governor. Arizona Constitution, art. 6, secs. 36 and 41.

24.   Ibid., secs. 36, 37, and 41.

25.   See, e.g., Ed Hendricks, "Merit Selection Is Worth Keeping," *Arizona Attorney* 36 (August–September 1999) 1: 24–25; Michael L. Piccarreta, "Supporting Merit Selection," *Arizona Attorney* 33 (December 1996) 4: 11–12.

26. Arizona Constitution, art. 6, sec. 42.

27. Ibid., art. 6.1, sec. 4. The commission was initially established as the Commission on Judicial Qualifications in 1970. It was renamed, enlarged, and given expanded powers in 1988.

28. The figures of formal disciplinary action do not fully measure the effectiveness of the commission, because some judges resign while investigative processes are still pending. Interview with E. Keith Stott Jr., executive director, Commission on Judicial Conduct (25 June 1998).

29. In many other states, this office is called the "district attorney's office."

30. Arizona Constitution, art. 2, sec. 30. (A defendant can waive this right under certain circumstances.)

31. Grand juries operate in every county and consist of 12 to 16 members. Arizona Revised Statutes, sec. 41-101. There is also a state grand jury that handles more specialized cases. Sec. 41-421 et seq. Arizona grand juries have subpoena powers and can investigate criminal activity on a wide-ranging basis. However, prosecutors usually guide the grand jury's investigation by presenting select witnesses and evidence.

32. On rare occasions, preliminary hearings may be conducted in superior court instead.

33. The grand jury system is often criticized on the ground that it gives prosecutors too much control—that jurors are little more than "rubber stamps." Some mistrust the grand jury's secrecy and its far-ranging power to summon third parties to testify. Defendants especially dislike the grand jury because their attorneys cannot take part by cross-examining witnesses or arguing to the jurors. (In fact, defense lawyers are not even present at most grand jury proceedings.) Nevertheless, grand juries do refuse to indict on some occasions, and JPs are not always impartial either. Because they are elected, they are vulnerable to political pressure in high-profile cases. Finally, grand jury secrecy serves at least three legitimate interests: (1) it protects the reputations of suspects who are not indicted and the privacy of witnesses who may be innocently caught up in the investigation; (2) it allows complex crimes to be more thoroughly investigated (without tipping off the suspects); and (3) it better protects the identities of undercover officers and informants.

34. The two alternatives are not entirely discrete. Sometimes after a criminal complaint is filed in JP court, the prosecutor will take the case to a grand jury and cancel the preliminary hearing. Alternatively, the prosecutor will sometimes take a case to a preliminary hearing after a grand jury has failed to indict.

35. If the defendant is in custody, this hearing must be conducted within twenty-four hours of the arrest. Arizona Rules of Criminal Procedure, Rule 4.1. At the initial appearance, the judicial officer also determines whether the defendant is eligible for release while the trial is pending and sets bail or other conditions.

36. U.S. Constitution, amend. 5; Arizona Constitution, art. 2, sec. 10.

37. When the prosecution rests its case, it is customary for the defendant's attorney to ask the judge to enter a judgment of acquittal. The defense argues that the prosecution simply failed to introduce sufficient evidence to meet its high burden of proof. If the judge grants the motion, the case ends. If not, the defense has the opportunity to present witnesses and evidence.

38. These reports typically cover the full circumstances of the crime, its impact on the victims, and the defendant's background and prior history of criminality.

39. Arizona Constitution, art. 2, sec. 2.1(4).

40. Ibid., art. 2, sec. 23.

41. Ibid., art. 6, sec. 27.

42. Jurors must be U.S. citizens. The law precludes felons, mental incompetents, and persons who have some connection to the case (e.g., blood relationships with the parties, witnesses

to the events) from serving. See Arizona Revised Statutes, secs. 21-201 and 21-203.

43. Arizona Constitution, art. 2, sec. 23 and Arizona Revised Statutes, sec. 21-201. Misdemeanor cases tried in JP and municipal courts use six-member juries.

44. Arizona Constitution, art. 2, sec. 23.

45. U.S. Constitution, amend. 5; Arizona Constitution, art. 2, sec. 10.

46. This constitutional privilege may not even be available in civil cases. For example, if the defendant had been previously acquitted on parallel criminal grounds, the privilege would evaporate.

47. Arizona Constitution, art. 2, sec. 23 and Arizona Revised Statutes, sec. 21-102.

48. The prohibition is even repeated in Article 18, section 6 of the state constitution.

49. The first hypothetical situation involves the defense of contributory negligence and the second, assumption of risk. Article 18, section 5 reads:

> § 5. Contributory negligence and assumption of risk
> The defense of contributory negligence or of assumption of risk shall, in all cases whatsoever, be a question of fact and *shall, at all times, be left to the jury* (emphasis added).

50. However, if the jury does award damages, the law now requires it to apportion its monetary award to the defendant's degree of fault. See Arizona Revised Statutes, sec. 12-2505. This is known as the doctrine of comparative negligence.

51. *City of Tucson v. Fahringer*, 164 Ariz. 599, 795 P.2d 819 (1990).

7 Local Government

1. As a condition of statehood, the U.S. government required Arizona to renounce jurisdiction over tribal land in its state constitution. See Article 20, fourth and fifth ordinances.

2. See, e.g., *Udall v. Severn*, 52 Ariz. 65, 79 P.2d 347 (1938). Governments that have home rule have greater power and autonomy.

3. Until recently local elections could be held at any time of the year. A new law now reduces the permissible election dates to select times in March, May, September, and November. Arizona Revised Statutes, sec. 16-204.

4. U.S. Bureau of the Census, *County Population Estimates for July 1, 1999*. 9 March 2000. <http://www.census.gov/population/www/estimates/co_99_1.html>.

5. Ibid.

6. The U.S. government owns 57.4 percent of the land, the Apache Tribe owns 37 percent, and the state owns 1 percent. This leaves a mere 3.7 percent in private hands as a property tax base for the county. *Community Profile: Gila County* (Phoenix: Arizona Department of Commerce, 1999). <http://www.azcommerce.com/county/gila.pdf>.

7. Prior to 1948, the state did not permit Native Americans living on the reservation to vote in state and local elections.

8. The majority of the nation's counties still use this organizational form. Since the turn of the century, however, many counties have switched to structures that consolidate power in either an elected or an appointed county administrator. See National Association of Counties, *Basic Forms of County Government*. <http://www.naco.org/counties/general/forms.cfm>.

9. Arizona Constitution, art. 7, sec. 15; art. 12, sec. 4; and art. 20; also Arizona Revised Statutes, secs. 11-402, 11-531, and 15-301.

10. These include a county administrator (who oversees the county's bureaucracy); a clerk of the board of supervisors (who performs administrative functions for the board); a county

engineer (who oversees the county's surveying, engineering, and road construction); a county medical examiner (who performs coroner functions); a county public defender (who provides legal representation for indigent defendants); and a county public fiduciary (who performs guardianship functions).

11. Alan Ehrenhalt, "Good Government Bad Government," *Governing* (April 1995): 18–24.

12. Sheriff Joe Arpaio quoted in Ehrenhalt, "Good Government Bad Government," 20.

13. See, e.g., *Associated Dairy Products Company v. Page*, 68 Ariz. 393, 206 P.2d 1041 (1941).

14. Although user fees, state funds, and sales taxes have taken up some of the slack, the counties are continually cash-starved. See generally Dan A. Cothran, "Local Government in Arizona," in *Politics and Public Policy in Arizona*, 2d ed., ed. Zachary A. Smith (Westport: Praeger, 1996), 61–63.

15. Arizona Constitution, art. 12, secs. 5–9.

16. For example, the proposed Maricopa County charter would have created a more powerful county administrator, expanded the size of the board of supervisors, switched to nonpartisan elections, and allowed the voters to determine whether any or all of the seven elected offices should be eliminated. Maricopa County, *Voter Publicity Pamphlet: Charter Government Election*, 5 November 1996.

17. Ibid.

18. Technically, the supervisors were functioning as the governing board for the stadium district, not the county, when they levied the controversial quarter-cent sales tax. The tax expired on 30 November 1997 after $238 million (67 percent of the total stadium cost) had been raised. (The Arizona Diamondbacks financed the remaining construction costs.)

19. See generally Alan A. Lew and R. Dawn Hawley, "The Open Range on the Urban Fringe: Land-Use Planning in Arizona," in *Politics and Public Policy in Arizona*, 207–22; and Bradford Luckingham, *Phoenix: The History of a Southwestern Metropolis* (Tucson: University of Arizona Press, 1989).

20. Between 1990 and 1998, Phoenix was the fastest growing large city in the nation. Chandler (with 78 percent growth) was second for all midsized cities, and Scottsdale (50 percent), Glendale (32 percent), and Mesa (25 percent) were in the top twenty. U.S. Bureau of the Census, *Population Estimates for Cities with Populations of 100,000 and Greater*. 30 June 1999. <http://www.census.gov/population/estimates/metro-city/SC100K98-T2-DR.txt>. Arizona's smaller communities (Gilbert, San Luis, Goodyear, Oro Valley, Prescott Valley, and Surprise) experienced even greater levels of growth—with percentage increases in the triple digits. U.S. Bureau of the Census, *Population Estimates for Cities with Populations of 10,000 and Greater*. 30 June 1999. <http://www.census.gov/population/estimates/metro-city/SC10K98-T4-DR.txt>.

21. Ibid.

22. I.e., they were not legally incorporated. In fact, only 21 of Arizona's 87 cities and towns were incorporated prior to statehood. See *Local Government Directory* (Phoenix: League of Arizona Cities and Towns, 1999).

23. *Community Profile: Gilbert* (Phoenix: Arizona Department of Commerce, 1999). <http://www.azcommerce.com/comm/gilbert.pdf>.

24. Arizona Revised Statutes, secs. 9-101 and 9-271.

25. Arizona Constitution, art. 4, pt. 2, sec. 19. However, the legislature is permitted to classify cities by size. This enables it to circumvent the special law barrier by enacting general laws that apply only to cities with a certain minimum population ("one million or more").

26. Ibid., art. 13, sec. 2.

27. These include Avondale, Bisbee, Casa Grande, Chandler, Douglas, Flagstaff, Glendale, Goodyear, Holbrook, Mesa, Nogales, Peoria, Phoenix, Prescott, Scottsdale, Tempe, Tucson,

Winslow, and Yuma. *Charter Government Provisions in Arizona Cities* (Phoenix: League of Arizona Cities and Towns, 1996).

28. Council members typically have staggered four-year terms, while mayoral terms are either two or four years. Election cycles vary from city to city.

29. Arizona Revised Statutes, sec. 9-303.

30. See generally Luckingham, *Phoenix: The History of a Southwestern Metropolis* and Ehrenhalt, "Good Government Bad Government."

31. Technically, this wasn't a pure council-manager government because the council members also individually supervised various city departments.

32. The city manager's powers and tenure were enhanced, and the council was expanded to seven members (including the mayor), with all members elected at large.

33. In 1993, Phoenix won the international Carl Bertelsmann Prize, identifying it as one of the two best-run cities in the world. In 2000, it was the only major American city to receive an "A" in a prestigious management study. Katherine Barrett and Richard Green, "Grading the Cities: A Management Report Card," *Governing* 13 (February 2000): 22–91.

34. See, e.g., Hal Mattern, "Symington Jolts School System, Pushes Dramatic Reforms, Self-governing Campuses, No Education Agency," *Arizona Republic*, 30 September 1995, sec. A, p. 1.

35. Arizona Revised Statutes, sec. 15-351. According to the language of the statute, these councils are intended to "ensure that individuals who are affected by the outcome of a decision at the school site have an opportunity to provide input into the decision making process."

36. See, e.g., Elizabeth Greenspan, "Keegan Skeptical of Site Councils," *Arizona Republic*, 9 July 1999, sec. B, p. 1.

37. In the 1998 general election, for example, eight west valley school districts failed to attract sufficient candidates to run for school board seats. See Lori Baker, "Too Few School Board Candidates; Some Districts Have More Seats Than Takers," *Arizona Republic*, 11 September 1998, sec. A, p. 1.

38. Some contend that the cuts were due to fiscal mismanagement because the district apparently overlooked some available funds.

39. The school board president dismissed complaints about the board's composition, stating, "I don't want to downgrade parents, but parents tend to have a narrow view of what's going on. The number one issue for the district is to make it run efficiently and bring us into the modern era with technology." Quoted in Lori Baker, "No Dysart Parents on School Board," *Arizona Republic*, 16 November 1998, N.W. Valley Community section, p. 1. See also Ryan Konig, "Forum Looks at Loss of Dysart Employees, Hispanic Teachers, Staff in 'Exodus,'" *Arizona Republic*, 8 May 1999, Sun City/Surprise Community section, p. 1. In May 2000, however, voters in the Dysart school district approved the first budget override in a decade. The superintendent credited the school board for winning the support of fellow retirees. Connie Cone Sexton, "School Budget Overrides OK'd," *Arizona Republic*, 17 May 2000, sec. A, p. 16.

40. *Roosevelt Elementary School District No. 66 v. Bishop*, 179 Ariz. 233, 877 P.2d 806 (1994).

41. *Hull v. Albrecht*, 192 Ariz. 34, 960 P.2d 634 (1998).

42. Operational costs (e.g., teacher salaries) are funded by local property taxes and supplemental state money according to a complex formula that attempts to equalize the districts. However, there are many loopholes that permit disparities among districts.

43. Arizona Revised Statutes, sec. 15-183(e)(5). For general information about Arizona's charter schools see Arizona Department of Education, *Arizona Charter Schools Handbook* (January 2000) <http://www.ade.state.az.us/schools/charter-schools/handbook/toc.htm> and Arizona Department of Education, *FAQ's about Charter Schools* <http://www.ade.state.az.us/

schools/charter-schools/faqs.html>.

44.   U.S. Charter Schools, *Overview of Charter Schools.* 19 February 2000. <http://www.uscharterschools.org/>.

45.   Arizona Revised Statutes, sec. 15-1421 et seq.

46.   Arizona Constitution, art. 13, sec. 7.

47.   The debt limitations are discussed in chapter 3.

Photograph Credits

Index

About the Author

Toni McClory teaches political science at Glendale Community College. Before assuming her current teaching career she practiced law in Arizona for over eighteen years. She served as an Arizona assistant attorney general from 1976 to 1991, a period spanning six governors. Her practice focused on constitutional law, election issues, public records, local government, and consumer fraud. A clerkship with the U.S. Court of Appeals for the Ninth Circuit and a brief stint as a judge pro tem for the Arizona Court of Appeals provided additional opportunities for observing the inner workings of government. She has resided with her husband and children in Phoenix since 1973.